Sacred Journeys

A Woman's Book of Daily Prayer

Sacred Journeys

A Woman's Book of Daily Prayer

❖

Jan L. Richardson

UPPER
ROOM BOOKS
NASHVILLE

Upper Room Ministries® Website: http://www.upperroom.org

UPPER ROOM®, UPPER ROOM BOOKS® and design logos are trademarks owned by Upper Room Ministries®, Nashville, Tennessee. All rights reserved.

Unless otherwise designated, the Scripture quotations contained herein are from the New Revised Standard Version Bible, © 1989 by the Division of Christian Education, National Council of the Churches of Christ in the U.S.A. Used by permission.

Scripture quotations designated RSV are from the Revised Standard Version of the Bible, copyrighted 1946, 1952, and © 1971 by the Division of Christian Education, National Council of the Churches of Christ in the U.S.A. Used by permission.

Scripture quotations designated JB are taken from the *Jerusalem Bible,* published and copyright © 1966, 1967, and 1968 by Darton, Longman & Todd Ltd. and Doubleday & Co. Inc., and are used by permission of the publishers.

KJV is used to identify quotations from the King James Version of the Bible.

For additional acknowledgments, see page 435.

Cover art: "Wise Women Also Came," by Jan L. Richardson; an
    original paper collage
Cover design: Susan Scruggs
Fourth printing: 2000
ISBN: 0-8358-0709-6
Library of Congress Catalog Card Number: 94-60658

Printed in the United States of America

For the New Year's Eve sisterhood
and for all who journey

—— ❖ ——

Mujeres, a no dejar que el peligro del viaje y la immensidad del territorio nos asuste—a mirar hacia adelante y a abrir paso en el monte *(Women, let's not let the danger of the journey and the vastness of the territory scare us—let's look forward and open paths in these woods).* Caminante, no hay puentes, se hace puentes al andar *(Voyager, there are no bridges, one builds them as one walks).*

—Gloria Anzaldúa in *This Bridge Called My Back*

and in the remembering of
Edward DeLoach McCool
1961–1994
on the journey still

I'll praise my Maker while I've breath. . . .

Contents

— ❖ —

—— ❖ ——

Acknowledgments

— ❖ —

MANY KIND FOLKS BLESSED ME AS COMPANIONS AND COCREATORS in this journey. My family—Judy and Joe Richardson, Sally Richardson Carncross, and Scott Richardson—first awakened my love of stories and in many ways made it possible for me to write this book. I first gave voice to my dream of this book over a meal with Sue Joiner, and she has continued to provide sustenance and to keep the vigil along the way. For sacred space, nourishing and challenging conversations, encouragement; and in many cases for reading portions of the manuscript or providing other technical or spiritual assistance, I am grateful to and celebrate Carolyn Abrams, Tammy Adams, Betsey Brogan, Lesley Brogan, Linda Ellis, Tom Frank, Charlene Kammerer, Kary Kublin, Lori Leopold, Brenda Lewis, Leslee Lyndon, Carolyn Mathis, Scott McReynolds, Andy Oliver, Laura Rasor, David Schoeni, Dorri Sherrill, Sandra Smith, and Carol Wilson.

I am deeply grateful to Helen Bruch Pearson, Don E. Saliers, and Luther E. Smith, Jr., faculty members of the Candler School of Theology at Emory University, who agreed to read and discuss the manuscript, but who did much more. Their comments, questions, suggestions, and insights helped shape the text, and their friendship continues to grace and shape my soul.

Octavia Wilkins provided "a room of one's own" for me during my first year of writing, and her graciousness and that of those who share her household were gifts along the journey. Helen Neinast came along at a critical time, helping me believe that I could be a pastor and a writer at the same time and also providing assistance with the questions for reflection. I am grateful to my home church, Trinity United Methodist in Gainesville, Florida, for the stories we have shared; and to the staff and congregation of St. Luke's United Methodist Church in Orlando, where I am serving, for the way they have welcomed me into their community.

Lynne Deming, formerly of Upper Room Books, received my proposal with heartening enthusiasm and companioned the manuscript through much of its journey. Rita Collett was a wise and sensitive editor. Sarah Schaller-Linn devoted enormous energy toward securing the numerous copyright permissions and grieved with me the voices lost from this book because permission was not available.

Getting Started

❖

FIRST, A STORY. . . .

Once upon a time, when I lived in Atlanta, there was a park down the street from my home. Flowing through that park was a stream, and by that stream was a spot where I spent a good bit of my life during those years in Atlanta. I kept returning to that space, where the land gently curves and the stream comes down a small waterfall. The rhythms of the water became a constant in my life. I knew I hadn't come to Atlanta to stay—that I was journeying through—but it became home in many ways. The place by the stream offered itself as sacred space along the journey, as refuge in the often intense flow of life there. It was a place of welcome even when I was long absent, even when I was grumpy, even when I changed. I kept coming back, often stretching out on a blanket and reading, eating, pondering, writing, snoozing, or simply watching the moving water. Sometimes I shared the space with another, the water's rhythms unchanging through both pleasant conversations and hard ones. It was one of the first places I discovered when I moved to Atlanta, and it was one of the last places I visited before I left.

❖

This book is not so much a collection of devotional pieces as it is a story, and stories. It is a story of my longing to have, in a single devotional book, language, images, prayers, stories, and other expressions of faith that record women's search for the holy throughout the centuries.

And it is stories. These pages tell the stories of some of the women I have encountered in my own journey—women I have sought or stumbled into; women I have invited in or been surprised by; women who live close by or in a vastly different place and time; women who have stretched me with their stories, their questions, their lives, their sacred journeys.

Many of these women I encountered in the liturgies, prayers, and rituals of various communities of which I have been a part. Like my space by the stream, the space of those communal experiences offered a place of refuge as well as challenge as the language and stories both widened my vision and also rang true to my own experience. The words, prayers, stories, and songs of women from different cultures, times, and lives became a living stream to which I and others could return, to rest, to celebrate, to remember, and to come away from strengthened for the journey ahead.

When I came to my solitary times of devotion, I had a more difficult time finding the kinds of resources that have become available for worshiping communities. Frustrated by my attempts to adapt such resources for my own use, I began to dream of what such a book would look like. I wanted a book designed for individual use yet through which would flow a concern for the wider community and creation.

Out of this dream, *Sacred Journeys* began to emerge. The women of these pages have become companions along my own journey these past two years, teaching me much about prayer, devotion, worship, faith, celebration, stillness, and struggle. I have learned that prayer and action are not separate entities; rather they flow in the same stream. Our solitary acts of devotion are linked intimately with the larger community, and vice-versa.

Bärbel von Wartenburg-Potter writes in *We Will Not Hang Our Harps on the Willows*, "Once my spiritual self has been formed, it is often too late to incorporate justice in it. It is while the dough is being kneaded that everything has to go into it. Meditation, prayer, struggle all belong together, they do not neatly come one after the other." These women have taught me that if I am truly part of the body of Christ, then I am connected spiritually to, and affected by, the prayers of a mystic living in the Middle Ages, the writings of a woman killed in the Holocaust, the struggles of the Mothers of the Disappeared who march in the Plaza de Mayo in Argentina, the stories of homeless women living in the streets of my own country. I am connected intimately also with the ancient stories of Hagar and Sarah, of Mary and Elizabeth, of women from our own sacred texts whose names we know as well as those whose names we do not remember. These stories flow in the stream too.

It has become important for me to remember that while I cannot physically be everywhere and while I cannot touch the wounds of every sister who shares the journey, neither can I pray or worship with my back turned to them and to their stories. And so these women summon us to the stream, to sit by its life-giving waters. They invite us to gather with them, to feast, to celebrate, to rest, to listen to one another's stories. And then we go, returning to wherever we are called to bear our gifts.

They also tell us that the journey can be difficult. We may discover places along the way and in these pages, where we don't feel at home; places that make us uneasy. That's okay! As my friend Don Saliers wisely pointed out, "It's never been otherwise in the presence of God. Yet we don't shrink from the slippery places. Don't be fearful!"

―――― ❖ ――――

I am completing this manuscript while on a journey in Alaska. From the window of this "upper room" that I inhabit in Anchorage, I look out onto Mt. Susitna, "The Sleeping Lady." According to legend, Susitna was a maiden who lay down to sleep while waiting for her fiance and the other men of her village to return from their attempt to peacefully avert an attack from another village. The men of her village were killed, but her people did not want to disturb Susitna's slumber. Susitna still sleeps, waiting for peace to come again.

As these days unfold, may we who dream of peace awaken anew to the Spirit of God who calls us to pursue our dreams in concrete ways. May God continue to bless us with wisdom, with wellsprings of rest, and with passion for our paths. And one day we may gather with all creation at the place where the mountains dance and the river flows with peace, with justice, and with delight in all our sacred journeys.

—Jan L. Richardson
July 1994

Using This Book

——— ❖ ———

ALONG THE JOURNEY THROUGH THIS BOOK you will find certain markings in the landscape each week. The *Invocation* welcomes you into the space you have created for prayer and devotion. A biblical *Text* appears each week; some weeks employ a series of daily scripture readings. The *Context* portion sketches out the space of that week, providing biographical information on the woman or women or background information on the chosen theme.

In the readings for each day, you will hear the voices of women from around the world and throughout the centuries. They bid you to hear their stories, their songs, their struggles, their prayers. The questions or thoughts that follow each daily reading invite you to *Reflect* and call you into a time of prayer, pondering, journaling, conversation, meditation—however you choose to dwell with this text. You may read the *Meditation* daily or at the end of the week. It is here that I weave together images and insights from the words of the week, and some of my own story emerges here. The *Blessing* offers a word of hope and sends you on your way.

I wrote all pieces not attributed to another writer—specifically, the invocations, meditation pieces, blessings, and seasonal introductions. I am grateful to the writers who either shared the daily readings with me or made them available for me to find along my journey. I encourage you to seek out the sources included in these pages to discover the paths they open to you.

Birthing the Holy

The Season of Advent and Christmas

THE JOURNEY BEGINS WITH ADVENT. Advent is a dance set to the rhythm of waiting. We wait for the holy, we wait for the birth, we wait for the light. In our haste to make it to Christmas, we often fill our waiting with frantic steps. We may dance a frenzied tarantella of shopping, baking, Christmas card writing, decorating, and caring for others. We wear ourselves out in the process and then wonder why our spirits sink after the holidays. Or we may dance a slow, painful dance of aloneness, wishing that the images of happy, prosperous families and friends would hurry up and pass for another year.

In this season, Mary reminds us that Advent waiting is an intricate, intimate process of receiving and bringing forth, of movement and stillness, of pain and joy, of darkness and light, of solitude and community. In pregnancy, one does not choose between these extremes; they are not opposites to be separated. Rather, pregnancy is a constant process of incorporating, of embodying, of integrating. In the intimate darkness of the womb, God continually weaves new life.

Advent reminds us that we are a pregnant people, for God calls each of us to bring forth the Christ. Conception and birthing of the holy do not depend on physical pregnancy. Women's capacity for birthing extends beyond biological reproduction, despite what some would tell us. Birthing encompasses the wide range of our creative abilities—abilities that enable us to bring forth such gifts as children, dreams, hopes, relationships, art, music, new ways of living, and our selves.

The strong, creative women of these Advent stories call us to ponder what it means to bring forth the holy. They show us that the most important activity may *precede* the birth. Their stories tell us that waiting is neither passive inactivity nor frantic motion. Rather, it is a purposeful dance that begins with opening, with actively choosing to receive God. Our choosing does not guarantee that our dance will be without pain. But in our choosing to be partners with God we find strength, and in our strength we find new life.

Blessed be our Advent journey. Blessed be our dance!

A Prayer for the Beginning of Advent

—— ❖ ——

No one knows what lies ahead when we say yes to God! To accept God's invitation to a creative relationship requires learning different rhythms. These rhythms sustain us and pull us into a dance set to the heartbeat of God.

You may light a candle.

God of new creating,
who beckons us
to the dance of birthing
and sustains us
in our laboring,
hear this prayer:

From fear of the unknown
deliver me.
From doubts of my creativity
deliver me.
From ridicule by those around me
deliver me.
From my excuses about my abilities,
   my age, my education,
   my looks, my status
deliver me.

With your promise of companionship
comfort me.
With your creative spirit
bless me.
With your pledge of sustenance
strengthen me.
With your embrace of all of me
heal me and set me to motion.

You who called me to life
that you may be born again in me,
blessed be in this and all seasons!
—Jan L. Richardson

1 Partnership with God
The Annunciation to Mary

Invocation: *Here am I, God. In this season of waiting and wondering, I open myself to you. Let us share our strength as we embrace each day.*

Text: Luke 1:26-38

Context: In speaking of the journey that led her to become an Episcopal priest, Barbara Brown Taylor once remarked, "If I claim one guiding principle for my life, it is to say yes to unusual propositions and see what happens." Taylor's words, recorded in *Women of the Word: Contemporary Sermons by Women Clergy,* reveal her as a kindred spirit to a foresister who received an unusual proposition of her own generations earlier. The proposition was not merely unusual but unbelievable. Unimaginable. Almost inconceivable.

Mary of Nazareth. Mary, barely beyond childhood herself, called by God to bear a child of her own. Mary, who by her own account had not known the touch of a man, was asked to perform the intimate task of carrying a child within her own body.

Often persons have interpreted Mary's response to the angel Gabriel's invitation as unquestioning obedience and humility. Often they lift up Mary as a model of passivity for all women. Yet when we listen closely, we can hear the voice of a strong, active woman—a woman who dared to question Gabriel, a woman whom Gabriel did not leave until she had spoken her words of acceptance.

Let it be. The words sound like whispers to ears that have always heard them as inevitable, as the only possible response to a demanding God. But if we draw closer, if we draw back the veil that has obscured Mary's humanity, if we listen to the one who bore divinity out of her own womanliness, what will we hear?

—— MONDAY ——

In Luke's account, Mary's story begins with the greeting of an angel. Mary, then, is a woman who listens to angels. "Peace be with you," the angel says to her. Mary is receptive to something magnificent, and God is receptive to her. The act of divine interest and grace contains two promises. First, God will share strength with Mary. Second, the very name Yahweh is a promise of strength and an assurance of fidelity. It is given in this one phrase "I stand by your side with all that I have and all that I am, with all my strength" and "you will always be able to count on me!" With such promises in safekeeping, who could fail to be strong? This, then, is the basis of Mary's strength and daring.

—Bärbel von Wartenberg-Potter, from "The Old, New Visions" in *The Power We Celebrate*

Reflect

❖ What unusual propositions have you received in your life?

❖ How have you responded?

❖ What does it mean to "share strength" with God?

——— **TUESDAY** ———

To many of us, reading or hearing the story of Mary is like reading or hearing a story of which we already know the ending. We know that Joseph is not going to abandon her and that he is not going to throw her to the wolves. The penalty for a betrothed virgin being with child by a third party was, after all, death. We know everything is "going to be all right."

Therefore, there is not sufficient awe in us at the incredible courage of this young woman, who said what she said: "May it happen to me as you have said."

—Marianne Katoppo in *Compassionate and Free: An Asian Woman's Theology*

Reflect

Imagine the story as if you didn't know the ending.

❖ What do you think of the danger of Mary's decision—the risk she took of being ridiculed, ostracized, killed?

❖ How does this danger change the impact of her response?

——— **WEDNESDAY** ———

Annunciation (excerpt)

This was the minute no one speaks of,
when she could still refuse.

A breath unbreathed,
                    Spirit,
                              suspended,
                                        waiting.

———————————

She did not cry, "I cannot, I am not worthy,"
nor, "I have not the strength."
She did not submit with gritted teeth,
                                   raging, coerced.
Bravest of all humans,
                    consent illumined her.
The room filled with its light,
the lily glowed in it,
                    and the iridescent wings.
Consent,
          courage unparalleled,
opened her utterly.
—Denise Levertov in *Breathing the Water*

Reflect

- ❖ As you make difficult decisions, what are your thoughts and feelings?
- ❖ When has someone asked you to do something that seemed impossible, beyond your capabilities, or something that might alienate others?
- ❖ What consequences are you willing or unwilling to endure in making decisions?

——— **THURSDAY** ———

Magnificat of Acceptance (excerpt)

My soul trembles in the presence of the loving Creator
      and my spirit prepares itself to walk hand in hand
      with the God who saves Israel
      because I have been accepted by God
      as a simple helpmate.
Yes, forever in the life of humankind
      people will sing of this loving encounter;
      through remembering this moment, the faithful
      will know all things are possible in God.

Holy is the place within me where God lives.
God's tender fingers reach out from age to age
      to touch the softened inner spaces of those
      who open their souls in hope.
I have experienced the creative power of God's embracing arms
      and I know the cleansing fire of unconditional love.
I am freed from all earthly authority
      and know my bonding to the Author of all earthly things.
—Ann Johnson in *Miryam of Nazareth*

Reflect

- ❖ What encounters have enabled you to know the possibilities in God?
- ❖ What places within you long for God's touch?

——— FRIDAY ———

Whether or not we ever experience physical pregnancy, God calls us to give birth to the holy in our lives. Therefore, we are sisters of Mary and share in her sacred creativity. Like Mary, God invites us to be "cocreators" as we continually seek to bring Christ into the world. Dorri Sherrill, in her sermon "The Annunciation," writes, "God invites us all to be God-bearers, to reveal God's love and grace, to embody God to the world. . . . We are invited to continue the incarnation, which was not a once-and-for-all event, but rather a process; something that continues still, a continual coming of God in Christ to be present to us."

God *invites* us. And, like Mary, we choose. The call to bear Christ in us does not ask for passive acceptance, for passivity will not provide the strength to survive the birth. The call does not demand conformity or un-questioning submission, because, as Mary discovered, agreeing to bear the Christ often requires stepping outside societal boundaries and asking, "How can this be?" In the shadows of Mary's assent to "let it be" lies the pos-sibility that she—or we—can choose to let it *not* be. God leaves the choosing to us.

—Jan L. Richardson

Reflect

- ❖ Cocreating with God, being in partnership with God, bringing forth the Christ . . . what do these images mean?
- ❖ How do these images challenge, affirm, disturb, or welcome you?

What about the man who is to marry her [Mary]? He stood by Mary because he too has heard the voice of God and he too believes that Mary's submission to God's purposes will bring new life to the whole human community.

Joseph too is going against custom and tradition when he takes a pregnant woman for wife. We never stop to think how embarrassing his own position is. What will his parents say? What will his friends say?

Here is a man who stood in solidarity with a woman he loved and trusted. A man who had an ear tuned to what God is saying to him and to the world.

Does the story have a message for us?

—Mercy Oduyoye in *Who Will Roll the Stone Away?*

Reflect

❖ What men stand in solidarity with you, going against custom and tradition to be with you or work with you?

❖ Where do you find support for your decisions?

—— **SUNDAY** ——

When all is said and done, in the tradition, angels are messengers of God. Winged words. Hovering visitations. They are the medium through which God touches our lives. But we must be alert for their arrival, open to hear their words.

In this season especially, we are invited to be alive to their nearness, anticipating their arrival in our time. Who then are our angels that come to us, as it were, out of the clear blue sky? Who in our lives are the messengers of God? Who are those around us—spouse, children, parents, friends, colleagues, members of the congregation, strangers—who come to us as the medium through which God wishes to touch our lives? Have we eyes capable of the simple vision and hearts capable of the wonder needed to discern what they have to say?

—Wendy M. Wright in *The Vigil*

Reflect

❖ What are you feeling at the close of this first week of Advent?

❖ In the midst of the advertisements, activities, and frantic pace that accompany the holiday season, how do you prepare a place within yourself to hear the news of the season—that the Christ is coming and seeks to be born in you?

❖ Who brings this message to you?

—— **Meditation** ——

The Message

Take this message back:
       that when the angel left I wept
       that I thought I was insane
       that I sat in the dark for three days
       that I dreamed of stones
       that I dreamed of angry crowds
       that I dreamed I spread my arms to meet them.

Say on the third day
       a wind through the door
       say the smell of perfume
       say fire
       say ancient, familiar music
       say I opened
       say I laughed
       say just a bit.
—Jan L. Richardson

—— ❖ ——

Blessing: *God is with you, favored one! As this sacred season begins, may you know God as an intimate partner. May your knowing enable you to imagine the unimaginable and to conceive the unexpected. Let it be.*

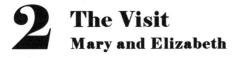

The Visit
Mary and Elizabeth

Invocation: *God of all journeys, visit me with your peace in this time of reflection. Help me remember those who have graced my journey with their accepting arms and words of blessing.*

Text: Luke 1:39-55

Context: Luke's account of Mary's visit to Elizabeth immediately follows Gabriel's departure from Mary. Having boldly assented to bear the Christ, Mary finds herself suddenly alone. Young and unwed, Mary's awe at Gabriel's invitation probably gives way to fear, dismay, and a sense of isolation. Who will believe her? Who will listen to her? Who will comfort her?

Elizabeth. We do not know whether Mary decides to visit Elizabeth because they have been close kinswomen and friends for a long time or because Mary simply has no one else to whom she can turn. But we do know, as does Mary, that her elder relative has experienced, as has Mary, a miraculous conception of her own. This fact alone may have prompted Mary to act decisively once again and journey, alone and "with haste," to see Elizabeth.

Surely Elizabeth's welcome assures Mary that she has done well to turn to her kinswoman. Blessed by Elizabeth for her faithfulness, Mary breaks forth into a song full of praise for the liberation that God has brought. We know this song as the Magnificat.

A. M. Allchin has noted in his book *The Joy of All Creation* that this meeting of Mary and Elizabeth is, in one sense, the beginning of Christian liturgy. He observes that in liturgy we meet not only God but also one another. The blessing, praise, and liberation that flow out of Mary and Elizabeth's meeting serve as a model for how we, in worship and all of life, should bless and call forth one another's gifts.

—— **MONDAY** ——

[A] lesson to be learned was how to receive a blessing that caused more problems than it solved.

"How can this be?" the words kept going through Mary's head as she sat in her chambers on another side of the country. . . .

Mary—a peasant girl, unmarried and untutored—was to be the mother of the Christ.

To be pregnant is one thing.

To be pregnant with the Christ is something altogether different.

How could this *happen*? This was not the way Mary had planned her life.

"How do you defend a blessing you cannot explain?" she asked herself. "How do you live with a blessing that creates more problems than it solves?"

Besides, who would believe her? Joseph? Absolutely not. The townswomen? Hardly. Elizabeth, her relative? Perhaps. . . .

At least Elizabeth was married. Still, Mary needed someone to talk with. Someone who knew what it meant to grapple with God's intentions. Someone. A woman, pregnant like herself. Mary's mind kept going back to the old woman Elizabeth. Suppose her kinswoman did not believe her? It was a chance Mary had to take. She needed to talk with another woman.
—Renita J. Weems in *Just a Sister Away*

Reflect

❖ What blessings have you received that you cannot explain, that caused more problems than they solved?

❖ Is it easy or difficult for you to turn to someone else when you feel isolated and overwhelmed?

❖ To whom do you turn?

——— **TUESDAY** ———

Elizabeth's greeting affirms Mary's faith. With this show of solidarity from another woman, Mary's . . . lingering doubts disappear. . . .

Yes, blessed is she who believes that the promise made her by the Lord will be fulfilled. What reassurance! What a gift! How significant this was for Mary! how often do we need reassurance when we are challenged, or required to face difficult situations, or to carry heavy responsibilities! Is this what we mean by building solidarity among women?

With this assurance Mary feels liberated. She is liberated from her fears and misgivings, from her feelings of weakness and of inadequacy. She is liberated from what she was taught as a woman. Suddenly she sees the significance of Gabriel's message. She realizes what it actually means to be empowered by the Holy Spirit and how such power can reverse all so-called natural human order.

Then Mary, like Hannah before her, is filled with joy and gratitude and breaks out in a hymn of praise to God, her Savior.

—Marie Assaad, from "Reversing the Natural Order" in *New Eyes for Reading: Biblical and Theological Reflections by Women from the Third World*

Reflect
❖ When has someone else empowered you to bring forth something that needed release?

—————— **WEDNESDAY** ——————

Where are these words coming from? She is no politician, no revolutionary; she just wants to sing a happy song, but all of a sudden she has become an articulate radical, an astonished prophet singing about a world in which the last have become first and the first, last. What is more, her song puts it all in the past tense, as if the hungry have *already* been fed, the rich *already* freed of their inordinate possessions. How can that be? Her baby is no bigger than a thumbnail, but already she is reciting his accomplishments as if they were history. Her faith is in things not seen, faith that comes to her from outside herself, and it is why we call her blessed.

—Barbara Brown Taylor, from "Magnificat" in *Mixed Blessings*

Reflect
❖ When have you been surprised by what has emerged from you?
❖ How do you see your creativity—in whatever form it takes—as a sign of faith and of God's liberation?

—————— **THURSDAY** ——————

It is Mary, a peasant girl, who talks about the restructuring of social orders and religious and political and economic institutions. Mary is talking about more than shaking the rugs and dusting off the furniture. She's talking about a thorough cleaning that shakes the very foundation of all that is familiar and comfortable. It is Mary, the *mother* of Jesus, who speaks this kind of strident message, *before* God's child is born—and before Jesus had the power of speech, Mary had already said it! Mary hits every note of life with her song, for she sings about a new creation—a new way of taking risks—a new way of committing ourselves to the world and to each other. Mary's "yes" sings of revelation and liberation and transformation.

—Helen Bruch Pearson in "Saying Yes to God"

Reflect

Read Mary's song again.

- ❖ Where do you see yourself in it?
- ❖ Is it a song of comfort or discomfort, of affirmation or challenge for you?
- ❖ How do you think Mary's vision and life influenced Jesus as he grew?

——— **FRIDAY** ———

Blessed art thou for thou believest that which the Lord has told thee and why this wonderful benediction shall be fulfilled.

These words have to do with the power of the faith that makes the impossible possible. In order to struggle, to confront the enemy who oppresses, courage, strength and devotion are necessary for these alone make faith concrete.

In her canticle, Mary incorporates the experience of another woman, Hannah, the mother of the prophet Samuel, a woman who gave her sons to build the history of her own people.

The rural woman in Guatemala is capable of renouncing a life of tranquillity in order to link her life with the historical destiny of her people. For this reason, Mary is the typical image of the woman of faith.

The working-class woman and the professional woman have been renouncing their normal future—a quiet family life and immediate fulfillment—in order to join the struggle for justice and peace.

The sense of devotion, of total availability, of hope against all hope, of faith which makes possible the impossible, which submits the only thing one has—one's life—all this in order to collaborate with the future of one's people, makes liberation possible.

—Julia Esquivel, from "Liberation, Theology and Women" in *New Eyes for Reading*

Reflect

- ❖ How does this image of Mary compare to yours?
- ❖ How can women, living far removed from one another, hear and

bless one another so that liberation for all becomes possible, so
that each can sing Mary's song in her own land?

—— **SATURDAY** ——

Meditation on luke 1

It is written that mary said
my soul doth magnify the lord
and my spirit hath rejoiced in god my savior
for he hath regarded the low estate of his handmaiden
for behold from henceforth
all generations shall call me blessed

Today we express that differently
my soul sees the land of freedom
my spirit will leave anxiety behind
the empty faces of women will be filled with life
we will become human beings
long awaited by the generations sacrificed before us

It is written that mary said
for he that is mighty hath done to me great things
and holy is his name
and his mercy is on them that fear him
from generation to generation

Today we express that differently
the great change that is taking place in us and through us
will reach all—or it will not take place
charity will come about when the oppressed
can give up their wasted lives
and learn to live themselves

It is written that mary said
he hath shewed strength with his arm
he hath scattered the proud
he hath put down the mighty from their seats
and exalted them of low degree

Today we express that differently
we shall dispossess our owners and we shall laugh

at those who claim to understand our feminine nature
the rule of males over females will end
objects will become subjects
they will achieve their own better right

It is written that mary said
he hath filled the hungry with good things
and the rich he hath sent empty away
he hath holpen his servant israel
in remembrance of his mercy

Today we express that differently
women will go to the moon and sit in parliaments
their desire for self-determination will be fulfilled
the craving for power will go unheeded
their fears will be unnecessary
and exploitation will come to an end
—Dorothee Sölle in *Revolutionary Patience*

Reflect

❖ When those who have been oppressed come into their power, how can they avoid exploiting other groups?

❖ How could you express the song of Mary differently today, in your own words, in your own context?

—— SUNDAY ——

I don't know who wrote these words, but I first heard them in the haunting voice of Enya on her album, Shepherd Moons. *I have played them often, both in days of rejoicing and in times when I thought it was impossible to sing.*

Whoever we are, we are called to sing; not necessarily to sing well but to give expression to the call upon us to bear hope in the midst of struggle and peace in the presence of pain. We are the beloved of God, invited into partnership with the holy. How can we keep from singing?

How Can I Keep from Singing?

My life flows on in endless song, above earth's lamentation;
I hear the real, though far-off hymn, that hails a new creation.
Through all the tumult and the strife I hear its music ringing;
It sounds an echo in my soul; how can I keep from singing?

When tyrants tremble in their fear and hear their death knell ringing,
when friends rejoice both far and near, how can I keep from singing?
In prison cell and dungeon vile our thoughts to them are winging,
when friends by shame are undefiled, how can I keep from singing?
—Traditional folk song

Reflect
- ❖ What songs sustain you?
- ❖ What song can you not keep from singing?

—— **Meditation** ——

Generation to Generation

From generation to generation
women meet in common spaces,
sharing sacred places
in the journeys of our lives.

From generation to generation
women call to women-kin,
yearning deep within
to be seen with Spirit-eyes.

From generation to generation
women risk, their fears confessing,
and seek out words of blessing
to melt away the scorn.

From generation to generation
women sing out of the shadows
and labor in the echoes
for the holy to be born.
—Jan L. Richardson

—— ❖ ——

Blessing: *In your journeying may you find the embrace of acceptance; in your acceptance may you find your song; in your song may you find liberation: the holy coming to birth in you.*

3 Weaving Threads of Waiting
Elizabeth and Mary

Invocation: *Creating God, you too know the rhythm of pregnancy. Share this dance of waiting with me as I embody rest and work, discomfort and hope.*

Text: Luke 1:56

Context: As my sister neared the end of many weeks of bed rest during a difficult pregnancy, I flew up to be with her. Sally soon resumed "normal" activities, and we thought the baby would come immediately. Many days later, the baby still had not arrived, and it seemed that Sally would be pregnant forever. The weight of waiting became palpable in the house.

Was it this way too for Mary and Elizabeth? Did they, like all who struggle to create, sometimes feel they would never be delivered of their waiting?

Luke's brief words belie the intensity of Mary and Elizabeth's waiting. So we must imagine what happened during those hours, days, and weeks they shared together. What hopes and fears took form in their hearts and minds as their children took shape in their wombs? How did these women help prepare each other for the births that lay ahead? What stories did these kinswomen weave as they worked and waited?

Perhaps in their waiting these women remembered other women who also knew what it meant to wait, strong women remembered by their people: Tamar, Rahab, Bathsheba, and Ruth. The stories of these women distinguish them as ones who crossed society's boundaries as they responded to God's call. Perhaps in remembering these women who had brought forth life by embracing challenges, Mary and Elizabeth gained the strength to sustain them in their own waiting.

—— **MONDAY** ——

Read Genesis 38.

> Sister Tamar, wait with us;
> bring your thread of deepest brown

like the earth that holds your husbands,
like your hope spilled on the ground.

Bring your dark-hued thread of longing
that gave you strength to wait no more,
to cloak yourself with justice
and claim the promise that was yours.

Bring the thread you spun anew
from the strands of severed trust;
weave it through our sacred longings,
bless it now, and wait with us.
—Jan L. Richardson

Reflect

❖ When have you waited so long for something that you took desperate action?

—— **TUESDAY** ——

Read Joshua 2; 6:15-25.

Sister Rahab, wait with us;
bring your fiery crimson thread
spun from the stalks of flax
where you kept your visitors hid.

Bring the thread as dark as blood
that you risked for their lives spared,
as deep as your saving passion
for those whose lives you shared.

Bring the thread of intuition
that transformed time and fate;
weave it through our changing lives,
bless it now, and with us wait.
—Jan L. Richardson

Reflect

❖ When have you received protection from an unexpected source?

Read 2 Samuel 11–12.

> O Bathsheba, wait with us;
> bring your thread of blue so pale,
> color of your cleansing waters
> carried from devotion's well.
>
> Bring out the tough-spun thread
> that wove a heavy cloth
> streaked with your tears of terror
> and stained with streams of loss.
>
> Bring the thread of wellsprings clear
> birthed anew from sorrow's dust;
> weave it through our birthing waters,
> bless it now, and wait with us.
> —Jan L. Richardson

Reflect

The text leaves Bathsheba almost completely silent as David's actions cause her to lose her husband, her child, and the life she has known.

- ❖ What do you imagine in the gaps of the story—what was happening in Bathsheba's spirit?
- ❖ How is your own spirit responding to this story?

—— **THURSDAY** ——

Read the Book of Ruth.

> Sister Ruth, please wait with us;
> bring your thread of burnished gold,
> hue of sun that lit your path
> on a strange, uncertain road.
>
> Bring the thread of warm compassion,
> of fierce vows spun from tender care,
> of the fires of springtime harvest,
> of the passion you found there.
>
> Bring the thread of bold devotion
> that drew you through a foreign gate;

weave it through our sacred journey,
bless it now, and with us wait.
—Jan L. Richardson

Reflect

❖ When has your love for a friend or companion led you to journey
to an unknown place?

 **FRIDAY**

I sit here on the porch as if in a deep sleep waiting for this unknown child. I
keep hearing this far flight of strange birds going on in the mysterious air
about me. This time has come without warning. How can it be explained?
Everything is dead and closed, the world a stone, and then suddenly
everything comes alive as it has for me, like an anemone on a rock, opening
itself, disclosing itself, and the very stones themselves break open like
bread. . . .

How can it be explained? Suddenly many movements are going on
within me, many things are happening, there is an almost unbearable sense
of sprouting, of bursting encasements, of moving kernels, expanding flesh.
Perhaps it is such an activity that makes a field come alive with millions of
sprouting shoots of corn or wheat. Perhaps it is something like that that
makes a new world.

—Meridel Le Sueur, from "Annunciation" in *Salute to Spring*

Reflect

❖ How does waiting affect the way you experience and move
through time?
❖ What images come to mind when you think about waiting—for a
change, for a child, for the realization of a dream?

SATURDAY

A friend is building a house. As we discussed the highs and lows of such an
undertaking, she said she could hardly wait to be settled into the new place.
But she also commented that she is really trying to enjoy the *process* as
well.

Afterward, I compared her project to my pregnancy. I admit I haven't
put a lot into enjoying the pregnancy. I have been enduring it—just wanting
to be done and have that healthy baby in my arms and get started. But I

realize the waiting is an important time too—anticipating, wondering about this new person growing inside me, savoring the undivided time with my son who is two and a half and knowing that spring comes to this far reach of New England with the birth of my child.

With my friend's insight I hope I can focus on this waiting time as a worthy journey in its own right—a fine place to be now.
—Sally Richardson Carncross

Reflect

❖ What do you enjoy about waiting?

❖ For what or whom do you now wait?

—— SUNDAY ——

We must acknowledge that not all waiting ends in the birth of new life. Babies arrive stillborn. Dreams disperse. Revolutions die.

At these times, community becomes particularly important. Awkwardness and uncertainty may sometimes dull a community's response when a long-awaited birth ends in brokenness. Yet communities with skill in healing know that what sustained us in waiting will sustain us in grief. Our wounds begin to heal as they are bound by strong threads of connection: spirits that recognize and know our inner beings, voices that bless, arms that hold our rage and embrace our sorrow.

We are sustained by hands that span the ages, that contain the strength of generations of women who have waited and who assure us that through our remembering, no life is forever gone, no dream is completely lost, no loss goes untransformed.
—Jan L. Richardson

Reflect

❖ When has your waiting ended in loss?

❖ Where have you found sustenance and healing?

❖ How did the loss influence the dreams and plans you carry now?

—— Meditation ——

Waiting

Waiting
like spinning
motion and stasis

darkness and light
into one strand
fine
and strong

Waiting
like weaving
body and spirit
like threads across the loom
stretched to breaking
aching
for release

Waiting
like folds of cloth
around an ages-old stone
for something,
    anything to hold onto
    in the labor:
    for crushing
    for breaking
    for bringing forth
    grain
    bread
    rivers
    a world.
—Jan L. Richardson

———— ❖ ————

Blessing: *May the presence of all who wait be with you. In your waiting may you deeply feel the strong, sacred, ancient threads that connect you with those who wait: threads of longing, of justice, of devotion, of compassion.*

 4 A Celestial Sign
The Woman Clothed with the Sun

Invocation: *O God who hears all birthing cries, be with me in the wilderness. Nourish me, attend me, be my companion, I pray.*

Text: Revelation 12:1-9, 13-17

Context: The celestially clad woman of Revelation remains rather mysterious. Some scholars consider her an image of Mary (indeed, the Roman Catholic church reads this text on the Feast of the Assumption of Mary); others see her as a symbol of the church itself. Susan Garrett, in "Revelation" from *The Women's Bible Commentary,* perceives her as the people of Israel, who "gave birth to the Messiah *and* to the church." The dazzling array of sun, moon, and stars that surround the woman link her to ancient images familiar to John and his contemporaries.

Whoever he understands her to be, in his vision John witnesses deep truths of the birthing process. The woman clothed with the sun embodies the dangers that often accompany birth, and women the world over intimately know the demons that would destroy what they seek to create: poverty; hunger; war; oppression; isolation; the risk of separation from or death of the child, dream, or hope.

In John's vision, the woman labors alone to bring forth her child. As we witness the revelation, she invites us to attend the birthing, to accompany her in the wilderness, to comfort her pain, to touch her fear, to heal the separation. The revelation calls us to hear those women who know her pain in their own bodies and spirits. In this season of Advent, we look forward to the time when no woman will labor without support.

—— **MONDAY** ——

Early Morning Woman

early morning woman
rising   the sun
          the woman

bending and stretching
with the strength of the child
that moves
in her belly

early morning makes her
a woman that she is
the sun
is her beginning
it is the strength
that guides her child

early morning woman
she begins that way
                    the sun
                    the child
are the moving circle
beginning with the woman
in the early morning
—Joy Harjo in *What Moon Drove Me to This?*

Reflect

❖ What gives you strength and warmth when you are carrying a dream, an idea, a child?

❖ How does your creativity link you to creation?

❖ How does your creativity link you with other creative women?

───── **TUESDAY** ─────

Maria [a Brazilian woman] was only thirty-two years old, and this was her eighth pregnancy. She had had three miscarriages, and the doctor had advised her not to have another baby. But because she suffered from malnutrition, the birth control pills the doctor had given her (which Maria had hidden from her husband) didn't work. So she was pregnant again. Also she was very weak. After spending hours in labor, she finally delivered a baby girl. But Maria was not recovering. She was bleeding too much. I had never before seen death and life so closely linked. The baby girl was screaming "life," and Maria, who had brought forth life, who had given life, was dying.
—Wanda Deifelt, from "Of Gardens and Theology: Women of Faith Respond" in *The Power We Celebrate*

Reflect

- ❖ What are some dragons that attend the process of birth?
- ❖ How do attitudes toward motherhood affect a woman's ability to give birth to herself or to others?
- ❖ What social realities affect women's choices regarding birth, mothering, and other creative acts?

—— WEDNESDAY ——

"Ah, sisters," the elder said as she gazed at the woman huddled in their midst. They had found her at the edge of the wilderness, bleeding and nearly dead beside the shallow stream. She had the appearance of one who had journeyed far at too great a pace, and though she bore the marks of childbirth, there was no child to be seen.

"Ah, sisters," she repeated. "We were prepared, but we were not prepared for this."

Water was brought. The woman grimaced with pain, but she remained silent as they washed her wounds. Strange streaks, like a claw mark, ran scarlet across her belly. Brilliant burns laced her body.

Someone placed a jar of fragrant ointment in the elder's hand. Moving to anoint the woman's wounds, the elder stopped at the sound of the woman's voice.

"Mother," she whispered haltingly. "Who can heal the wound of a woman torn from her child?"

—Jan L. Richardson

Reflect

- ❖ What kind of place in the wilderness do you imagine God prepared for the celestial woman?
- ❖ What wildernesses have you inhabited, or do you inhabit now?
- ❖ What did you find within them that would enable you to provide a place of comfort for this woman?

—— THURSDAY ——

Nov. 9, 1982
Beth greetings,

Very happy you wrote. . . .

I'm praying a way will be made for me to get the needed Bond money together. I haven't seen my Son for over a year now. Each second I'm away from him the lonely feelings I endure Becomes worse. I try to remain strong, at times it's difficult. When I'm at the lowest, I usually hear from beautiful people such as you.

Cold weather is now here. I missed the entire summer. I was on lock from July 9th till a week and a half ago. They put me on lock for defending a young girl that was being used and abused. They now have me on Closed Custody, that's a little better than what I was on. At least I'm allowed phone calls now. I get 2 hours out of my cell.

I've had plenty of time to really know myself. I meditated a lot, and steadily prayed.

—Rita Silk-Nauni, from a letter in *A Gathering of Spirit: A Collection by North American Indian Women*

Reflect

❖ What are some of the wildernesses where women live?

❖ What similarities do you find in Rita's story and that of the woman from Revelation 12?

—— **FRIDAY** ——

Woman of South Africa (excerpt)

You who watch
Your children
Die of hunger
Because there is no food to eat.

You who watch
Your children gripped by fear
And lack of hope
As they see no way out.

You who watch your children
seized and murdered
When they dare to rise up
Against the Oppressors.
You who watch
Your children
Detained by Security
For months and months
Without a trial

. . . .

You who watch
With courage
But are refused a reason
For all this suffering.

I salute You
Woman of South Africa!
—Celene Jack in *Creation Fire: A CAFRA Anthology of Caribbean Women's Poetry*

Reflect

Salute. The word comes from the Latin and conveys a wish for good health. More than a gesture, in this context it conveys the recognition of a world of pain and of dreams.

❖ What is your connection with these women?
❖ How is their good health linked with yours?
❖ In what ways can you dare to dwell in the wilderness together?

—— SATURDAY ——

Music began, softly at first and then pulsing deeper and more loudly. A woman who had grown up in Saudi Arabia stepped into the center of the circle. She was robed in the traditional dress of Saudi women who are midwives to a woman in labor. She began the birthing dance—rhythmic, throbbing. Her body undulated with the music, first slowly, then faster and faster. The circle swayed back and forth; we rang the traditional bells, emphasizing the birthing beat. Her long hair flew round her head as she twisted and bent her body. Hers was the body of woman. Hers was our body. The dance was ours. . . . There was One Woman in the room and she was dancing the creation dance.

At the end of the dance the dancing woman carried a basket of red roses into the circle of women and, giving a rose to each woman, proclaimed:

"You are a Birthgiver, clothed in the Sun."

And with that gift the worship was complete.
—Christin Lore Weber in *WomanChrist*

Reflect

❖ What rituals, worship services, plays, concerts, or other events

that celebrate the creativity of women have you experienced?
- ❖ What names have these experiences enabled you to claim?

Vision

And a great portent appeared:
    a pregnant woman
    crying out in birth pangs
    in the agony of giving birth.

And another portent appeared:
    three women
    approaching her
    and encircling her.

One held the woman,
    and the warmth of her touch
    clothed her through the long night.

One wept with the woman,
    and their tears became as stars
    giving them vision in the shadows.

One sang to the woman
    until the baby's head crowned
    like a new moon in a midnight sky.

The woman named the child Compassion,
    and laughter filled the place
    where earth and heaven embraced.
—Jan L. Richardson

Reflect
- ❖ When have you been a midwife, giving support to someone who was laboring to give birth to a dream, an idea, a vision, a child?
- ❖ How have others participated with you in bringing something to birth?
- ❖ In the midst of the Advent season, how do you envision the birthing of a new creation?

Kyrie

Woman birthing alone:
    sun have mercy.
Woman in travail:
    moon have mercy.
Woman crying out:
    stars have mercy.
Woman in flight:
    wind have mercy.
Woman in the flood:
    earth have mercy.
Woman in the wilderness:
    creatures have mercy.
Woman in mourning:
    God have mercy.
Woman in our midst:
    let us have mercy.
—Jan L. Richardson

—— ❖ ——

Blessing: *In labor, may God give strength. In danger, may God give protection. In the wilderness, may God give presence. In mourning, may God give companions. In time, may God give you life anew.*

5 **Birther of the Holy**
Mary

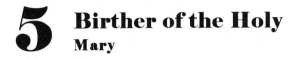

Invocation: *Birthing God, be with me as I labor to bring forth what is within me.*

Text: Luke 2:1-7

Context: "Give me a call if anything breaks," my brother said to my sister and me as we concluded our phone conversation. "Like Sally's water."

I turned to look at my pregnant sister as Scott and I chuckled. Sally's mouth was agape but not with laughter. The phone dropped from her hand as she pulled at her skirt.

"We'll call you back!" I sputtered to my brother.

It was time. The weeks and months of waiting, wondering, and planning quickly dissolved into water, blood, groans, and deep cries as Sally and the baby labored together into the night. Nurses poked and monitored her; my brother-in-law and I plied her with wet rags, ice chips, and soothing music; we held her as she pushed.

She remembers little of this. She had a baby to birth. A shattering groan, a final great push, a rush of blood and water and . . . Baby Scott.

And I wonder . . . as this woman's groans gave way to a new child's cries, did the stars dance in ancient recognition? Did they remember a scene that our gleaming nativities and depictions of pastel-garbed Mary, Joseph, and Jesus belie: a scene of laboring, of groaning, of birthing's "great pure effort"?

What emotions must have gripped Mary and Joseph as Mary lay, homeless and a stranger, in the labor of birthing? As her child strained against her flesh, did Mary regret her choice? From where did she draw her strength? Did anyone hear her cries? Today do we hear the cries that rise from isolated, impoverished, makeshift places?

—— **MONDAY** ——

Another outcome of the kind of sex education, if you can call it that, I had received, was that, even at this late stage, the birth process was still somewhat of a mystery to me. I had heard of women screaming, breaking furniture, calling out to the beasts, the men who had inflicted the pregnancy on them. In the throes of giving birth, they called on them so they could kill them for making them go through such agony. Alone. It was with much trepidation that I awaited my turn in that special hell for women.

Therefore, the morning I woke up feeling a slight heaviness not unlike that announcing the advent of my periods, I took little notice. I suffered severe period pains as a young woman. What I felt that morning, compared to what I was used to, really hardly registered as pain. Never mind Labor Pains.

By evening, I happened to mention this to Mother who had popped in for a quick visit. . . .

Mother, herself veteran of eight live deliveries and at least one miscarriage I have vague recollections of—I have never heard it mentioned except when it was actually happening and immediately thereafter—sent for the midwife.

—Sindiwe Magona in *To My Children's Children*

Reflect

❖ What silences, tales, traditions, and stories about birthing did you encounter as you grew up?

—— **TUESDAY** ——

Suddenly the coming is upon you, and time dissolves. There is only the present in its gleaming, stark clarity. No past, no future, there is only now—this time which is strangely timeless in its intensity. There are as many different experiences of birth as there are women, but for all of them the waiting is over. The promised one bursts forth, new life sings out, the primal rush of blood and water carries the miracle into our arms. It is a moment whose mystery is timeless.

—Wendy M. Wright in *The Vigil*

Reflect

Think of experiences of birthing and other acts of creativity.

❖ What images or words stand out in your memory?

❖ What was your sense of time during the laboring? during the creating?

❖ How did your creation compare with your expectations?

The Midwife's Song

The inn is shut against the cold,
all the guests are warm inside;
but from the hearth so crowded
I could hear your birthing cries.

So little can I give you—
some strips of cloth, some firelight;
but young one, you have greater needs
as you labor through this night.

I cannot take your pain,
but your body I have worn;
to its core my flesh remembers
the ache of new life's being born.

We'll share our strength, my sister,
born from ages of women wise,
till all creation joins the song
born of your birthing cries.
—Jan L. Richardson

Reflect

- ❖ Where do we find similar conditions of birthing today?
- ❖ What details of the birthing scene and story do you imagine Luke left out?

—— **THURSDAY** ——

Magnificat of the Stable

My soul rests confidently in the animal warmth
    and the lantern light of this simple place, Yahweh,
    and my spirit rejoices in the privacy of this time of birthing
    we share with you, O God of Creation,
    for you come alive again tonight
    in the blood and water of your people.
Yes, this is the time we have waited for.
    This is the moment of blessing.

Holy is birth,
>   and you shall show yourself from age to age
>   in those who enter into creation with you.

You have shown the power of a dream enfleshed
>   and we are humbled.

You have pulled down all our strivings
>   and lifted up this simple, common moment.

This stable is filled with good things,
>   new life and happy people.
>   Are those in the inn rooms as satisfied?

You have come to Israel,
>   mindful of our shared nature,
>   . . . according to the promise of Eden . . .
>   mindful of our nature to seek the wisdom of new life together
>   as long as we walk the earth.

—Ann Johnson in *Miryam of Nazareth*

Reflect

- ❖ The power of a dream enfleshed . . . what happens beyond the birthing, beyond the creating?
- ❖ How do you imagine Mary in the moments and days after she gave birth to Jesus?
- ❖ What was in Mary's mind and emotions . . . what did she think, feel, pray, remember?

FRIDAY

And finally, human birth is a bearing. In spirituality this places before us the questions of what we are bearing in our spirituality. It poses the question of what we are willing to bear for the sake of Transforming ourselves and the face of the Earth. Birthing would say we bear bodiliness, enfleshment, new life; passion, emotion, and feeling; blood and water; labor and pain. Birthing would teach we bear human selves and remind us that genuine spirituality always leads in this direction too. The giving birth to our own selves and to other selves for the sake of one another is giving birth to dreams and customs and spiritualities that make life human for all the people of the world. Birthing would remind us that every new creation means the entire Universe must be ready to shift and make room; it makes midwives of us all. Birthing would teach, finally, that we are called to give birth to the God waiting to be born from us, that we are, in Meister Eckhart's description:

"Mothers of God; for God is always needing to be born."
—Maria Harris in *Dance of the Spirit: The Seven Steps of Women's Spirituality*

Reflect

❖ How do you sense God's being born through you?
❖ How do you work with others to birth God into the world?
❖ What transformations take place within you in this process?

—— **SATURDAY** ——

Newborn

Like the layered heat of
a summer sun, you awaken early.
Soft, your cries reach in-

to my dreams and motion me awake
to rock you. Your skin
bunches warm, elastic. Quick,

your small mouth stretches
wide around my tender breast. I tense,
a burn like flash-fires.

Slowly, I melt into the rhythm pull,
giving. This makes the pain
bearable as you tug me towards some

semblance of where we both
began. I think I am awake and watching
your eyes flicker sparks

that stare, unfocused. I imagine
you still see the cloudy,
enclosed waters from the place you were

before you passed through me,
to air. Unseen, like wind shifts, you
are sudden breath, a panting

deep that opens fear up in my heart. I
have to hurry, feeling
your lips set and hardening, feeling

your jaws lock and your tongue
sticking, before you get too used to flesh.
Before you learn to bite

down hard, I must teach you how
to eat of the earth
and how to drink the water.
—Valerie Jean in *Double Stitch: Black Women Write about Mothers
and Daughters*

Reflect

❖ How do you nourish what you have created?

❖ How does the relationship change?

—— **SUNDAY** ——

A Psalm of Bringing to Birth

Leader: Women, what will we bring to birth
            in the world of the new creation?

All: Wisdom and justice,
            peace and compassion,
            concern for all God's little ones,
            for the homeless and the destitute,
            the hungry, and all who bear the brunt
            of indifference and oppression.

Leader: Women, what will we bring to birth
            on the earth of the new creation?

All: A deep respect for our planet,
            its windsong and its waters,
            its topsoil and its forests,
            and a oneness with the wilderness
            that is image of our soul.

Leader: Women, what will we bring to birth
            in the church of the new creation?

All: A total disdain for power
            that diminishes or destroys,
            divestment of wealth and status,

a sharing of human resources
based on mutuality
and the sudden surprise of grace.

Leader: Women, what will we bring to birth
in the hearts of the new creation?

All: An unbreakable bond in the Spirit
that binds as one all brothers and sisters,
transcending class, color, culture,
religion, race, and gender,
that treats no personal preference,
no physical or spiritual difference
as aberration or handicap.

Leader: One has been born among us
Who heralds such liberation.
Human liberation,
women's liberation
have taken flesh among us
and in Spirit dwell with us.

All: Holy the woman who helped this happen.
Blessed are we when we give birth
to the Word made flesh
in us.

—Miriam Therese Winter in *WomanWord*

Reflect
❖   What visions, creations, and birthings have these days and weeks
of expectation brought you?
❖   Where have you encountered surprising grace this Advent?

—— **Meditation** ——

Thanksgiving

And on the night in which Mary delivered,
she placed her hands over her round, full womb
and whispered,
"Flesh of my flesh,
this is my body

which I willingly opened to you.
May you always remember
to feed on the bread of integrity."

In the same manner, she whispered,
"Child,
you share my blood;
freely shall I shed it
in bringing you to birth.
May you always remember
to drink deeply from the cup of wisdom."

O Mary, we remember these your gifts,
and we join our hearts to yours in rejoicing,
    Glory to the God of generations!
    For heaven and earth have met
        in the womb of a woman.
    Peace to all people
        who bring forth the Christ.
—Jan L. Richardson

—— ❖ ——

Blessing: *Peace to you, God-bearer, God-birther. May you create with integrity and wisdom, and may your creating connect you with all who labor to bring forth a new creation.*

6 Wise Midwife of the Community
Anna

Invocation: *Loving God, you allowed many to share in your birth. Grant me wisdom to recognize and care for you as you are birthed in the community that I share.*

Text: Luke 2:22-24, 36-38

Context: Angels. Shepherds. Wise men. Simeon. The Gospels tell of many who greeted Jesus in the months following his birth. These accounts testify not only to the wonder of the incarnation but also affirm that birthing does not end with the physical delivery of the child. We are born into a community. The community acts as midwife and "othermother" as it prepares for the child, receives the child, and nurtures the child in her or his growth. (Patricia Hill Collins defines "othermothers" as "women who assist blood-mothers by sharing mothering responsibilities." See "Bloodmothers, Other-mothers, and Women-Centered Networks" in her book *Black Feminist Thought.*)

Anna plays a significant role in the birthing of Jesus into the community. We find her in the temple, the heart of the life and worship of the Hebrew community and the place to which Mary, Joseph, and Jesus have come to fulfill the obligations following the birth of a child. Anna's status as a prophet indicates her wisdom in divine matters, a wisdom enhanced by, and perhaps born of her long life and her complete devotion in the temple. This wisdom enables Anna to be receptive to God and to perceive instantly the significance of Jesus' arrival in the temple.

According to scripture, Anna is the first witness to Jesus as God's earthly bearer of redemption. Not only does she receive Jesus into the community, but she also takes the good news of his arrival out to the community. In doing so, Anna demonstrates that women's gifts as vessels of life do not depend solely on biology but on receptivity and strength, present at any age. In her rhythm of receiving Jesus into the community and taking him out to it, Anna is bearer and birther, midwife and mother.

---

* *If this is the first Sunday after Epiphany, use Week 7.*

Caroline's Baptism

On Thanksgiving Day I baptize her with water and words, speaking of the far-flung community that surrounds my niece in this moment. We scooped the water from the lake that carried so many stories for us, holding our memories in its depths. So many of us who dwelt near its shores have scattered now, but on this day of welcoming we know and celebrate the familiar contours of our community.

And we who have just shared in the Thanksgiving feast welcome our newest member with water and words. We continue our feasting with the breaking of bread and the sharing of the cup. And we remember the One who brought each of us to birth. We know that on this day, our community includes not only those who have gathered within the walls of this small church. We remember, in the water and the words, in the loaf and the cup, that we share this day with all who have gone before—with those who shaped this land and shaped these lives, with those who walked on the sacred shores before us.

With water and words, we bless Caroline and those who hold her on this Thanksgiving Day. And in the silences I wonder what other words she will know, what other feasts will attend the passages still to come. I want words with which to bless her as she becomes a woman, words that will surround her in her turnings and returnings—words to help her know the stories that flow through her community, words to help her know how blessed she is, what a feast this life is, how freely she may choose.
—Jan L. Richardson

Reflect
* ❖ Into what community were you born?
* ❖ How you were received, and by whom?

—— **TUESDAY** ——

Child care is a responsibility that can be shared with other childrearers, with people who do not live with children. This form of parenting is revolutionary in this society because it takes place in opposition to the idea that parents, especially mothers, should be the only childrearers. Many people raised in black communities experienced this type of community-based child care. Black women who had to leave the home and work to help provide for families could not afford to send children to day care centers and such centers did not always exist. They relied on people in their communities to help. Even in families where the mother stayed home, she could also rely on people in the community to help.

This kind of shared responsibility for child care can happen in small community settings where people know and trust one another. It cannot happen in those settings if parents regard children as their "property," their "possession."

—bell hooks in *Feminist Theory: From Margin to Center*

Reflect
- ❖ Beyond your immediate family, who cared for you as you grew up?
- ❖ Who decides who will care for the children in your community?
- ❖ How are children treated and included in the community?

—— **WEDNESDAY** ——

If we suffer from too many myths about Mary, we hardly know Anna exists. And yet she brings a gift to the birth of Jesus that is just as precious as the one Elizabeth and Mary bring. She brings her gift of witness. In the day and age in which we live, witness is sometimes seen only as a very personal and non-threatening activity, one in which Christians should engage for the good of their souls. This is true but we all know witness is much more than that....

Remember the gift of witness given to us by Peggy Hutchison, one of the defendants in the sanctuary trial who was convicted of violating immigration laws for helping Central Americans fleeing their homelands. She received a suspended prison sentence and five years probation. She had taken a job in a project that the church said was important—helping refugees fleeing persecution. Little did she know or understand where her witness would take her—or the price she would have to pay.

—Haviland C. Houston, from "The Gifts of the Three Wise Women" in *engage/social action*

Reflect
- ❖ How does our care for others in our community witness to God's care for us?
- ❖ What risks does this caring for others in our community involve?
- ❖ What price do you think Anna might have paid for her witness?

I use prophecy, and the word "prophetic," as the Hebrew Bible does. . . .
The Hebrew prophets were women and men who had come face-to-face
with a God of justice, Who felt sorrow and pathos over the human
condition. And these original prophets spoke the word of this grieving
God, providing a model for others who attempt to do that today. . . .

I think the prophetic spirit can be found today in one question that
illuminates all the others: "What about the children?" The first person I
heard asking that question was Molly Rush, mother of six, grandmother
of two, and director of the Thomas Merton Peace Center in Pittsburgh.
Because of her directorship she was often asked to join community
efforts and demonstrations protesting the proliferation of nuclear arms,
nuclear warheads, nuclear missiles, and nuclear submarines—the whole
array of lethal weapons our society has created. And her response was
always the same. She would think of her family of six and say, "I'm
sorry; I can't go with you—*what about the children*?" But one day she
heard her own question with reference not to the time given for the
protest, but with reference to the impact of the weapons and what they
could mean for her own children and the children of the world. And so
she began to say no [to the weapons]. Publicly. Both in communion and
community. . . .

This is the impact of prophetic speech as a discipline, spoken in
community. It arises from our acknowledging the brokenness in life, and
from our attending to the agonies of children. But it also arises from the
sense of what makes a *complete* spirituality, one that is personal and
communal and awake to our call as humans to move toward healing and
wholeness. That healing and wholeness are not just our own; they are
also the healing and the wholeness we might offer, as women, to a
bruised, bent, and broken world.

—Maria Harris in *Dance of the Spirit: The Seven Steps of Women's
Spirituality*

Reflect

❖ What dangers attend the birthing and growing of a child in the
community?

❖ In your past or present community, who has acted as a prophet in
the midst of these dangers?

Wise One Welcoming

I long to see
what in your eyes he perceived:
stars of all those
nights of prayer,
sun of all those
mornings of devotion,
flames of wisdom
born of all those years of waiting.

Oh to see,
to be borne
in the gaze of
the wise one welcoming
the wise one welcoming
the wise one welcoming home.
—Jan L. Richardson

Reflect

❖   What practices help you welcome others into your community?

——— SATURDAY ———

People praying together is a beginning—and still the Earth is asking more of us. She is asking that we take one another's hands and that we grow gardens together, that we put aside the idea of "my" garden and "your" garden. It is "our" garden. Look at some of the old people living around you. Whatever they are doing or not doing, they have done more than you—and they have something to say. When society falls flat, when the culture is dying, the elders are disrespected and we forget how to give or receive. There are things that one can *live*, not just pray and think about. . . . These things we have forgotten, and that forgetting is the sickness of the time. We have all been given clear direction as to what right life, right action is, and yet it has come to the point now where many even doubt that the family is something to be preserved. Family is the circle of humanity. Everything is our relative. . . . The family becomes the clan and the nation and the whole planet.
—Dhyani Ywahoo in *Voices of Our Ancestors: Teachings from the Cherokee Wisdom Fire*

Reflect

❖ Whom do you consider to be part of your family?

❖ How do people of different ages in your family share wisdom?

❖ What price do we pay for the sin of forgetting?

—— SUNDAY ——

The poet Barbara Mor writes in *Crow Call* that an old woman's hand "is the first hand of earth." I wonder what Jesus felt in the touch of this old woman's hand as they met in the temple. Did his infant skin feel the hollows of time in the creases of her flesh? Did he who had just passed through the birthing waters sense the years of her waiting, flowing like rivers across her palms? Did he whose limbs ran with holy human blood perceive the landscape of the holy on earth in the veins that laced her hands? Did he feel the heartbeat of creation in the tips of her fingers?

This first hand of earth, greeting the hope of the world enfleshed and cradled in his mother's arms—what must have passed between them; what must have been passed on?

—Jan L. Richardson

Reflect

❖ What do you imagine Anna carried in her hands after eighty-four years of living?

❖ What wisdom might Anna have handed to Jesus in a touch of his cheek or in a cradling embrace?

❖ What wisdom might Anna hand to us as we seek to widen the circle of our community?

—— Meditation ——

Canticle of Anna

Rejoice, O sun!
Sing out, O moon!
For God has made wide
creation's womb.
A child, a child;
make way, make room!
Our wholeness is coming;
salvation is soon.

Give praise, O stars!
And dance, O earth!
For all are bid come
to share in the birth.
Take hands, join hearts,
be whole, be free!
And all shall be mothers
of divinity.
—Jan L. Richardson

———— ❖ ————

Blessing: *May you be open to the wisdom of the ages in unexpected places. May you know the touch of many hands as together we care for the holy in our midst.*

Wisdom's Journey

Epiphany and the Season Following

THE EARLIEST CHRISTIANS CELEBRATED EPIPHANY as one of the three primary holy days of the liturgical year. Deriving from the Greek word *epiphaneia*, meaning "appearance" or "coming," Epiphany more so than Christmas celebrated the manifestation of divinity on earth through Jesus Christ. The celebrations that occurred during Epiphany found their origins not only in Jesus' birth but also his baptism and his first recorded miracle, the turning of water into wine at the wedding feast in Cana. For Christians in the East, Epiphany remains the primary holy day in this season.

As Christianity developed, those of the West focused more specifically on the birth narratives and began to associate the celebration of the Incarnation primarily with Christmas. Epiphany became a less celebrated holiday and focused mainly on the journey of the Magi, the wise ones, to honor the newborn Jesus. Western Christians began to observe the celebration of Jesus' baptism on the Sunday following Epiphany.

It is not necessary to choose one meaning of Epiphany over another. The traditions of both East and West remind us that our journey does not end on Christmas Day; rather, it begins there. Often we in the West forget that Christmas is not one day but twelve. Even when Epiphany, the last day, passes, it has but prepared us for the journey through the year to come.

The journey of the wise ones, which characterizes our Epiphany celebrations in the West, calls to mind the journey of Wisdom through portions of Hebrew scripture. Personified as a woman, Wisdom, or *Hokmah* in Hebrew, appears in such places as Proverbs and in the apocryphal books Sirach and Wisdom of Solomon. Wisdom offers us an image of God's wisdom enfleshed. As we see Wisdom preparing her feast, delighting with God in creation, giving instruction, pondering the mysteries of God, and inviting us to follow the holy path, we glimpse ways in which we too can draw closer to God and walk with wisdom in our sacred journeys.

During Epiphany and the season that follows, we will journey with some women who have embodied attributes of Wisdom as recorded in the Hebrew scriptures. Some weeks we will accompany one particular woman; other weeks we will explore an attribute through the perspectives of a variety of women. Through sharing in their journeys, may we perceive Wisdom's movement through our own lives.

A Prayer for the Beginning of Epiphany

*Along the journey come times of pausing, of surprise, of wonder at what
we discover on the way. We may be so intent on what lies ahead that we
find ourselves occasionally amazed by one who has journeyed toward us,
who meets us by chance or by purpose with a word, a gesture, a touch we
most need to receive. Epiphany is such a time. In the midst of the journey
we pause to ponder, to listen, to marvel at the ways God appears to us.*

You may light a candle.

Maker of the universe, fashioner of the stars,
who dwells within time and beyond time,
hear this prayer:

if I have failed to perceive you
when you have appeared
in the face of a friend,
if I have neglected to feed you
when you have come
with the hunger of a stranger,
if I have not embraced you
when you have sought me out of
a sister or brother's poverty,
if I have not laughed and played with you
when you greeted me with the delight of a child,
forgive me.

Open my eyes, my hands, my arms, my heart
to know your appearing and to celebrate
the flesh-shaped mystery of Emmanuel,
God with us.

Make my heart a dwelling place ready to receive you
in even the bleakest spaces,
to delight at your appearing even as the animals
who made welcome for the birth of wonder.
—Jan L. Richardson

7 Wisdom Perceives Times
Rites of Passage

Invocation: *God of seasons and times, changes and cycles, days past and yet to come, be with me in this turning of time. May the wisdom of each passage free me from fear of what lies ahead.*

Text: Wisdom of Solomon 8:8

> And if anyone longs for wide experience, she knows the things of old, and infers the things to come; she understands turns of speech and the solutions of riddles; she has foreknowledge of signs and wonders and the outcome of seasons and times.

Context: In the liturgical year, this week marks the baptism of Jesus by John the Baptist. In Matthew's account (Matt. 3:13-17), this public act is the first time we see Jesus as an adult. His baptism begins a rite of passage from his former life to his public ministry. But baptism does not complete the rite nor does the descent of the Spirit. Matthew tells us that Jesus then goes into the wilderness, where he fasts for forty days and nights and endures temptations from the devil. This time of wilderness fasting and temptation is a passage for Jesus. It is a time of gaining clarity, of shedding other concerns, of intuiting, of claiming vision for his unfolding life.

Passages mark our lives, signaling a turning in our journey. They herald our entry into a new phase of life, a different relationship with our community, a keener awareness, a deeper wisdom. The passage may be slow or speedy, solitary or communal, celebrated or unrecognized. Rarely can we rush it. Our own bodies tell us this, as in the larger cycle from birth to death and in the periodic cycles we experience for a season of our lives, we come to know intimately the spiraled shape of time's passing.

What prompts these turns in our journey, these rites of passage? And what sustains us in the wildernesses that often accompany them? Perhaps what sustains us is the whisper of Wisdom, the knower of seasons, saying, "It is time." Perhaps Wisdom reminds us of what Jesus knew: even in the wilderness one may encounter angels.

Beginning

Exiled upon this ledge
   I stand
naked with unknowing,
facing winds that blow
hurricanes within me.

Standing as I was held
(their world beginning where
mine ended)
shrivelled, wet and crying—
Mama why did you expel me,
left me abandoned upon this
ledge of
beginnings?

You smiled,
exulting in my newness
as I fumbled to train
uncertain steps
to balance on edges.

You said that learning
begins with falling off
of this ledge.
—Jennifer Rahim in *Creation Fire: A CAFRA Anthology of Caribbean Women's Poetry*

Reflect
❖   Where in your life have you found passages, ledges of beginnings?

—— **TUESDAY** ——

My name became a matter of importance. I wanted her [my grandmother's] name to be mine. I wanted to be called by her name, not the name I had been called since birth. I had asked my mother several times why she gave me my first name, and she said she was reading a book at the time I was born, and she liked the name of the little girl in the story. She hoped I'd be a girl like the storybook character. I had never been especially fond of my name, but I had never thought about it very much—until then. Since my middle name was the name of my grandmother, I decided that I would be "Elizabeth" from then on. . . . I informed my parents of my decision. I felt that what I was doing was right. They were stunned, I am sure, but they asked me why I wanted to change my name after all these years—nine of them! I said that I wanted to think it over for a little while, but I knew that I wanted to be called after my grandmother. Her name of "Elizabeth" meant something to me, but the other name—the one I'd been called—was a name from a storybook, and it didn't have any real meaning for me. . . .

At breakfast the next morning, I told them it was final—from that moment on, I was "Elizabeth."
—Elizabeth Welch in *Learning to Be 85*

Reflect
- ❖ Where does your name come from?
- ❖ What rites of passage have involved your name—through changing it or claiming it?

——— WEDNESDAY ———

In my second year at [Hebrew Union College], in a wonderful old classroom overlooking 68th Street [in New York City]. . . . Rabbi Kravitz said, "There is no important moment in the lifetime of a Jew for which there is no blessing." And then I realized that it was not true. There had been important moments in my lifetime for which there was no blessing . . . like when I first got my period. There in the classroom overlooking 68th Street I became again the thirteen year old girl running to tell her mother she had just got her period. And I heard again my mother tell me that when she got her first period my grandmother slapped her. I could almost feel the force of my grandmother's hand on my mother's face, the shame, the confusion, the anger. I remembered my grandmother's explanation when I asked her why; she answered, "Your mother was losing blood, she was pale, she needed color in her cheek, the evil eye, poo poo poo." And, as I thought back to that time, I understood that there should have been a blessing—*sh'asani eisha, she'hechianu* [Thank you, God, for having made me a woman]—because holiness was present at that moment.
—Laura Geller, from "Encountering the Divine Presence" in *Four Centuries of Jewish Women's Spirituality*

Reflect

- ❖ What do you remember about your first period?
- ❖ Whom did you tell, and how did she or he respond?
- ❖ What rites of passage in your life do you long to have recognized and blessed by your community?

——— THURSDAY ———

I left home when I was twenty-two years old. I would like to say that my reasons for leaving were the same as any young adult's, but that would not be true. I wanted my independence, as everyone says, but what independence meant for me as a disabled woman was more than wanting to live closer to my job or having a social and sexual life unhindered by my parents. (The absence of sexual activity was then so total that I regarded myself as nearly neuter.) I left because I feared the alternative: living with my aging parents, possibly for the rest of my life. I needed to find out whether or not I could take care of myself. . . .

The next morning [after moving into a dim, barely-accessible apartment in Boston's Back Bay] was Sunday. I awoke at nine and lay there on my bed, blissfully surveying my books, clothes, couch, walls, floor, ceiling, and door, luxuriating in my splendid squalor. I could let people in or out. I could buy the food I wanted, eat when I wanted, go to bed or stay up when I wanted, go out when I wanted. *I* would choose. I no longer had to come home early because my parents liked to go to bed early. I no longer had to ask my father to drive me anywhere. I could experience whatever presented itself, without asking my parents if it was all right with them. That was real independence. I thought of all that freedom and the new life I had begun. As I threw back the covers—I remember as if it were this morning—an incredibly wide grin streamed across my face.

—Cheryl Davis, from "Disability and the Experience of Architecture" in *Rethinking Architecture: Design Students and Physically Disabled People*

Reflect

- ❖ If you have left home, in what ways was that leaving a rite of passage?
- ❖ How did your leaving affect your relationship with the various members of your family?
- ❖ What challenges did the leaving involve?

Mother

I wish that I could talk with her again.
That's what I thought of when I thought of home,
Always supposing I had a home to come to.
If she were here, we'd warm the Chinese pot
To brew a jasmine-scented elixir,
And I would tell her how my life has been—
All the parts that don't make sense to me,
And she would let me talk until the parts
Fitted together.

That will never be.
She couldn't wait for me to come to her—
Ten years away. I couldn't wish for her
To wait, all blind and helpless as she was.
So now I have come home to emptiness:
No silly welcome-rhyme, no happy tears,
No eager questioning. No way to get
An answer to my questions. Silence fills
The rooms that once were cheery with her song,
And all the things I wanted to talk out
With her are locked forever in my heart.

I wander through the rooms where she is not.
Alone I sit on the hassock by her chair,
And there, at last, I seem to hear her voice:
"You're a big girl now. You can work things out."
—Bea Exner Liu in *Looking for Home: Women Writing about Exile*

Reflect

❖ As both you and your mother (or whoever cared for you as a child) have aged, what changes have occurred in your relationship?

—— **SATURDAY** ——

And then there is *intentional celebration*. I have known for a long time now that life is sustained when life is sacrament. When our lives become a ceaseless process of transforming the ordinary into the sacred then hope is forever renewed. Celebration is not always happy or joyous, but it is always meaning-filled and often redemptive. It is no small thing to celebrate a person's life in this midst of mourning death. It is painful to celebrate the leaving of a home, even in the face of a promising move. It is a challenge to celebrate the gifts of a relationship, knowing its end was not your choice. Our celebrations remind us that the sacred touches us in this moment, has touched us in the past, and will touch us in the future. . . . Whether we light candles in remembrance, prepare a meal in celebration of another's birth, or write our check to Greenpeace in quiet silence, we are a people called to *celebrate*.

—Chris Smith, from "Feminist Spirituality" in *Wellsprings: A Journal for United Methodist Clergywomen*

Reflect

❖ What are you going to do about a passage in your life that has gone uncelebrated, unmarked?

❖ What celebration or ritual of remembrance might you create to honor its importance, whether it was a grievous or joyous passage?

—————— **SUNDAY** ——————

Initiation is not a predictable process. It moves forward fitfully, through moments of clear seeing, dramatic episodes of feeling, subtle intuitions, vague contemplative states. Dreams arrive, bringing guidance we frequently cannot accept. Years pass, during which we know that we are involved in something that cannot be easily named. We wake to a sense of confusion, know that we are in dangerous conflict, cannot define the nature of what troubles us. All change is like this. It circles around, snakes back on itself, finds detours, leads us a merry chase, starts us out it seems all over again from where we were in the first place. And then suddenly, when we least expect it, something opens a door, discovers a threshold, shoves us across.

—Kim Chernin in *Reinventing Eve*

Reflect

❖ Where are you now in your journey—in the passage? on the threshold? emerging into a new place?

Blessing

Blessed are you, O God, for having made me a woman.
In the intimate darkness of my mother's womb,
    you knew me and called me good.
Keeper of time, maker of seasons,
    you journey with me through each turning;
in my birthing, you are there
in my growing, you are there
in my bleeding, you are there
in my bearing, you are there
in my deepening, you are there
in my returning, you are there.

Bless these sacred seasons, O God,
    that each turning may bring me into Wisdom's arms.
—Jan L. Richardson

Blessing: *May you know many seasons; may each passage go well for you, bringing insight, bringing wisdom, bringing peace.*

8 Following Wisdom's Steps
On the Journey

Invocation: *Move with me, O God. Make me wise to your steps, to your paths, to your gifts along the way.*

Text: Sirach (Ecclesiasticus) 51:13-15

> While I was still young, before I went on my travels, I sought wisdom openly in my prayer. Before the temple I asked for her, and I will search for her until the end. From the first blossom to the ripening grape my heart delighted in her; from my youth I followed her steps.

Context: Christmas break. I practically fled to Tallahassee, looking for a place to regroup. Over pizza by candlelight on the shore of a lake, Kary listened as I tried to make some sense out of the last few months and sought to discern where my journey should lead. The stars overhead winked at me but gave me no obvious sign.

I saw Brenda on my way out of town, and she handed me a tape as we said good-bye. I popped it into the tape deck as I headed toward my parents' home, and the music kept me company as the trees rushed past. The Indigo Girls reminded me that at moments of decision along the journey, every step offers its own wisdom.

The theme of life as a journey helps us understand the movement of our lives, yet at times it also encourages us to devote more attention to reaching our destination efficiently than to savoring the path. Wisdom is born of openness to the adaptations, improvisations, and detours often required or chosen in journeys, of the capacity to delight in what we can learn along the way. We pray for vision and for strength. And in our emerging lives, we also pray to recognize that in our openness, our questions, and our encounters, Epiphany happens along the way.

—— **MONDAY** ——

His [Jesus'] is a call that frees. But the call is only one part of the imagery

of the star's season into which the Christian community has lived. The call is not an ending but a beginning. The birth of the baby invites us into a search. I think the simple truth that is being held out here is that at its richest the Christian life is not so much a life lived as though all the answers were given, but a life lived as though all our answers are only gateways into deeper levels of answering, which in turn lead us into mystery where all answers give way to bended knee and adoration and praise. This truth was once presented to me in a form that I have never forgotten. A novice master of a Trappist monastery I once visited offered this observation: To be a Christian does not mean knowing all the answers; to be a Christian means being willing to live in the part of the self where the question is born.
—Wendy M. Wright in *The Vigil*

Reflect

❖ How willing are you to live with questions, with uncertainty, with mystery that lies beyond the answers?

❖ What questions and uncertainty are you living with right now in your life?

❖ What mystery are you discovering within yourself and beyond as you live in the part of yourself where the question is born?

------ **TUESDAY** ------

On that Dark and Moon-Less Night

On that dark and moon-less night

my mother opened the door
at the back of the house

quietly
quietly
so as not to waken
the others.

I stood by the door
looking out
into the snow-covered fields and mountains.

She had given me warm clothing and boots.
She had filled my knapsack with food for the journey.
The family dog would come as companion and guide.

My mother opened the door for me
that cold and snow-lit night

and set me free.

—Judy Scales-Trent in *Double Stitch: Black Women Write about Mothers and Daughters*

Reflect

❖ When and how did you begin to claim your journey as your own?

❖ What did you take with you as you set out on your journey—supplies, companions?

❖ What did you leave behind?

—— **WEDNESDAY** ——

Sister Mercy

Mercy is a sister
and she came to me one day
through a door that I had locked
and she softly called my name.
I said that I had nothing
to give a guest so fine,
and she laughed and lay beside me,
stroked my hair, and eased my mind.

Mercy is a sister
and she came to me one night,
fed me by a silver lake,
stars and flame our only lights.
When she asked me why I'd come there,
I said I really didn't know,
but for a space along the journey
she gave a place to call my own.

Oh Mercy, oh my sister,
all the times you came to me
when I thought I traveled singly
and was as lonely as could be.
By the blazing sun you found me,
by the shadows of the moon;

Sister Mercy, by your touch
you gave me strength to journey on.
—Jan L. Richardson

Written after hearing Cris Williamson sing L. Cohen's "Sisters of Mercy"

Reflect

❖   In your journey, who have been companions, your sisters of mercy?

——— THURSDAY ———

Journey

The dream of the journey comes repeatedly. Over the years the point of
departure in the dream varies; I begin in many different places, familiar or
foreign to my experience. But once in movement, the journey is always the
same. I travel for many days, leaving a great city, passing through ever
smaller towns into increasingly remote villages. I travel alone, driving a
small white car, carrying a small white puppy. Beyond the last village lies
an open, untracked landscape, the distance so vast and unarticulated that no
horizon can be seen. I leave the car and we walk into the space where earth
and sky are merged, perfectly united, each the other. We walk for a long
time. Gradually earth and sky separate and on the horizon a dark speck
appears. We walk toward the object which grows as we come to it.

The tree and the sea announce their identity simultaneously. The earth
ends in the sea; the tree grows at the edge. We continue walking toward the
great pine and enter the substance of the tree. In the darkness my dog disappears but this does not grieve me. I circle through the multiple concentric
rings of the tree, shrinking and aging within each ring. At last the spiraling
ends. I arrive at the small dark spot of origination. When I touch this inner-
most center I realize I am already there. I have been journeying to where I am.

—Meinrad Craighead in *The Mother's Songs: Images of God the Mother*

Reflect

❖   What dreams, insights, moments of epiphany have visited your
path, giving clarity to your journey?

——— FRIDAY ———

My final question, How will I know when I have reached the destination?
brings me full circle, and I face the Mystery again. Perhaps the truth is that

we never arrive, not because the journey is too long and too difficult but because we have been there all along. I am coming to believe that there is no final destination except to continue to be on the journey and to know that every place along the way is a holy place because God is present. I believe that God is calling us to stand on our own ground and know that it is holy and let our roots grow deep. And yet at the same time, the journey goes on. It is a paradox, I know, but perhaps we are traveling most faithfully when we know ourselves to be most at home.

—Judith E. Smith, from "This Ground Is Holy Ground" in *Weavings: A Journal of the Christian Spiritual Life*

Reflect

❖ How do you know when it is time to settle—to let your roots grow deep—or time to move on?

❖ What sense of home persists in the midst of your traveling?

—— SATURDAY ——

I believe that our aesthetic sense, whether in works of art or in lives, has overfocused on the stubborn struggle toward a single goal rather than on the fluid, the protean, the improvisatory. We see achievement as purposeful and monolithic, like the sculpting of a massive tree trunk that has first to be brought from the forest and then shaped by long labor to assert the artist's vision, rather than something crafted from odds and ends, like a patchwork quilt, and lovingly used to warm different nights and bodies. Composing a life has a metaphorical relation to many different arts, including architecture and dance and cooking. In the visual arts, a variety of disparate elements may be arranged to form a simultaneous whole, just as we combine our simultaneous commitments. In the temporal arts, like music, a sequential diversity may be brought into harmony over time. In still other arts, such as homemaking or gardening, choreography or administration, complexity is woven in both space and time.

—Mary Catherine Bateson in *Composing a Life*

Reflect

❖ What image besides that of journey helps you understand your life, connect its parts, and envision its future?

Creator of the Stars
God of Epiphanies
You are the Great Star
You have marked my path with light
You have filled my sky with stars
    naming each star
    guiding it
    until it shines into my heart
    awakening me to deeper seeing
    new revelations
    and brighter epiphanies.

O infinite Star Giver
I now ask for wisdom and courage
    to follow these stars
    for their names are many
    and my heart is fearful.

They shine on me wherever I go:
    The Star of Hope
    The Star of Mercy and Compassion
    The Star of Justice and Peace
    The Star of Tenderness and Love
    The Star of Suffering
    The Star of Joy
And every time I feel the shine
    I am called
    to follow it
    to sing it
    to live it
    all the way to the cross
    and beyond

O Creator of the Stars
You have become within me
    an unending Epiphany.
—Macrina Wiederkehr in *Seasons of Your Heart: Prayers and Reflections*

Reflect

❖ What are the names of the stars you follow?

❖ What to you in the created world testifies to God's "unending Epiphany"?

—— **Meditation** ——

This Is a Woman

This is a woman standing at the stove slowly stirring vegetables, spices, juices—reading the pot. This is a woman—hands in the soil, loving her garden, turning the earth. This is a woman stitching again and again across patches, across time—my grandmother—she gave this to me for cold nights. This is a woman on a journey.

This is a woman reaching in the darkness, praying night will give way to flesh. This is a woman dark house one light on waiting for a child a sound a shot. This is a woman outstretched hands with questions running through them like blood. This is a woman   this is a woman on a journey.

This is a woman spinning inward; this is a woman on the verge; this is a woman seeing, smelling, tasting, touching, hearing herself crying out WHY crying out YES this is a woman moving reaching leaving loving herself this is a woman   this is a woman   this is a woman on a journey.

—Jan L. Richardson

—— ❖ ——

Blessing: *May you know the mystery of open hands.*
May you stretch them out with longing
and touch the fire of unknowing.
May they teach you of fullness
and instruct you in emptiness.
May you reach toward the holy
and find yourself
in your own embrace.
May you know the mystery of open hands.

Written for Betsey, for the journey.

9 Wisdom Cries Out
Prophetic Women in Scriptures

Invocation: *God of visions, let me perceive you; God of deep thoughts, let me know you; God of bold speech, let your truth dance on my lips.*

Text: Proverbs 1:20-23 and daily readings

Context: This portrait of Wisdom in Proverbs 1 brings to mind prophets throughout scripture. While persons today often understand prophecy as the ability to predict the future, the prophets of scripture display more concern for their present situations. As noted in *Cruden's Complete Concordance,* they give less attention to *fore*telling than *forth*telling—speaking forth the truth regarding social, religious, and economic matters. Their persistent outspokenness in calling people to live justly often renders them unpopular.

Scripture identifies eleven women as prophets and alludes to others elsewhere (see, for example, 1 Corinthians 11:5). The Hebrew scriptures tell us about Miriam, Deborah, Huldah, Noadiah, and the unnamed prophet who conceives and bears the prophet Isaiah's child. In the New Testament we learn of Anna, the four unnamed daughters of Philip, and the woman identified as Jezebel.

The relative independence of these women prophets often opened them to mistrust, ridicule, and slander by those suspicious of powerful women. Even in places where they received respect, persons may have considered them exceptional cases rather than models for other women to emulate. One wonders to whom they turned for support and strength.

What might these prophetic women say if they gathered together? What might they share of their independence, their isolation, and their vision? What might they say about those suspicious of their power, of their strong voices, of their relationship with God?

—— **MONDAY** ——

Miriam—Read Exodus 15:20-21.
[*Bible scholars generally consider this song to be the most ancient song in*

Hebrew scripture. It probably provided the inspiration for Moses' similar but more lengthy song, which precedes it.]

I bring flame of celebration,
of singing with elation,
of dancing with abandon
on the shore of a new land.

Though the journey to be free
will lead through wilderness and sea,
we shall be strengthened for our dreaming
if we remember how to sing.
—Jan L. Richardson

Reflect

❖ How does celebration sustain you for the journey?

—— **TUESDAY** ——

Deborah—Read Judges 4–5.

I bring flame of fierce passion,
of spirits longing for release,
of bodies aching to move freely,
of souls and hearts that yearn for peace.

In the face of blazing rage
men of iron will melt away,
and the songs of once-bound people
will greet the dawning of the day.
—Jan L. Richardson

Reflect

❖ What do you think about the use of violence in fighting oppression?

❖ In working for freedom for all, which tools and methods of the oppressors are valuable and which are not?

—— **WEDNESDAY** ——

Huldah—Read 2 Kings 22:14-20; 2 Chronicles 34:22-28.

I bring flame of keen perception,
of insight sharp where shadows dim,
of knowledge passed from age to age,
of wisdom carried deep within.

To your queries I'll reply,
but as you listen, know this too:
that even for your comfort
I cannot spare the truth.
—Jan L. Richardson

Reflect
- ❖ How do you suppose King Josiah's messengers responded to Huldah's prophecy of destruction in their land?
- ❖ When has your truth-telling brought discomfort to others?

—— **THURSDAY** ——

Noadiah—Read Nehemiah 6:1-14.
[Verse 14 contains all we know of Noadiah. That Nehemiah mentions her by name indicates she has made a significant impact on him, one he considers worthy of punishment by God.]

I bring the flame of woman-boldness,
of uncompromising speech
that frightens those who think
we ought not work beyond their reach.

As we move into our power
worlds will doubtless start to crack,
so let us recreate the remnants,
for we are not going back.
—Jan L. Richardson

Reflect
- ❖ What do you imagine Noadiah said that made Nehemiah so fearful?
- ❖ How much responsibility do you take for others' responses to you?

—— **FRIDAY** ——

The mother of Isaiah's child—Read Isaiah 8:1-4.

[Only in these verses do we learn of the prophet who bore Isaiah's child, and the author does not tell us her name. We do not know whether her role as a prophet consisted primarily of bearing children or if this constituted a special alliance between prophets with similar responsibilities.]

I bring flame of creativity,
of birthing life from shadows deep,
of shaping meaning from the hollows
left by those who grasp, then leave.

We who live in silence
weave visions new from threads of pain
and will bring forth sons and daughters
to shout our forgotten names.
—Jan L. Richardson

Reflect
- ❖ How is childbirth a prophetic act?
- ❖ How do our sexuality, fertility, and creativity inform our visions for our world?

—— **SATURDAY** ——

The prophetic daughters of Philip—Read Acts 21:8-9.
[Luke does not describe the nature of the prophetic gifts of his host's daughters. He does describe, however, an encounter with the male prophet Agabus immediately after his mention of the daughters.]

We bring flames of sisterhood,
of a common work and life,
of strength found in shared vision,
of trust in our uncommon sight.

Though the disbelieving mock us,
and we may clash, as sisters will,
our bonds of blood sustain us
to lift our voices still.
—Jan L. Richardson

Reflect
Think of your companions, those who are as close as, or closer than, family.
- ❖ How do your connections with them enable you to handle tensions

that arise within your relationships and those that come from outside?

—— SUNDAY ——

Jezebel—Read Revelation 2:18-25.
[*Here John relates Christ's words to the church in Thyatira. Probably "Jezebel" is not the woman's real name but rather an epithet that John borrows from the story of a queen named Jezebel who persecuted prophets of Israel. (See 1 Kings 16:29-34; 18:1-20; 19:1-3; 21:1-25; 22:51-53; 2 Kings 9:1-13, 21-37.) While this woman, who claimed prophetic powers, indeed may have worked against the church in Thyatira, the nature of the accusations give pause for thought. Persons have used accusations of sexual immorality and satanism for hundreds of years to discredit independent women who live and give voice to different visions. What else might have been the real root of the venom heaped upon her?*]

I bring flame of self-naming,
of self-knowledge and self-claiming,
of defining what I understand
of things and things-to-be.

To all those so suspicious
of my power you think malicious,
here's a prophecy for you:
what you seek is what you'll see.
—Jan L. Richardson

Reflect
 ❖ How does what we look for in people influence what we find?
 ❖ When have you seen others distort and make suspect a woman's sexuality in an effort to hide the real issues?

—— **Meditation** ——

The Prophets' Watch

Watching the fire
    they sit hushed
watching the flames
    they barely touch

all words spent
   all visions rising
      into the night air

full moon rises bright
   crosses the sky
      rests behind the next hill
   still they sit
cry of wild animal
   still they watch

in the embers
   a final vision
eyes meet:
   each has seen
a woman rising
   glowing hot
over the next hill
   dawn comes dancing.
—Jan L. Richardson

——— ❖ ———

Blessing: *May the God who blesses you with wisdom, grant you strength to give voice to your visions. By your words, by your witness, by your longing, by your power, may you birth justice into these days.*

10 Wisdom Walks with Justice
Sojourner Truth

Invocation: *Grant me imagination, O God, as I ponder my own path. In these words may I hear the voice of one who, with boldness and passion, walked in partnership with you.*

Text: Proverbs 8:20

Context: Born into slavery in New York around 1797, Isabella Baumfree (Sojourner's given name) spent most of her life walking a relentless journey toward freedom. The second youngest child of Betsey ("Mau-mau Bett") and James Baumfree, Isabella had ten or twelve brothers and sisters. She knew of them only from Mau-mau Bett's recollections, for their master had sold all the children except Isabella and her younger brother Peter. In 1828, having been sold herself and later escaping, Isabella was emancipated and soon moved to New York City.

After living in New York City for over a decade with friends, Isabella felt called by the Spirit to travel and lecture. Her new name, Sojourner Truth, reflected the life she envisioned. "I left everything behind," she once said. "I wa'n't goin' to keep nothin' of Egypt on me, an' so I went to the Lord an' asked him to give me a new name. And the Lord gave me Sojourner, because I was to travel up an' down the land, showin' the people their sins, an' bein' a sign unto them. Afterward I told the Lord I wanted another name, 'cause everybody else had two names; and the Lord gave me Truth, because I was to declare the truth to the people."

A fiery orator, Sojourner commanded respect and effected change through biting humor and forthright speech. Susan B. Anthony, Harriet Beecher Stowe, Abraham Lincoln, and William Lloyd Garrison included themselves among her many friends and admirers. In her tireless pursuit for justice for all, Sojourner refused to bow to any obstacle as she lectured and preached. Once, when she learned of threats to burn down a building where she was to speak, she replied, "Then I will speak upon the ashes."

---

* *If this is the last Sunday after Epiphany, use Week 15.*

Sojourner continued to speak until shortly before her death in 1883. The following excerpts come from *The Narrative of Sojourner Truth*, first published in 1850 by her friend Olive Gilbert and reprinted in 1875 with additional notes by Frances W. Titus.

——— MONDAY ———

"Ye see we was all brought over from Africa, father, an' mother an' I, an' a lot more of us; an' we was sold up an' down, an' hither an' yon'; an' I can 'member, when I was a little thing, not bigger than this 'ere," pointing to her grandson, "how my ole mammy would sit out o' doors in the evenin', an' look up at the stars an' groan. She'd groan, an' groan, an' says I to her,

"'Mammy, what makes you groan so?'

"An' she'd say,

"'Matter enough, chile! I'm groanin' to think o' my poor children: they don't know where I be, an' I don't know where they be; they looks up at the stars, an' I look up at the stars, but I can't tell where they be.

"'Now,' she said, 'chile, when you're grown up, you may be sold away from your mother an' all your old friends, an' have great troubles come on ye; an' when you has these troubles come on ye, ye jes' go to God, an' he'll help ye.'

"An' I says to her,

"'Who is God, anyhow, mammy?'

"An' says she,

"'Why, chile, you jes' look up *dar*. It's him that made all *dem*!'"

Reflect

Look at the stars or see them in your mind's eye, and hear again the words of Sojourner's mother.

❖ What do they tell you about finding connections in the midst of separation and pain?

❖ What feelings do they prompt?

——— TUESDAY ———

As we have before mentioned, she [Sojourner] had ever been mindful of her mother's injunctions, spreading out in detail all her troubles before God, imploring and firmly trusting [God] to send her deliverance from them. Whilst yet a child, she listened to a story of a wounded soldier, left alone in the trail of a flying army, helpless and starving, who hardened the very ground about him with kneeling in his supplications to God for relief, until it arrived. From this narrative, she was deeply impressed with the idea, that if she also were to present *her* petitions under the open canopy of heaven, speaking very loud, she should the more readily be heard; consequently, she sought a fitting spot for this, her rural sanctuary. The place she selected, in which to offer up her daily orisons, was a small island in a small stream, covered with large willow shrubbery, beneath which the sheep had made their pleasant winding paths; and sheltering themselves from the scorching rays of a noon-tide sun, luxuriated in the cool shadows of the graceful willows, as they listened to the tiny falls of the silver waters. It was a lonely spot, and chosen by her for its beauty, its retirement, and because she thought that there, in the noise of those waters, she could speak louder to God, without being overheard by any who might pass that way. When she had made choice of her sanctum, at a point of the island where the stream met, after having been separated, she improved it by pulling away the branches of the shrubs from the centre, and weaving them together for a wall on the outside, forming a circular arched alcove, made entirely of the graceful willow. To this place she resorted daily, and in pressing times much more frequently.

Reflect

❖ Where have you found secret places of grace and hidden shelters for your soul?

—— **WEDNESDAY** ——

She [Sojourner] . . . went to listen further to the preachers [at a camp-meeting of those who believed in the "Second Advent" doctrines]. They appeared to be doing their utmost to agitate and excite the people, who were already too much excited; and when she had listened till her feelings would let her listen silently no longer, she arose and addressed the preachers. The following are specimens of her speech: —

"Here you are talking about being 'changed in the twinkling of an eye.' If the Lord should come, he'd change you to *nothing*! for there is nothing to you.

"You seem to be expecting to go to some parlor *away up* somewhere, and when the wicked have been burnt, you are coming back to walk in triumph over their ashes—this is to be your New Jerusalem! Now *I* can't see any thing so very *nice* in that, coming back to such a *muss* as that will be, a world covered with the ashes of the wicked! Besides, if the Lord comes and burns—as you say he will—I am not going away; *I* am going to stay here and *stand the fire*, like Shadrach, Meshach, and Abednego! . . . Do you tell me that God's children *can't stand fire?*" And her manner and tone spoke louder than words, saying, "It is *absurd* to think so!"

The ministers were taken quite aback at so unexpected an opposer, and one of them, in the kindest possible manner, commenced a discussion with her, by asking her questions, and quoting scripture to her; concluding finally, that although she had learned nothing of the great doctrine which was so exclusively occupying their minds at the time, she had learned much that man had never taught her.

Reflect

❖ When have your own experience and intuition come into opposition with those perceived to be in authority?

❖ When have you encountered suspicion or misunderstanding from others because your way of learning differed from theirs?

—— **THURSDAY** ——

The two excerpts that follow constitute Sojourner's famous "Ar'n't I a Woman?" speech, delivered in 1851 at a Woman's Rights convention in Akron, Ohio. The presider, Frances D. Gage, recounts the speech.

Slowly from her seat in the corner rose Sojourner Truth, who, till now, had scarcely lifted her head. "Don't let her speak!" gasped half a dozen in my ear. She moved slowly and solemnly to the front, laid her old bonnet at her feet, and turned her great, speaking eyes to me. There was a hissing sound of disapprobation above and below. I rose and announced "Sojourner Truth," and begged the audience to keep silence for a few moments. The tumult subsided at once, and every eye was fixed on this almost Amazon form, which stood nearly six feet high, head erect, and eye piercing the upper air, like one in a dream. At her first word, there was a profound hush. She spoke in deep tones, which, though not loud, reached every ear in the house, and away through the throng at the doors and windows: —

"Well, chilern, whar dar is so much racket dar must be something out o'kilter. I tink dat 'twixt de niggers of de Souf and de women at de Norf all a talkin' 'bout rights, de white men will be in a fix pretty soon. But what's all dis here talkin' 'bout? Dat man ober dar say dat woman needs to be helped into carriages, and lifted ober ditches, and to have de best place every what. Nobody eber help me into carriages, or ober mud puddles, or gives me any best place [and raising herself to her full height and her voice to a pitch like rolling thunder, she asked], and ar'n't I a woman? Look at me! Look at my arm! [And she bared her right arm to the shoulder, showing her tremendous muscular power.] I have plowed, and planted, and gathered into barns, and no man could head me—and ar'n't I a woman? I could work as much and eat as much as a man (when I could get it), and bear de lash as well—and ar'n't I a woman? I have borne thirteen chilern and seen 'em mos' all sold off into slavery, and when I cried out with a mother's grief, none but Jesus heard—and ar'n't I a woman? Den dey talks 'bout dis ting in de head—what dis dey call it?" "Intellect," whispered someone near. "Dat's it honey. What's dat got to do with women's rights or niggers' rights? If my cup won't hold but a pint and yourn holds a quart, would n't ye be mean not to let me have my little half-measure full?" And she pointed her significant finger and sent a keen glance at the minister who had made the argument. The cheering was long and loud.

Reflect

- ❖ What images of "woman" prevail in your community and in the larger society?
- ❖ How does Sojourner challenge notions of what it means to be a woman?

──── **FRIDAY** ────

Sojourner's speech continued

"Den dat little man in black dar, he say women can't have as much rights as man, cause Christ want a woman. Whar did your Christ come from?" Rolling thunder could not have stilled that crowd as did those deep, wonderful tones, as she stood there with outstretched arms and eye of fire. Raising her voice still louder, she repeated, "What did your Christ come from? From God and a woman. Man had nothing to do with him." Oh! What a rebuke she gave the little man.

Turning again to another objector, she took up the defense of mother Eve. I cannot follow her through it all. It was pointed, and witty, and solemn, eliciting at almost every sentence deafening applause; and she ended by asserting that "if de fust woman God ever made was strong enough to turn the world upside down, all 'lone, dese togedder [and she glanced her eye over us], ought to be able to turn it back and get it right side up again, and now dey is asking to do it, de men better let 'em." Long-continued cheering.

"Bleeged to ye for hearin' on me, and now ole Sojourner hadn't got nothing more to say."

Reflect

❖ When have you experienced women silencing, not listening to, or fearing their own sisters?

❖ Why does this happen?

SATURDAY

I [J. A. Dugdale, author of a letter to the *National Anti-Slavery Standard*] was present at a large religious convention. Love in the family had been portrayed in a manner to touch the better nature of the auditory. Just as the meeting was about to close, Sojourner stood up. Tears were coursing down her furrowed cheeks. She said: "We has heerd a great deal about love at home in de family. Now, children, I was a slave, and my husband and my children was sold from me." . . . Pausing a moment, she added: "Now, husband and children is *all* gone, and what has *'come* of de affection I had for dem? *Dat is de question before de house!*"

Reflect

❖ How are we to respond to Sojourner's question in a society in which families often are torn apart as they slip through the cracks for reasons involving economics, race, and other factors?

SUNDAY

Previous to the war, Sojourner held a series of meetings in northern Ohio. She sometimes made very strong points in the course of her speech, which she knew hit the apologist of slavery pretty hard. At the close of one of these meetings, a man came up to her and said, "Old woman, do you think that your talk about slavery does any good? Do you suppose people care what you say? Why," continued he, "I do n't care any more for your talk than I do for the bite of a flea." "Perhaps not," she responded, "but, the Lord willing, I'll keep you scratching."

Reflect

❖ What prompts you to "keep scratching" at dreams that others consider inconsequential?

—— **Meditation** ——

Thumbing through my thesaurus one day, I came upon the word woman.
*The synonyms listed there inspired this piece, which includes some of
those words plus others that have been used to describe women.*

Womanwords

Ball and chain it said
there in black and white it was
number two (*wife* being number one)
and I thought of you
and the chains you'd left behind

See my arm, you say,
ar'n't I a woman?

Doxy it said
(I had to look it up)
"floozy, prostitute" it meant
little woman was there too
and *old lady*

and I thought of your great height
and your persistent vision

Hear my voice, you say like thunder,
ar'n't I?

And words came pouring in
weaker sex   misbegotten male   jezebel
but you say
planter   birther   bearer   worker
see my scars
my thirteen children somewhere
ar'n't I?

Temptress they say
Devil's gateway   tease   wench   bimbo   chick

Mother   you cry   *creator*
lover   lifegiver   wisewoman   partner
see my gardens
ar'n't I?

Nag! they protest *hag!*
shrew! whore!

SISTER! you thunder *SEER!*
DREAMER HEALER SAGE PROPHET SOJOURNER
watch me walk
ar'n't I
WOMAN?
ar'n't I!
—Jan L. Richardson

———— ❖ ————

Blessing: *Woman of God, may you be strengthened to claim the names that belong to you. By the names you are and by the names you choose, may you bless and be blessed.*

 Wisdom Rejoices at Creation
Women and Creativity

Invocation: *May I know your playful ways, O God; in my delighting, in my creating, may we experience each other more intimately.*

Text: Proverbs 8:22-32

Context: "Happy are those who keep my ways!" exclaims Wisdom after telling of her delight in creation. In the midst of calling us to justice, insight, and maturity, Wisdom reminds us that pleasure, delight, and play are part of the divine path also.

Through her creative partnership with God, Wisdom reminds us that creativity happens in community. My friend Kary often invites me to "come out and play!" Kary is a musician; I am a writer. Hearing Kary's music breathe life into my words or weaving my words into her music, I better understand Christin Lore Weber's reflection in *Blessings: A WomanChrist Reflection on the Beatitudes* that "Creation is the process by which God becomes embodied."

This process has more to do with the meaning of creativity than does the final product. The often mysterious workings of imagination, vision, and improvisation required for what we term "art" apply also to creative forms such as sewing, quilting, cooking, and decorating a home as well as to less tangible creations such as friendships, families, partnerships, and new ways of living—creations on which women spend an enormous amount of often unrecognized energy.

Wisdom's call to delight in creation invites us to embody the sacred with creativity in all our living. Come out and play!

—— MONDAY ——

Egg

My infant body contained all the eggs which would spill out during the

---

[*] *If this is the last Sunday after Epiphany, use Week 15.*

months of the fertile years. So, too, some childhood experiences contained the shape of my future years.

The first picture I can remember coming out of my imagination was of a snake and a bird bound together. My mother recalled a time, one summer in my third year, when I spent each morning rolling balls of mud in my hands. She said I called them "eggs" which were "full of things." I remember the cardboard box I filled with these eggs, the muddy hole I sat in, the hot Texas sun on my body.

I have never conceived, but whether or not a woman does conceive, she carries the germinative ocean within her, and the essential eggs. We have a spirituality, full from within. Whether we are weaving tissue in the womb or pictures in the imagination, we create out of our bodies.

—Meinrad Craighead in *The Mother's Songs: Images of God the Mother*

Reflect

❖ What is your earliest memory of creating?

—— **TUESDAY** ——

Womanwork

some make potteries
some weave and spin
remember
the Woman/celebrate
webs and making
out of own flesh
earth
bowl and urn
to hold water
and ground corn
balanced on heads
and springs lifted
and rivers in our eyes
brown hands shaping
earth into earth
food for bodies
water for fields
they use
old pots

broken
fragments
castaway
bits
to make new
mixed with clay
it makes strong
bowls, jars
new
she
brought
light
we remember this
as we make
the water bowl
broken
marks the grandmother's grave
so she will shape water
for bowls
for food growing
for bodies
eating
at drink
thank her
—Paula Gunn Allen in *A Cannon between My Knees*

Reflect
❖ How have you or women you know used or reused materials at hand to fashion new creations?

—— **WEDNESDAY** ——

Like everyone, my life is made of experience, memory, and dreams. Years ago something happened that briefly allowed me to have an experience of what I will call "the whole" although that is a puny, inadequate word borrowed from others. The perception was of a convincing order to all things—an order that is in no way limited to those systems imposed by human need; not geometry, nor language, nor any mathematical theory. The event is a memory now and is as hard to reconstruct as a dream, but it was as real at the time as being born. Every drawing I have made since then has been made in the hope that I can recapture that moment and recompose within the small space of a piece of paper the infinite greatness of its perfection. Every image has started out as a symbol of that harmonious whole, but between the mind and the hand an essential something has gotten lost. In the process of trying to draw that particular phenomenon, I have instead drawn other memories, other images. Over the years I have tried to analyze why one memory will emerge on the paper and not another. I might say to myself, "I have drawn a snake because . . . ," and then give myself various reasons ranging from the sacred to the profane. What I tell myself is only as true as the interpretation of my dreams. I don't know why I dream or why I draw, and I can't be certain of the meaning of either. There is a usefulness, however, to try to find meaning, but that usefulness is purely selfish. It helps me to live.

—Susan Cofer, from the essay in her "Drawing from Experience" exhibition catalogue, 1992, Atlanta, Georgia

Reflect

❖ What is the usefulness of your creating?
❖ What frustrations do you encounter in the process of creating?

—————— **THURSDAY** ——————

Some years ago, I spent an afternoon caught up in a piece of sewing I was doing. The waste basket near my sewing machine was filled with scraps of fabric cut away from my project. This basket of discards was a fascination to my daughter Annika, who, at the time, was not yet four years old. She rooted through the scraps searching out the long bright strips, collected them to herself, and went off. When I took a moment to check on her, I tracked her whereabouts to the back garden where I found her sitting in the grass with a long pole. She was affixing the scraps to the top of the pole with great sticky wads of tape. "I'm making a banner for a procession," she said. "I need a procession so that God will come down and dance with us." With that she solemnly lifted her banner to flutter in the wind and slowly she began to dance.

—Gertrud Mueller Nelson in *To Dance with God*

Reflect

❖ Who has been a wise bearer of creativity in your life, inviting you to dance with God?

The Possible (excerpt)

This teacher tells us we must ride the unknown. She has made many pots. She says we cannot rely on a formula. . . . We must follow our hands, she says, the clay will speak to our hands; the clay has qualities of its own, and we must yield to the clay's knowledge. She says every rule we have memorized, the roughing and the wetting of edges, for instance, to where the clay will be joined, every law must yield to experience. She says we must learn from each act, and no act is ever the same. . . .

For an instant we must admit we do not know the future, and we are afraid. Yet our hands are wet and coated with clay and they continue to work, despite our fear, they continue and this particular clay speaks to them. And now as our hands give us knowledge, fear becomes wonder: we are amazed at this shape we have never seen before which we hold now in our hands. . . .

Suddenly, we find we have a new language.
—Susan Griffin in *Woman and Nature: The Roaring inside Her*

Reflect
❖   What have you had to learn on your own?
❖   What new language have you found in your creating?

—— **SATURDAY** ——

I Want to Write

I want to write
I want to write the songs of my people.
I want to hear them singing melodies in the dark.
I want to catch the last floating strains from their sob-torn throats.
I want to frame their dreams into words; their souls into notes.
I want to catch their sunshine laughter in a bowl;
fling dark hands to a darker sky
and fill them full of stars
then crush and mix such lights till they become
a mirrored pool of brilliance in the dawn.
—Margaret Walker in *October Journey*

Reflect
❖   What does your creativity have to do with your community?

I talked recently with a woman struggling to discern God's will for her life.

"What do you most love to do?" I asked her.

"I love to do things with my hands," she answered quickly. "I love to paint, to sew, to garden."

"What longing underlies that love?" I asked.

This took more thought, and her answer came more slowly: "I really want to feel that I am making something beautiful, and that I have become part of that beauty."

"What longing lies beneath *that*?" I probed. "Try to *feel*, to sense that longing at your deepest core."

She closed her eyes, and there was a long silence. Then she answered softly: "I want to be part of God while God creates. My whole body, my whole self wants to be part of that power, part of that mighty river. It feels very fierce, very joyous."

She opened her eyes. "Is this really what God wants for me, too? I've always been a bit ashamed that what I really liked to do was material and physical. I never thought that was spiritual enough. Perhaps my hands knew it before I did—that God made me to be a creator in my own way. Maybe I'll begin to see other ways, too, in which I can create."

—Flora Slosson Wuellner, from "Transformation: Our Fear, Our Longing" in *Weavings: A Journal of the Christian Spiritual Life*

Reflect

❖ In what ways—physical, tangible, and ways that are less so—do you create?

❖ What creating spirit do you bring to forming relationships, to creating welcoming spaces, to fashioning your life, to transforming the world around you?

—— **Meditation** ——

Creation

Moving turning whirling inward
darkness I can barely see
I reach out wet earth meets me
slips through fingers stiff and trembling

Nervously I roll it on my palms

it takes me back to when
Playdoh was my medium
look a cup a snake a flower

Left those back behind who knows where
now I bid my memories teach me
once again to break to mash
to smooth flat trusting shape to come

Barely do the shadows trace it
barely do I realize
the lines my fingers form, remembering
dark earth giving way to flesh

Moon comes searching, lights this figure
colored deep like fire like blood
she stands, we press our palms together,
heaven-blessed, and start to dance.
—Jan L. Richardson

———— ❖ ————

Blessing: *May you journey to the place where your creativity is born. May you dwell there with wisdom, trusting sense and shape. May you come out with dancing, delighting in the sacred creative partnership you share with God.*

12 Wisdom Prepares Her Feast
Women and Food

Invocation: *Let me share your table, Hostess of the Feast, where in the presence of you and many, all hunger turns to bread and all thirst becomes wine.*

Text: Proverbs 9:1-5

Context: Ever since Eve picked the fruit of knowledge, women have had an intimate and complex relationship with food. Most often it has been women who have understood the power of food as they have gathered it, shopped for it, prepared it, shared it, begged for it, binged on it, starved for lack of it, or given it up as they sought to match society's image of a perfect body. Often women live in the tension between society's expectation that women do the feeding and its lack of recognition that preparing a meal is a creative, and therefore sacred, act.

Many women know from experience what theologian Mary Hunt observes in *Waterwheel*: "Food . . . does what theology talks about. It nurtures and nourishes, it occasions celebration, and it mirrors how the community divides up its resources." Mary's words prompt memories woven of tastes and smells and images that continue to influence my understanding of community, of communion, of life in common: Thanksgiving dinners shared with most of my hometown in our community park, Christmas dinners at my grandmother's, lingering long at tables with friends, sharing a cookie with my nephew, a meal offered by an estranged friend, serving meals in a soup kitchen in downtown Atlanta, meals eaten on the run, pictures of people starving in Somalia while tons of food wait at the harbor, the array of different languages and skin colors and fascinating foods at the Farmer's Market.

In this week, let us bring both memory and foresight to Wisdom's table as we ponder what it means to share the fruits of Earth.

If this is the last Sunday after Epiphany, use Week 15.

—— MONDAY ——

Blessing

O God, we know
that this food we are about to share
has already been blessed
by you
by those who planted it
by those who tended it
by those who gathered it
by those who prepared it.

So bless us, O God,
that we may taste and know
its blessedness
as we feast with one another
at this table you have prepared.
—Jan L. Richardson

Reflect
- ❖ Why bless food?
- ❖ What mealtime blessings do you remember?

—— TUESDAY ——

The Taste of Mother Love (excerpt)

III. LEARNING EXPERIENCE

I sit in my mama's kitchen, watching her cook.

Did you brown the meat before you set it in the oven?
How much onion did you put in that dressing?

Do you use milk or water in your cornbread? any eggs?
And how many spoons of sugar did it take to make the potatoes this
sweet?

What made your stew go from thin to thick like that?
Sometimes mine never does, no matter how long and slow I cook it.

My mother is a patient woman;
she cooks and answers,

if I keep pinning her down.

Later, I stand in my own kitchen, trying to cook.
I do it just so, remembering and following exactly everything mama
said.

BUT THEN, MY FOOD JUST WON'T TASTE LIKE HERS.

That's why when anybody says
cooking is a science,
I know better.

Ever been served contentment in a laboratory?
And any fool can tell you:
Real mother love don't grow on trees.
—Gloria T. Hull, from "The Taste of Mother Love" in *Double Stitch:*
Black Women Write about Mothers and Daughters

Reflect

❖ What are your earliest memories of watching your mother or
someone else cook?

❖ What was distinctive about her cooking?

❖ What did you learn from her?

—— **WEDNESDAY** ——

*In 1992 Kary and I took a trip to Montreal and spent time with three
different sets of her friends. Kary and I spent much of our time at the table,
sampling the marvelous variety of tastes that Montreal offers. Her friends
welcomed me warmly, and coming to know them in the breaking of bread
was a powerful experience. Those table-times provided refuge in the midst
of a profound exhaustion I couldn't explain but which the doctor later
would diagnose as mononucleosis. I spent our final night in Montreal
collapsed on a sofa in our hosts' sun room, looking out over the city as
Kary played their piano. Reflecting on the tables of the past week, I felt a
peace and healing that I had rarely known settle into my spirit and body.*

So Many Fine Tables
For Kary

Stories in crevices of cobblestone streets,
tales for the telling around every turn.

Looking out over this city we've shared,
how can I tell you of what I have learned?

So deep was the laughter, so warm the embrace,
so welcome the fire of the friends you have shared.
How deep was my hunger, how well I was fed
at so many fine tables prepared.

Passing the peace was never so holy,
breaking the bread was rarely so sweet;
for a body quite broken and a spirit well-worn,
oil for the healing ran free in these streets.

So deep was my longing to see with new eyes
so deep was my hunger, and I unaware
till ache turned to bread and thirst became wine
poured out at so many fine tables prepared.
—Jan L. Richardson

Reflect

❖ What meals particularly stand out in your memory?
❖ How were they times of communion, of healing, of grace?

—————— **THURSDAY** ——————

In the traditional way of life gardens were a ceremonial event for all, an opportunity to give to the Earth as well as to receive. The seeds of good food are also the seeds of good relationship, so caretaking the garden is symbolic of caretaking all beings. The garden can be an offering to all.
—Dhyani Ywahoo in *Voices of Our Ancestors: Teachings from the Cherokee Wisdom Fire*

Reflect

❖ What gardens have you tended or planted?
❖ What have you learned of creation, of caretaking, of cultivating life?

—————— **FRIDAY** ——————

The Lord's Prayer from Guatemala (excerpt)

And forgive us, Lord,
for not knowing how to share the bread

which *you* have given us,
as we forgive those
who have taken from us *your* bread
which is *ours*.
Forgive us for separating ourselves from our brothers,
forgive us, Lord, for our lack of faith and courage
which prevents us from surrendering ourselves as living hosts
to do *your will*,
which is to take what is yours
and share it with everyone right now.
Forgive us when out of fear
we remain silent
and do not say what *you* want us to say.
Forgive and destroy
our tiny kingdoms
and our useless struggles
which delay and obstruct our victorious march
toward the New Dawn. . . .
—Julia Esquivel in *Threatened with Resurrection*

Reflect

For Julia, "bread" includes not only food but also education, housing, medical assistance, land, freedom, and peace in a war-torn country.

❖ What do you consider to be as essential as food in sustaining life?

❖ From the local to the global level, how does the distribution of food connect with the availability of other resources?

—— SATURDAY ——

In Jewish, Christian, and other religious traditions, many adherents practice fasting as a spiritual discipline. Typically referring to abstinence from food, we may understand fasting in a broad sense as refraining from any activity for the purpose of gaining clarity and reorganizing priorities.

I Want a Fast

I want a fast from fast fast food
made in haste and eaten thus,
greasy quickly slickly packaged,
gobbled guzzled bolted gulped.
I want a fast from images

that set my body's boundaries:
SKINNY   CURVY   PERFECT SIZE 8
FLAWLESS   FEMININE   FAT-FREE.

I want a fast from gluttony
of nations, systems, policies
that feed some well while others starve
for grain, for bread, for dreams, for peace.

I want a fast, a long, slow fast
that lets us savor feasts, reclined
at tables newly dreamed and set
with justice for bread and peace for wine.
—Jan L. Richardson

Reflect

❖   What pattern do your own eating habits take?

❖   What images of food and eating do you encounter in the media and elsewhere?

❖   What do those images suggest about power, sexuality, body image, and community?

—— SUNDAY ——

Blessing the Bread: A Litany (excerpt)

Then God, gathering up her courage in love, said,
"Let there be bread!"
And God's sisters
her friends and lovers
knelt on the earth
planted the seeds
prayed for the rain
sang for the grain
made the harvest
cracked the wheat
pounded the corn
kneaded the dough
kindled the fire
filled the air
with the smell of fresh bread

And there was bread!
And it was good!

We the sisters of God say today,
  "All shall eat of the bread,
  And the power.
  We say today,
  All shall have power
  And bread.
  Today we say,
  Let there be bread!
  Let there be power!
  Let us eat of the bread
  and the power!
  And all will be filled
  For the bread is rising!"
—Carter Heyward in *Our Passion for Justice*

Reflect

❖ When have you participated in the making of bread and how did that affect your feelings when eating it?

❖ What blessing would you offer for the feast of life, of justice, of power restored?

—— **Meditation** ——

Comm(on)union

Sifting measuring pouring mixing
kneading rising baking breaking:
the choreography of feeding
is as common as our common lives

common sensing, common sharing
common is as common does
common loaf bears revelation
common crust can feed us all
—Jan L. Richardson

— ❖ —

Blessing: *Gathered, kneaded, rising, broken,*
you who eat are yet the feast.
Fashion wide your banquet table;
by your lives may all be fed.

13 Wisdom Seeks God's Mysteries
Julian of Norwich

Invocation: *God of the mysteries, in this time of reflection may I know you deeply. Enable me to trust the wisdom that is born of my relationship with you.*

Text: Wisdom 8:4 (Jerusalem Bible)

Indeed, [Wisdom] is an initiate in the mysteries of God's knowledge.

Context: We know few historical facts about Julian, the English mystic who lived during the fourteenth and early fifteenth centuries. It is likely that she took the name Julian from the church where she lived a solitary life within a faith community, the Church of St. Julian in Conisford at Norwich.

Most of what we know of Julian comes from the *Revelations of Divine Love* (commonly called *Showings*), her account of the revelations that came to her on May 13, 1373. Julian tells us that she desired "three graces by the gift of God": a recollection of Christ's passion, a bodily sickness, and three wounds (the wounds of contrition, compassion, and "longing with my will for God"). At the age of thirty and a half, Julian became ill; just as she thought herself at the point of death, the pain suddenly left. Not only were the other two graces granted her, but she also received sixteen revelations, which she recorded in a short text and then, after as much as two decades of reflection, in a longer text.

Julian emphasizes that she did not receive the revelations through her own merit but through the graciousness of God who desires that "all things [be] well" for all. Fifteen years after the revelations, Julian received the following message: "Know it well, love was [your Lord's] meaning. Who reveals it to you? Love. What did he reveal to you? Love. Why does he reveal it to you? For love."

------ **MONDAY** ------

And in this he showed me something small, no bigger than a hazelnut, lying in the palm of my hand, as it seemed to me, and it was as round as a ball. I looked at it with the eye of my understanding and thought: What can this be?

---

[*] *If this is the last Sunday after Epiphany, use Week 15.*

I was amazed that it could last, for I thought that because of its littleness it would suddenly have fallen into nothing. And I was answered in my understanding: It lasts and always will, because God loves it; and thus everything has being through the love of God.

In this little thing I saw three properties. The first is that God made it, the second is that God loves it, the third is that God preserves it. But what did I see in it? It is that God is the Creator and the protector and the lover. For until I am substantially united to [God], I can never have perfect rest or true happiness, until, that is, I am so attached to [God] that there can be no created thing between my God and me.

—From the First Revelation

Reflect

❖   How does God come to you as Creator, protector, and lover?

—— TUESDAY ——

For God is everything that is good, as I see; and God has made everything that is made, and God loves everything that [God] has made. And [the one] who has general love for all . . . fellow Christians in God has love towards everything that is. For in [humankind] which will be saved is comprehended all, that is to say all that is made and the maker of all. For God is in [humans] and in God is all. And [the one] who loves thus loves all.

—From the First Revelation

Reflect

❖   Whom do you find difficult to love?

❖   How do the challenges to loving draw you closer to God?

—— WEDNESDAY ——

God wishes us to know that [God] keeps us safe all the time, in sorrow and in joy; and sometimes a [person] is left [alone] for the profit of [that person's] soul, although [that person's] sin is not always the cause. For in this time I committed no sin for which I ought to have been left to myself, for it was so sudden. Nor did I deserve these feelings of joy, but our Lord gives it freely when he wills, and sometimes he allows us to be in sorrow, and both are one love. For it is God's will that we do all in our power to preserve our consolation, for bliss lasts forevermore, and pain is passing, and will be reduced to nothing for those who will be saved. Therefore it is not God's will that when we feel pain we should pursue it in sorrow and mourning for it, but that suddenly we should pass it over, and preserve ourselves in the endless delight which is God.

—From the Seventh Revelation

Reflect

❖ How do you understand pain and sin in light of God's desire for our consolation and delight?

❖ Which do you hear more about in the church?

—————— **THURSDAY** ——————

For he [Christ] still has that same thirst and longing which he had upon the Cross, which desire, longing, and thirst, as I see it, were in him from without beginning. . . .

For as truly as there is in God a quality of pity and compassion, so truly is there in God a quality of thirst and longing; and the power of this longing in Christ enables us to respond to his longing, and without this no soul comes to heaven. And this quality of longing and thirst comes from God's everlasting goodness, just as the quality of pity comes from [God's] everlasting goodness. And though [God] may have both longing and pity, they are different qualities, as I see them; and this is the characteristic of spiritual thirst, which will persist in [God] so long as we are in need, and will draw us up into [God's] bliss.

—From the Thirteenth Revelation

Reflect

❖ What do you long for, and where does your longing lead you?

❖ How do your longings connect you with God's own longing for you?

—————— **FRIDAY** ——————

Prayer unites the soul to God, for though the soul may be always like God in nature and in substance restored by grace, it is often unlike [God] in condition, through sin on [humanity's] part. Then prayer is a witness that the soul wills as God wills, and it eases the conscience and fits [humans] for grace. And so [God] teaches us to pray and to have firm trust that we shall have it; for [God] beholds us in love, and wants to make us partners in [God's] good will and work.

—From the Fourteenth Revelation

Reflect

Imagine God's beholding you in love, beckoning you to partnership.

❖ How does this invitation make you feel?

❖ How do you respond to God's invitation?

─── SATURDAY ───

But our passing life which we have here does not know in our senses what our self is, but we know in our faith. And when we know and see, truly and clearly, what our self is, then we shall truly and clearly see and know our Lord God in the fullness of joy. And therefore it must necessarily be that the nearer we are to our bliss, the more we shall long, both by nature and by grace. We may have knowledge of ourselves in this life by the continuing help and power of our exalted nature, in which knowledge we may increase and grow by the furthering and help of mercy and grace. But we may never fully know ourselves until the last moment, at which moment this passing life and every kind of woe and pain will have an end. And therefore this belongs to our properties, both by nature and by grace to long and desire with all our powers to know ourselves, in which full knowledge we shall truly and clearly know our God in the fullness of endless joy.

—From the Fourteenth Revelation

Reflect

❖ How does knowledge of yourself draw you deeper into relationship with God?

❖ How does knowledge of God draw you deeper into relationship with yourself?

─── SUNDAY ───

As truly as God is our Father, so truly is God our Mother, and [God] revealed that in everything, and especially in these sweet words where [God] says: I am [God]; that is to say: I am [God], the power and goodness of fatherhood; I am [God], the wisdom and the lovingness of motherhood; I am [God], the light and the grace which is all blessed love; I am [God], the Trinity; I am [God], the unity; I am [God], the great supreme goodness of every kind of thing; I am [God] who makes you to love; I am [God] who makes you to long; I am [God], the endless fulfilling of all true desires. For where the soul is highest, noblest, most honourable, still it is lowest, meekest and mildest.

—From the Fourteenth Revelation

Reflect

- ❖ How do Julian's images of God fit with or challenge your own images of God?
- ❖ Create your own litany born of your experience of God—who is God to you?

—— **Meditation** ——

Taming Wisdom
   To Julian

When I have pursued Her,
sweating, bleeding,
seeking to capture
comprehension

When I have sought to lure Her
with food prepared by other hands,
thinking that its sight
would please her

When all that I have grasped
are my own knuckles
white with urgency

and all that I have tasted
are my own teeth
clenched in agony

You dance toward me,
hold out your hand,
and bid me see what God has made.
—Jan L. Richardson

—— ❖ ——

Blessing: *Woman of wisdom, may you delight in your createdness. Know that the God who longs for you strengthens you for your journey.*

14 Wisdom Renews All Things
Esther

Invocation: *Search my hidden places, O God, that they may become wellsprings of strength. In your wisdom renew me, that I may in turn make all things new.*

Text: The Book of Esther and Wisdom of Solomon 7:27, 30

> Although she is but one, she can
>> do all things,
> and while remaining in herself,
>> she renews all things;
> in every generation she passes
>> into holy souls
> and makes them friends of God,
>> and prophets;
>
> . . . .
>
> against wisdom evil does not prevail.

Context: The Book of Esther constitutes one of the five scrolls (in Hebrew, *megillot*) read during the primary Jewish holy days. The Book of Esther belongs to Purim, the two-day feast in the month of Adar (February-March) known particularly for the gaiety of its festivities. What may have begun initially as a pagan festival was transformed, through the story of Esther, into a celebration of the Jews' victory against forces of persecution and death.

Although the book never mentions God, Esther exhibits clear awareness of her identity as a woman in partnership with the God who delivers God's people. This identity does not rest on her youth, beauty, virginity, or the hiding of her Jewish heritage. While these things may have secured her position as queen, Esther soon learns that they will not preserve her or her people. Responding to her cousin Mordecai's urgings, Esther realizes her choice: claim her identity and speak for her people—or die.

---

[*] *If this is the last Sunday after Epiphany, use Week 15.*

Esther's decision to act—which in itself puts her at risk of death—speaks to those in power who, through identifying with those with the least power, make possible the new: new life, new visions, new structures, new hopes, new relationships. Esther's choice speaks to all who live in fear of claiming their identity and history in the face of ridicule, persecution, and even death. In claiming that she might indeed be coming to power and voice "for such a time as this," Esther already begins to prepare the festive celebration of fear and hatred transformed.

——— MONDAY ———

It is not insignificant that it is through Queen Esther's memoirs that we even hear of the courageous queen by the name of Vashti. If Queen Esther had chosen to ignore the memory of the woman who preceded her on the throne, Queen Vashti might have been lost to history. . . .

But the king's second wife, Esther, had much for which to thank Vashti. King Ahasuerus might not have been so predisposed to forgive Queen Esther her brazen disobedience had not his first wife taught him that, like it or not, some women will make their own decisions. At least with Esther, the king was willing to hear her out. . . .

As sisters, it is our responsibility to remember the women, both single and married, who have worked to clear and pave the way for us, at the risk of health, sanity, comfort, reputation, family, and marriage.

If the truth be told, we today are who we are—if we are anybody—because some woman, somewhere, stooped down long enough that we might climb on her back and ride piggyback into the future.
—Renita J. Weems in *Just a Sister Away*

Reflect
- ❖ Who are the Vashtis in your life, the women who made a path for you?
- ❖ For whom are you making a path?

——— TUESDAY ———

Esther was a Jewish woman living in Persia. She was in that land through the same circumstances that Black people came here: by enslavement. . . . It was a secret, however. If the truth had been known, they [Esther and Mordecai] would have been killed.

Have you ever felt that you had to hide your identity? Have you not been able to let yourself be known? I mean, you were not able to let folks know who you really were and what you really believed because you knew that there would be a great risk involved? It's hard when you want to be honest and truthful with folks and let them know all about you, but you really can't. It's terrible when you're in the midst of a multitude of people and can't find anyone around who's like you to whom you can talk. Many people go to church trying to find the "right" church where they can let things out. It's sad when even in the church of God, you feel all by yourself. Oh, it's a terrible feeling.

—Suzan D. Johnson Cook, from "God's Woman" in *Those Preachin' Women: Sermons by Black Women Preachers*

Reflect
- ❖ When have you felt that you had to hide your identity?
- ❖ What risks were involved in hiding your identity? in revealing it?
- ❖ How has the church helped or hindered your claiming who you are?

―――― **WEDNESDAY** ――――

In the article from which this excerpt comes, Lynn Gottlieb writes about the Marranos, Jews who pretended to be Christians during the Spanish Inquisition in order to avoid persecution. In a time when claiming one's Jewish identity meant the risk of torture or death at the hands of Christians, many Jews, particularly Jewish women, related strongly to the story of Esther. Lynn notes that "because of their lack of knowledge about the Jewish tradition women did assume major leadership roles in the community. They led communal prayers, performed marriage ceremonies, and developed rituals around the Fast of Esther, which became a major conversos *[converts'] holiday."*

The Secret Jew (excerpt)

Every day for six hundred years
people hid their faith
from the Inquisition.

　　And the seasons pass
　　saintly Esther
　　my soul stays hidden
　　speaking softly
　　words praising Adonai
　　time forgetting time

eyes forgetting light
we hide in order to survive
living in brief moments
whispering the truth to shadows
I am a woman and a Jew
Saintly Esther
how did you endure those long months
of living what you were not
of embracing what you loved not.
As I enter this house of wood and stone
give me
your poor handmaiden
strength enough to pass through
this night of fear.

. . . .

Seasons pass
saintly Esther
and yet
this time
of dark
burning fires
has given me a place
to praise the name of the Lord Adonai.
Though I hide my true self from the outside world
my people learn
the passion of my faith
for I am needed to remember the past.
I lead my people Israel in prayers my mother taught me
as we lit the Sabbath candles in the cellar.

Blessed be the name of the Lord Adonai forever amen,
who brings the light of morning to the afternoon
and from afternoon carries it to evening
and from evening until dawn
and from dawn brings light to the morning.
[from the Marrano liturgy]

Every day
for six hundred years
people hid their faith

from the Inquisition.
But in the tradition of Esther
we survived the secret.
—Lynn Gottlieb in *Conservative Judaism*

Reflect

❖ What has sustained you when you felt it necessary to hide your identity?

------ **THURSDAY** ------

For Esther the real power came when she invited others to join with her in fasting and prayer. This meant that not only would she get power but also others would get power. It meant that others trusted her enough to join with her, for they needed power too. When you unveil yourself and take off all the disguises so that you can be God's woman (or God's man), then you become a mirror for others so that they can also see the glory of God. Somebody wrote a song with the lyrics "Walk together, children, and don't you get weary." We can't run this race all by ourselves. We need others to walk and run with us.
—Suzan D. Johnson Cook, from "God's Woman" in *Those Preachin' Women*

Reflect

❖ How did those who joined Esther in fasting and prayer enable her to confront the king?
❖ What does it mean to share power?
❖ How does the sharing of power in a community enable its members to live their lives openly?

------ **FRIDAY** ------

In the process of accomplishing the larger task of saving her people, Esther began to change the way in which the laws functioned. She recognized the limits of the rigid hierarchical system that governed Persian culture, and she proposed a solution that would shift the internal power balance. Instead of urging the king to break the restrictions on his own legal system, Esther suggested that the Jews be allowed to defend themselves on the day authorized for their slaughter. . . .

We are not used to choosing chaos as Esther did. It is untidy and unpredictable. Esther did not try to control the results or even the process.

She asked for a kind of contained chaos! She was extending her own internal experience of opening to the possibility of death to the external realm. She could make her proposal "on faith," remembering God's faithfulness in the history of her people and the promise that they would not be obliterated. Esther knew she was called only to be faithful in doing her piece of a larger design that God was creating.

Looking at our lives with God's perspective (however we understand that statement), we can let go of having to be "in control" and, at the same time, take responsibility for doing our particular part on behalf of a larger vision. The ability to act, as Esther did, without needing to be in control depends upon doing the inner work of facing the threat of spiritual or physical death and coming to know God.

—Marjory Zoet Bankson in *Braided Streams: Esther and a Woman's Way of Growing*

Reflect

❖ How comfortable are you with chaos?

❖ How does your relationship with God enable you to integrate or pursue change in your life and in your surroundings?

—— **SATURDAY** ——

The Age of Gerontocracy [the exercise of political power and influence by society's rapidly growing population of older persons], a once-in-history occurrence with its geriatric echo creating a long shadow into the future, can turn the world around. It does not seem plausible to think that this "gray power" has happened by accident—that for this one time in history such a potential for achievement and enrichment of the society is here by chance. Rather, it seems that we, as that Larger Generation, that longevity revolution, are here at this particular time and place in history marked as a people of destiny, a people called to a purpose and a mission all our own. Certainly, it is at such a time as this that the story of [Esther] carries real meaning. . . .

How do we know that we are not here just for this time? This we do know—we have stepped into history as have millions of others of our elders, and we will be here in growing numbers as an expanding force to effect change of some sort. If we . . . fail to re-engage ourselves in the dynamic process of living and accomplishing—if we "retire," then we leave a retired world as our legacy, and we leave the world as its debtor.

—Elizabeth Welch in *Learning to Be 85*

Reflect

- ❖ Like Esther, like Elizabeth, do you have a sense of being called or led or pulled to some particular work or place "for this time"?
- ❖ How do your history, your experiences, your dreams, your community, and your visions make you particularly suited to live out this calling?

 **SUNDAY**

Dancing in Front of the Guns

[Written on the verge of the Gulf War. Dedicated to the people of Russia and the Republics.]

We're facing the guns again,
we have faced them before
Humanity's longing after so many deaths
for something more human than war
But part of me whispers,
Take your body and run away
Leave the vision to somebody else
Then I hear myself say

I'd rather be dancing
At the edge of my grave
I'd rather be holding you close as we
march forward loving and brave
I'd rather be singing
in the face of my fear
I'd rather be dancing in front of the guns
as long as I'm here.

Life is so dangerous
That there's little to fear
Life is so possible, every breath a frontier
And they've brought out the guns
once again cause they haven't a clue
That we could be dancing, the whole
human race, each one must choose
And I'd rather be dancing . . .

To the drum of my heartbeat

Pounding up through my feet
With millions of lovers urging me on
as we take to the streets
As we face the terror,
If I leave here before my time
One thing's for certain
I'll go dancing, and I'll go alive

And I'd rather be dancing . . .

I'd rather be dancing in front of the guns
as long as I'm here.
Dance with me as long as I'm here.
—Libby Roderick in *Thinking Like a Mountain* (CD)

Reflect

As Esther and her people knew, celebration plays a vital role in the ongoing process of making all things new.

❖ Where in your life do you need a feast, a celebration, to renew your soul and to restore healing rhythms to the work of transformation?

❖ When will you do this, and how?

—— Meditation ——

Wisdom's Query

When all who see differently are gone
    and all who think differently are gone
    and all who speak differently are gone
When all who pray differently are gone
    and all who live differently are gone
    and all who love differently are gone
who shall be left to keep the feast?

Surely the day is coming
when all hearts shall know and be known,
and the souls who live in secret
will hang their fears for all to see.

Surely the night is coming
when the fires of compassion shall burn long,

and those who come to warm themselves
shall eat the bread of tenderness
and all shall freely
walk in these streets.
—Jan L. Richardson

———— ❖ ————

Blessing: *May the God who makes all things new, strengthen you to know and claim who you are. May you journey without fear or shame, clearing a path for many and preparing a table for the feast.*

15 Wisdom Gives Knowledge
Remembering Women Teachers

Invocation: *Teach me your ways, O God; lead me in the path of wisdom.*

Text: Wisdom of Solomon 7:17-22

> For it is [God] who gave me unerring knowledge of what exists, to know the structure of the world and the activity of the elements; the beginning and end and middle of times, the alternations of the solstices and the changes of the seasons, the cycles of the year and the constellations of the stars, the natures of animals and the tempers of wild animals, the powers of spirits and the thoughts of human beings, the varieties of plants and the virtues of roots; I learned both what is secret and what is manifest, for wisdom, the fashioner of all things, taught me.

Context: This week we celebrate the Feast of the Transfiguration, commemorating Jesus' dazzling mountaintop encounter with Moses and Elijah, wise men of his tradition. (See Matthew 17:1-8.) Peter, one of those who accompanied Jesus, tried to contain the experience by building dwellings for Jesus, Moses, and Elijah. Yet Jesus defied such containment of the holy.

Jesus' teaching in this moment left the disciples transfigured as well. In this mountaintop experience, perhaps Peter, James, and John learned something of dwelling in mystery, of letting go their need to make the holy manageable and easily contained.

Wisdom appears as one who both dwells in God's mysteries and teaches us from within them. In this week, she invites us to remember women who, by their teaching, have challenged and broadened the limits of our understanding. Who has given birth to wisdom by enabling you to dwell with your questions? Who are those teachers who have transformed and transfigured you as they accompanied you in the search for answers?

—— **MONDAY** ——

A parent often wonders what lessons her child will remember. Other teachers must wonder too. As with parenting, it probably is not what one would expect.

She was my English teacher in my senior year of high school. Sallie Taylor. Strong-willed, bright as her copper hair. The sheer excitement of words to her was evident as she read poetry aloud to us. She pushed us; she challenged us; she called us up short when we needed it.

We wrote sonnets. We used all twenty words from "It Pays to Enrich Your Word Power" in one paragraph! We memorized. What good is knowing the whole prologue to *The Canterbury Tales* in the original Middle English? Or those snippets from Shakespeare, Milton, and other poets?

"De gustibus non est disputandum" . . . just a tidbit she threw out one day, but something that intrigued me and which, forty years later, still helps me to keep certain things in perspective. (*Latin* meaning "There is no disputing concerning tastes.") There is pure satisfaction and power in being able to pull one of those words out when I want it. It's fun too! The appreciation of words. . . .

Lessons from Sallie Taylor. Lifelong, life-enriching gifts. Jesus enjoyed words. The Word. The word. May my child remember.
—Judy Scott Richardson

Reflect

❖ What words or phrases, life-enriching gifts, do you remember from your childhood?

❖ Who gave them to you, challenged you to find them and make them your own?

—————— **TUESDAY** ——————

Education is dangerous. Those who have sought to keep persons or classes or races in bondage, physically or mentally, have been keenly aware of this. They have known all too well that for others to have free access to books, thoughts, ideas, and the means by which to write and speak of their own lives gives them the dangerous ability to see beyond the horizon and to question the way things are. In times of war and repression, the writers, the poets, the teachers, the thinkers are among the first to be imprisoned or killed.

Sylvia Dannett, in her book *Profiles of Negro Womanhood,* tells the story of a woman named Milla Granson who, although enslaved in Mississippi, tasted as a child, the freedom that education provided. Later Granson offered education, at risk to her own life, to hundreds of other enslaved people. Milla opened her night school in a little cabin in a back alley. "After laboring all day for their master," Sylvia writes, "the slaves would creep stealthily to Milla's 'schoolroom,' carrying a bundle of pitch pine splinters for light as the door and windows of the cabin had to be kept tightly sealed to avoid discovery." Milla taught twelve students at a time, graduating each class when she had taught them all she knew to teach. Many of the students she taught to write went on to write their own passes and escaped to Canada.

The discovery of her school forced Milla to suspend classes for a time. Her case reached the state legislature, which passed a law making it legal for enslaved people to teach one another. Milla reopened her school and a Sabbath School as well.

—Jan L. Richardson

Reflect

❖ What dangerous gifts has your education given you?

❖ Can you recall a time in your life or the life of another when the ability to read or speak encouraged a questioning of life?

❖ For what persons is gaining an education still a risk?

—— **WEDNESDAY** ——

A Teacher Taught Me

I

a teacher taught me
more than she knew
patting me on the head
putting words in my hand
—"pretty little *Indian* girl!"
saving them—
going to give them
back to her one day . . .
show them around too
cousins and friends
laugh and say—"aye"

II

binding by sincerity
hating that kindness
eight years' worth
third graders heard her

putting words in my hand
—"we should bow our heads
in shame for what we did
to the American Indian"
saving them—
going to give them
back to her one day . . .
show them around too
cousins and friends
laugh and say—"aye"
—Anna Lee Walters in *Voices of the Rainbow*

Reflect
❖ What hard memories do you have of teachers?
❖ What lessons did you learn from them—perhaps despite them?

—— **THURSDAY** ——

The need to sustain human growth should be a matter of concern for the entire society, even more fundamental than the problem of sustaining productivity. This, surely, is the deepest sense of homemaking, whether in a factory or a college or a household. For all of us, continuing development depends on nurture and guidance long after the years of formal education, just as it depends on seeing others ahead on the road with whom it is possible to identify. A special effort is needed when doubts have been deeply implanted during the years of growing up or when some fact of difference raises barriers or undermines those identifications, but all of us are at risk, not only through childhood but through all the unfolding experiences of life that present new problems and require new learning. Education, whether for success or failure, is never finished. Building and sustaining the settings in which individuals can grow and unfold, not "kept in their place" but empowered to become all they can be, is not only the task of parents and teachers, but the basis of management and political leadership—and simple friendship.
—Mary Catherine Bateson in *Composing a Life*

Reflect
❖ Who are your teachers now?
❖ What and where are you learning?

In a spirituality of teaching, the teacher is also a kind of priest, ordaining the learner into a world of responsibility. Dwelling in such a relation, women—and men and children too—can accept power and know the moment of ordination into it in response, feeling themselves close to [Ntozake] Shange's Lady in Purple [From the play *For Colored Girls Who Have Considered Suicide When the Rainbow Is Enuf*], who acknowledges "A layin' of hands: the holiness of myself released." This is the grace of power which a spirituality of teaching leads to: recognizing the holiness and power of ourselves released and sent forth into the world.

—Maria Harris in *Women and Teaching*

Reflect

❖ Who among your teachers revealed the power within you and sent you forth into the world with your holiness and power released?

—— **SATURDAY** ——

For Mary McLeod Bethune

Great Amazon of God behold your bread
Washed home again from many distant seas
The cup of life you lift contains no lees
No bitterness to mock you, in its stead
So many, gone this brimming chalice fed
And broken hearted people on their knees
Look up to you and suddenly they seize
On living faith and they are comforted.
Believing in the people who are free
Who walk uplifted in an honest way
You look at last upon another day
That you have fought with God and man to see.
Great Amazon of God behold your bread,
We walk with you, and we are comforted.

—Margaret Walker in *October Journey*

Reflect

Gather the images, the memories of those teachers, if any, who have been the "Great Amazons of God" in your life—offering their bread, walking with you. Give thanks and taste their gifts again.

Remembering is an incomplete step . . . if the only voices, the only lives, the only silences we commemorate are those of women. In fact, one test of the genuineness of our care for an appropriate spirituality of teaching will be our remembering other unheard voices: those silenced because of race, sexual orientation, economic hardship or political choices; the silences of men, bruised . . . by structures and systems which fail to liberate. . . . Communal Remembering should impel us to incorporate into our teaching not only other human beings, but the earth itself, and to imagine as we educate what relation our work has to the entire non-human universe: land, water, fire, air, as well as the other animals with whom we share the planet. Such remembering will be sacramental in that it respects the teaching power in all creation: of oil, incense, wax; of animals toward humans; of a cactus, a hurricane, a wren, a thornbush.
—Maria Harris in *Women and Teaching*

Reflect
Sit quietly for a while in respect for the teaching power that resides in all God's creation. For this moment, be present to the wisdom that permeates the world.

—— **Meditation** ——

On the Feast of the Transfiguration

To those who dwell
with the questions,
Mother Eve comes anew,
bearing fruit
in her hands.
The tree still stands,
burning at the roots
to become something new.
—Jan L. Richardson

—— ❖ ——

Blessing: *By all you learn, by all you teach, by all you dream, by all you pass on, may generations be blessed, and may the wisdom of God dwell delightfully in you.*

Remembering Our Wounds

❖

The Season of Lent

WISDOM MARKS OUR FOREHEADS WITH ASHES as we leave the season after Epiphany and begin the journey through Lent. She intuits what these forty days (forty-six, including the Sundays) may hold in store for us and tries to prepare us. Remembering Jesus' forty days in the wilderness, she knows the trials, temptations, and vulnerability one encounters in seeking to reflect, to shed, to open oneself, to prepare. She remembers the wounds that come.

As we journey through Lent, the shadow of the cross falls upon our path. All too often the church has viewed the cross of Christ as the only location of God's saving activity. A belief that our salvation depends solely upon Christ's death ignores God's saving activity in Christ's birth, life, teaching, and healing. It also risks the glorification of suffering, leading us to believe that suffering *in itself* brings us closer to Christ. Such a belief can make us complacent in the face of suffering, encouraging us to focus on its seeming benefits rather than healing its origins.

During Lent, Wisdom beckons us to remember the root meaning of sacrifice, which is to make holy, to make whole. Wisdom knows that the only true sacrifice is the one given freely.

In this season of reflection and repentance, we remember women whose dreams, hopes, and in many cases, lives were offered by others as unholy sacrifices toward their own ends. In these stories we encounter women whom history has dis-membered more often than re-membered. In remembering and in touching the wounds of these women, we remember and touch our own. Such remembering will lead us through painful places, yet this very remembering gives strength. The remembering itself is a sacrifice, an act of making whole.

Phyllis Trible, in her book *Texts of Terror,* likens the process of remembering difficult stories to Jacob's struggle with God in Genesis 32:

> To tell and hear tales of terror is to wrestle demons in the night. . . . We struggle mightily, only to be wounded. But yet we hold on, seeking a blessing: the healing of wounds and the restoration of health. If the blessing comes—and we dare not claim assurance—it does not come on our terms. Indeed, as we leave the land of terror, we limp.

And, like Jacob, we are named anew.

A Prayer for the Beginning of Lent

❖

Our word Lent *comes from a word meaning "lengthen," probably referring to the lengthening daylight of this season. These days may seem longer as we remember, as we prepare, as we begin to touch the wounds that have emerged along the journey. As we move into this season, remembering that we are elemental creatures, made of dust, we pray for strength for the journey and for endurance to wrestle a blessing from these days.*

You may light a candle.

God of the journey,
who calls us to travel with faith,
who reminds us we are dust
yet breathes into us the breath of life,
hear my prayer:

Bearer of the Sun,
draw me into your heart of fire,
that I may have light to uncover
the unremembered stories
and strength to endure their telling.

Creator of the world,
awaken me to the blessedness of earth,
that I may honor those who once dwelled
along these paths that I now travel.

Spirit who hovered
over the face of the deep,
lead me to your life-giving waters,
that I may give my tears to the depths
and find refreshment and delight.

Helper who breathes life
into each new generation,
surround me with the winds of your spirit,
and may I hear with tenderness
the stories that they bear.
—Jan L. Richardson

16 An Inhuman Sacrifice
The Unnamed Daughter of Jephthah

Invocation: *Accompany me, O God, in this perplexing season. Breathe through me, Tender Presence, when this journey of remembering takes me along painful paths.*

Text: Judges 11:29-40

Context: Unwittingly caught in her father's bargain with God to secure a victory against the Ammonites, this daughter's only recorded words are her assent to the deal and a request for two months in the mountains with her companions. Did she weep? Did she protest? Did she become angry with her father, with God? What happened on the journey? Who accompanied her? The text invites the reader's imaginings.

The Jewish people created stories to answer questions raised by scripture. By creating such a story, called a *midrash* (plural, *midrashim*), one could imagine the details that a text left out. While the scribes assembled many of the original, oral *midrashim* into written texts, to this day people still create *midrashim* by bringing their imaginations to the original stories. Many of the women of the scriptures, whom we often know through only a few verses, have come to life as others, individually and in groups, have imagined their lives and created *midrashim*.

And so we enter this season with a story, a *midrash*. As we begin our Lenten journey, we travel with the daughter of Jephthah and her companions into the mountains. From the perspective of one of the women who accompanied her, we imagine, we improvise, we mourn, and we remember. So let us hear *The Tale of She-Who-Remembers*—the story of Miriam, told by one who remembers.

—— MONDAY ——

We called her Miriam. Her father Jephthah had named her Mara, meaning "bitter," because her mother died in bringing her to birth. Although no one begrudged Jephthah his grief over such a loss, it soon became apparent that Mara was hardly an appropriate name for such a daughter as this. From an early age, she displayed a passionate love of singing, dancing, and making music. Someone once remarked that surely she had been touched by the spirit of Miriam, our foremother who led the women in rejoicing with timbrels and with dancing when our people passed safely through the sea during the Exodus. The name stuck. Miriam she was.

Miriam and I were the same age; and from the time before we could walk, we were the closest of friends. We were sisters, really, and Miriam was a member of my family almost as much as my brothers or I. Jephthah was an important man, a mighty warrior, and was away from the town quite often. With his power and wealth, Jephthah gave Miriam more than enough in the way of servants and possessions, but she didn't like being at home during her father's absences. So she usually stayed with us. These were my favorite times . . . times of whispered stories and secrets late at night when we should have been asleep, times of sneaking away when we had chores to do, times when Miriam's music filled the house. My parents loved to hear Miriam sing, so they overlooked the giggles and the missed chores. More than once one of us had to jump to grab a bowl or other object in midair as Miriam swung around in some spirited dance, timbrels flying, her voice so strong it seemed it would crack her open.

—Jan L. Richardson

Reflect

❖ Who whispered late at night with you when you were young?
❖ Who shared your secrets?

——— TUESDAY ———

Occasionally I was jealous of Miriam, it's true. My parents' eyes became a bit brighter when she was around, and they always went on and on about her music, about her dancing, about her sense of humor, about her beauty, about how if they had such a daughter as Jephthah had, they surely would not leave her so frequently. For a long time I wished I were more like her. Most especially I wished I had her voice. Mine seemed froglike in comparison, and one time I commented on this to her.

"How can that be?" she asked. "My songs don't come from inside me. They blow through me. Before me is the song; after me is the song. I catch it for a little while, dance with it, set it free. Singing isn't about how you sound, sister. How can you sound bad when the Spirit sings through you?"

The only time that Miriam stopped in the middle of a song was when Jephthah would come home. She knew before anyone else; it was like she had a special sense about it. She would stop, cock her head, and take off with hardly a good-bye. Even before he reached the gates of the town, she would be in her house, dressing herself and preparing to dance out to greet him. I resented Jephthah deeply for this—that he could go away so often for so long, and yet Miriam would drop everything when he came home. I didn't see her much when Jephthah was home, and I didn't understand how she could be so much a part of my family and then leave it all to devote herself to Jephthah when he came home. I learned quickly not to ask, for it angered Miriam to be questioned about this, as if it were wrong to cherish the scattered moments with the only parent she had known.

—Jan L. Richardson

Reflect
❖ What prompts jealousy in you?

—— **WEDNESDAY** ——

The last time this happened, this homecoming of Jephthah, is burned into my memory. It was in our fifteenth year, and we were just clearing away the evening meal to the melody of Miriam's voice when she stopped abruptly, hastily bade us good-bye, and ran home. Word soon spread throughout the town that Jephthah had returned from a crushing victory against the Ammonites. The celebration began immediately, with people pouring outdoors as quickly as they could gather up their wineskins and fruit and whatever they had on hand.

I was startled when Miriam made her way to me through the crowd, moving slowly and with a somber look on her face. Without a word she drew me into the house and in a low voice told me what had happened following her greeting of Jephthah with a special song she had created for the victory she knew he would have—something about a vow, she whispered; a promise to Yahweh, a sacrifice, a burnt offering. I sank to the floor in horror as her words washed over me. Miriam . . . the burnt offering was to be *Miriam.*

—Jan L. Richardson

Reflect
Imagine you are Miriam's friend.
❖ What do you feel?
❖ What do you say?

I immediately started sputtering plans for flight, for escape, but she quickly silenced me and told me that she had asked Jephthah to let her have two months in the mountains with her friends to "bewail her virginity." I almost laughed in spite of my horror. I'd never heard Miriam bewail much of anything, much less her virginity. Oh, she was admired by many young men in the town, and many mothers and fathers longed to have the daughter of the great Jephthah in their family, but she had laughed at the thought of submitting her independence to another's control. And she was all too aware of the dangers of childbirth. She had no desire to tempt the same demons that had attended her mother's birthing of her. But two months in the mountains . . . it was a brilliant excuse. I figured she had something planned, and this would buy us some time.

We parted company quickly—she going to visit some of our companions, and I to tell the others of what had happened. It was a blur. I didn't sleep that night, and just before dawn I slipped out of the house to meet the others. We gathered quietly, each carrying a pack with supplies for the two-month journey. Miriam's house was quiet. A few servants peeked out, but Jephthah was nowhere to be seen.

So we left, Miriam and her closest companions. Thirteen women who had known one another since childhood, who had shared our daily lives with one another in the town of Mizpah. We left, not quite knowing what had happened or what to expect in the days to come.
—Jan L. Richardson

Reflect

❖ If you were taking a final journey with your closest friends, where would you go?

❖ Who or what would you take with you?

—— **FRIDAY** ——

To say that it was not an easy trip would be almost comical. Life in Mizpah had barely prepared us for two months of travel, of making do with what little we had with us, of the dangers of the mountains, of constant togetherness. It was probably the latter that provided the greatest challenge. We learned quickly how to adapt physically. But it didn't take long for the emotional stress to show itself. Even when it wasn't talked about, we knew all too keenly the reason for our journey. And so Sarah would accuse

Hannah of taking more than her share of water, and Rachel would snap at Malkah for talking too much, and so on. I think Miriam and I fought the most bitterly. While she insisted that we would return to Mizpah, or that at least she would, I kept saying that we should keep going.

"*Why*, Miriam?" I asked for the hundredth time. "It would be *easy* never to go back. *Jephthah* made this stupid vow to Yahweh, not you. You shouldn't have to pay for it. If we don't go back, you'll live, and it'll let Jephthah off the hook. All we have to do is keep going. I'll come with you; we'll all come with you. It doesn't make sense to go back, Miriam. It doesn't make sense!"

Miriam would gaze at me, sometimes with great patience, and later, with little. "I don't have reasons, sister. At least not good ones, or any I can explain to you. I fear what would happen to my father if he broke his vow. It doesn't make sense, you're right. But sister, what are the odds of my surviving even if everything else were all right? If I did what people expected—got married, started having children? My own mother died doing that. I don't even know if getting married, if having me, were things she chose for herself. At least this will be a choice . . . *my* choice."
—Jan L. Richardson

Reflect
- ❖ What choices do you think Miriam has?
- ❖ What do you think of the choices she has made?

——— SATURDAY ———

Evenings were, by a common unspoken agreement, truce times. These were the times that enabled us to survive the journey. After the evening meal, we would linger around the fire. As the stars came out, we would tell stories that our mothers and grandmothers had passed down to us, stories of women who had survived journeys of their own. Each night as the moon rose and danced its arc across the sky, we would sing. All of us. And occasionally, just occasionally, between the songs I could hear a rushing wind, and the words seemed to come not from within us but from somewhere else, and I could physically feel them passing through me.

The nights passed quickly, and the days as well. All too soon we found ourselves, at Miriam's leading, circling back toward Mizpah. Before long, we knew we were within a day's journey of the town. Most of that day passed in silence as each of us contemplated what the return would be like—for Miriam, for ourselves, for we who had lived as a community for nearly two months' time and who had found in one another's hearts our true home.

We ate the evening meal in silence. When we had finished the meal and the moon had begun to rise, Miriam pulled a wineskin and some bread from her sack. She served the bread to each of us, and she said, "We are like this bread. We have sustained one another on this journey as bread enables a body to live. We are different from one another, yet together we are whole. When you break bread with one another, remember what we have shared. When you do this, I will be there with you."

Miriam served the wine to each of us, and she said, "We are like this wine. We have poured ourselves out to one another on this journey, satisfying one another's thirst in the way that wine can both bite and be sweet. We are different from one another, yet the blood of sisters flows through us. When you drink wine with one another, remember what we have shared. When you do this, I will be there with you."

We ate and we drank. We told stories of a foremother who had helped lead her people to freedom, who had been bold and fiery and spirited, who had not reached the promised land. We sang Mother Miriam's song, and we danced her dance. We huddled together, comfortingly, under the stars. That night I dreamed of passing through a great river, of turning around to see my friend Miriam behind me, of watching the waters pass over her as I touched the dry ground. I screamed, and she held me, silent, knowing.

—Jan L. Richardson

Reflect

❖ When did you share a final meal with someone?

❖ What sounds, smells, tastes, touches, sights, words do you remember?

——— **SUNDAY** ———

We rose and gathered our things the next morning, moving with quiet purpose. Before the sun had crested we were back in Mizpah. We walked toward Jephthah's house with a curious and somber crowd following after us. Jephthah sought to make Miriam's companions leave, that we might not witness his murder of our friend. But we stayed. Our journey was not finished. And Jephthah did with her according to the vow he had made.

Five years have passed since that time. Still our journey continues. Each year many of the women of Israel make a four-day journey into the mountains to honor Miriam. I have not married and do not plan to, but I have a niece who is old enough to make the journey this year. We will go, and we will visit some of the places we visited on the first journey with Miriam. We will tell the stories, we will sing the songs, we will dance, and we will break bread and drink wine. We will vow, for ourselves and for our daughters, *never again shall such a thing happen in the land of Israel. Never again shall such a thing happen to the daughters of the Holy One.*

And we will remember.

—Jan L. Richardson

Reflect

❖ How has this story affected you?

❖ How will you remember it, and what will you do with it?

—— **Meditation** ——

To the Moon

With my face to the moon
I confess,
and she hears me,
offering her comfort
as she glides
among the trees.
She doesn't need
my body,
and she doesn't want
my blood;
she just wraps me
in her brightness
and she tells me
I am good.
—Jan L. Richardson

—— ❖ ——

Blessing: *Blessed are you who struggle against forgetting, for the silenced sisters of the past will live in you.*

17   Her Body Broken for Many
The Unnamed Concubine

Invocation: *Abiding Spirit, accompany me in uncertain journeys. When I find the way filled with fear, may I know you as a faithful companion.*

Text: Judges 19

Context: In the story of the rape and murder of the unnamed concubine, we find a lesson in the cycle of domestic violence between spouses or partners. Those who have studied and/or lived with such violence have identified three phases that abusive relationships tend to follow: the stage of escalation, when tensions mount; the stage when an actual abusive episode occurs; and the "honeymoon" stage, when the abusive partner attempts to win the other partner back. This final stage may last a little or a long while, but in an ongoing abusive relationship, it rarely lasts.

The writer of the book of Judges relates this story with a significant amount of detail, but we never hear the woman's voice. We never even know her name. We do not know why she left her husband. But as the text unfolds, we witness the story of a bold, decisive woman who, by the end of the story, has been bartered to secure the life and the safety of her husband and his host.

In an unpublished paper entitled "Imaging a Christian Feminist Theodicy," Dorri Sherrill retells this story from the unnamed concubine's perspective. To a woman who has no voice in the text, Dorri gives voice through her own imagination. The readings for Monday through Friday will begin with an excerpt from this paper, so we may hear words the unnamed woman might have said or thought.

—— **MONDAY** ——

"You, O Yahweh, know how painful my life has been. I was bought—purchased, I was purchased—*as a concubine, and the man who 'owns' me does not honor me. At best, I am as any other of his possessions."*

A Woman Possessed

She is
a woman possessed
by pain
by despair
by aloneness
by desert
by wind
by dryness
by sorrow
by loss
by shame
by trouble
by him
by emptiness
by secrets
by silence
by choked breath
by fear-full hands
by hopelessness
by hesitation
by law
by unknowing
by stories
by possibilities
by the cusp
by the threshold
by the edge
by the verge
by flight.
—Jan L. Richardson

Reflect

❖ What possesses you?

—— **TUESDAY** ——

"My life at home with my father certainly wasn't great, but it will be better there than here with one who ignores me. I will return home to my father,

for there the pain and shame of being ignored is so familiar that maybe I won't even feel it."

This time is the most dangerous, they say. When I worked at the Council on Battered Women, they told me that when a woman is in the act of leaving an abusive situation, she faces the greatest threat of violence, even death. Because of this, you cannot tell a woman to leave. Because she may have no money, you cannot tell a woman to leave. Because she may have no emotional support or family or other resources, you cannot tell a woman to leave. Because children may be at risk, you cannot tell a woman to leave. Because, finally, a woman's life must be a woman's choice, you cannot tell her to leave.

And yet I longed to tell each one, *leave.* Leave, and come home with me. Leave, and I'll draw a hot bath for you and very gently wash your wounds, and you can stay in as long as you like. Leave, and I'll watch the door while you sleep through the night for the first time in years. Leave, and your children can gobble my food and jump on my bed and unlearn their fear. Leave, and I'll remind you each day of how talented you are, and how lovely. Leave, and you'll never have to wonder again, I swear, whether you could live without him, you now so fine and free.
—Jan L. Richardson

Reflect
Imagine you are the unnamed woman in this text.
 ❖ What has made you angry?
 ❖ Do you stay or leave? Why?

--- **WEDNESDAY** ---

"My God, no! He's here—and my father is delighted! He came today, and Father and he are sharing the best of our food and wine. I thought I was free from him and his arrogance and disrespect and abusiveness. But he has come for me. And I don't want to go! I know my father, though, and he won't even ask me what I want. He will give me back and not think twice about it. Why did I think I could get away? O God, why did I think it would get better? And where are you? Why does my life continue to be so unfair? I'm afraid. Don't abandon me. . . ."

I Wonder

Did she have a sister,

I wonder,
who brought thc news when he broke the horizon
who held her hand when he trespassed the door
who met his gaze, unflinching
who cried out to her father
who would not share their table
who held her every night
who offered to go in her place
who placed her only ring on her sister's finger
who packed her bag with bread
who breathed an ancient blessing into her ear
who watched her to the horizon
who remembered her after she left?
—Jan L. Richardson

Reflect

Imagine you are there at her father's house.

❖ Who else is there?

❖ What do you say to each other before she leaves?

——— **THURSDAY** ———

"There is some kind of commotion outside. I hear voices, lots of men's voices. What is it that these men want? What . . .—O God, he's coming for me! My husband, he has my arm, he's dragging me out—out to these men! I hear the man of the house say, 'Ravish her, do with her what seems good to you.' What is happening? Why are you doing this, my husband? I don't like being your property, but even so—protect me—I am your property! Oh, my God . . . it hurts! . . .O God, where are you? . . ."

Driving through town this evening, I flip on the radio to NPR. It's a report on domestic violence. They play an excerpt from a tape, a woman's call to a police station. She's screaming for help, screaming about her husband—then, no, "I just had a temper tantrum. It's okay. Don't come."

"Ma'am, do you need help?"

"No, really. No."

I can hear a man's loud voice in the background.

"Ma'am, if you don't need help, tell me a number between one and five."

A pause.

"Six."

And I wonder if behind that door in Gibeah where stood the husband, the host, the servant, and the virgin daughter, any counting went on as their companion called for help. Whether they were counting seconds between screams, counting the laughs of the crowd outside, counting their own blessings, counting sheep in order to fall asleep that night behind the door.

I wonder what they counted, and I wonder if somewhere, anywhere, someone heard the screams and cried out for the woman beyond the door who, in the eyes of that crowd, simply didn't count.
—Jan L. Richardson

Reflect
* ❖ How does it make you feel that no one did anything for the woman of this story?

—— **FRIDAY** ——

"Where am I? Oh, I hurt! I can't walk—what did they do to me? Am I safe now? . . . Where can I go? The house where he is—the one who gave me over to these men—it's over there . . . if I can just make it to the door. . . . It's not all that far—I had no idea we were so close to the house. That means he must have heard what was going on! . . . Just give me the strength to get to the door—I want him to see me. . . . Just a bit farther. . . . Just a few more feet. . . . Let them hear me knocking! . . . my body—how it aches! I'm feeling strange—God, are you here? God, if you can, take care of me! O God . . . "

She died with her hands on the threshold. This image is the most haunting of all for me. In a strange town, in an unfamiliar place, she goes to the only place she knows, this place of uncertain security. And with her hands on the threshold—of hope, of a touch, perhaps of revenge, perhaps of a final mercy, perhaps of a sister (what did happen to that virgin daughter whom the host offered?)—she dies.

I imagine her with her hands on the threshold, her fingers pointing west. I imagine her with her hands empty, having flung her spirit toward the house of the dying sun, toward the land of no-turning-back, toward the hills of the last light. I imagine her hands splayed in supplication to the guardians of the gates of night, may they draw her safely through. I imagine her pointing the way toward the Great Sea, the Mediterranean; toward salt, toward land's edge, toward water's birth, toward moon's rising, toward the

place where they wait for her, toward the home of safe return.
—Jan L. Richardson

Reflect

❖ To what does this woman point in her own life, in yours?

——— **SATURDAY** ———

When he had entered his house, he took a knife, and grasping his concubine he cut her into twelve pieces, limb by limb (Judges 19:29).

Parable (excerpt)

You ask me, my sister,
how have I made it this far?

It was really very simple,
to begin with
they removed one of my arms.

The man who thought himself most qualified
pulled the hardest.
He wanted to take it for himself
the very life force
which gave my arm strength
and movement.
And so he imposed on me
his macho right.

It was the same arm
that I had fraternally
shared with him
Light and Bread
when he was once in great need.

He had decided
to dominate
with that blind obstinacy
we women know so well.
While the others,
neutral,
watched
with "serene objectivity"

and concluded
that a woman's arm
lacked importance.

From the force exerted
the joint began to give way
until the limb parted from my body,
while the others,
still neutral,
watched until
the mutilation was complete,
choosing to keep
their united male silence.

Alone with God,
I dried my tears . . .
the hemorrhaging slowly stopped,
but the pain lasted for centuries.
—Julia Esquivel in *Threatened with Resurrection*

Reflect

❖ Where does this story leave you?
❖ What will you do with the pieces of this woman's life?

—— **SUNDAY** ——

Postscript

In Anne Michele Tapp's article "Virgin Daughter Sacrifice" in the book *Anti-Covenant: Counter-Reading Women's Lives in the Hebrew Bible*, she notes that in this story and that of Jephthah's daughter, doorways serve as a boundary between the "safety" of the home and the danger that lies beyond.

Only the male head of the household can pass through the doorway safely, and the well-being of his guests depends primarily on him. In these stories, the host protects the men in his home. The women are allowed, or pushed, through the doorway to deal by themselves with the dangers that await immediately outside. The doorway does not belong to the woman, yet it determines her fate.

The symbolism of the doorway reminded me of a letter I received from a friend in which she described a dream about a doorway of her own. My friend, who still deals with the wounds of childhood abuse, wrote,

I had a dream that I was building a door. It was a beautiful wooden door. It was partially open as I was working on it and the frame. Friends came by to help but it was my door—I was in charge and competent enough to build a door. And it wasn't a "keeping out" door, but it was a "going through" door. I think that's just where I am in my life. I need to claim me, my doors, and my ability to make them with the intention of going through them.

My friend's dream and her life speak to me of claiming our "doorways," our passages—turning them from other-owned openings to death into self-owned, self-fashioned passages to life, passages through which others may find safe space. Honest doorways that open into ourselves, into God.
—Jan L. Richardson

Reflect

Imagine your own doorway.

- ❖ What does it look like?
- ❖ Onto what space does it open?
- ❖ Whom do you let through?

—— **Meditation** ——

In Pieces

Piece by piece
they brought her forth;
piece by piece
they had gathered her
from the farthest corners.
In every land
where they had asked for her,
she was known by a different name.

Piece by piece
as they laid her out
piece by piece
they whispered her names:

Felicitas
    Christian slave who, along with Perpetua, was martyred by the

sword in Carthage, North Africa, in the third century.

Bridget Bishop
  convicted as a witch and hanged in Salem, Massachusetts, in 1692.

Kim Hak Sun
  one of the 80,000–200,000 Korean "comfort women" forced to be
  prostitutes for the Japanese Army during World War II. Raped
  repeatedly for months, Kim Hak Sun survived to speak out;
  thousands of others died or were killed.

Anne Frank
  young Dutch Jew killed in the Holocaust in 1945.

Anna Mae Pictou Aquash
  member of the American Indian Movement. When her unidenti-
  fied body was found in 1976 on the Pine Ridge Reservation in
  South Dakota, the cause of death was listed as "exposure." The
  FBI agent present ordered her hands severed and sent to
  Washington, D.C. for fingerprinting. After her family reported her
  missing, a second autopsy was performed. This time the coroner
  attributed her death to a bullet fired into the back of her head at
  close range.

Jean Donovan
  a Catholic lay missionary who, along with two Maryknoll sisters
  and one Ursuline sister, was raped and murdered by government
  soldiers in El Salvador in 1980.

And all the unnamed sisters,
known only by the earth
in all the places
you were buried:

Woman of Hiroshima and Nagasaki
  annihilated by manmade pillars of fire in 1945.

Woman of freedom
  who lived and died with "Before I'll be a slave,
  I'll be buried in my grave" on your lips.

Woman of South Africa
  still bearing the wounds of apartheid.

Woman of Bosnia
  on your body their war yet rages.

Woman of silence
  your voice beaten out of you.

Woman of hope

with your hands upon the threshold.

Piece by piece
they touched her skin
piece by piece
re-membering
the broken body
into flesh
the ancient wounds
into new life.
—Jan L. Richardson

———— ❖ ————

Blessing: *Blessed are you who re-member the ancient wounds, for through your remembering, broken bodies and broken stories will receive new life.*

18 Tender Anger
Mary and Martha

Invocation: *Sustain me, Fiery Power, when I journey through fields of anger. Make me wise to the lessons to be learned here and strengthen me, that my voice may be clear and life-giving.*

Text: John 11:1-6, 17-44

Context: I approach this story with hesitation. I hesitate because I wonder if I am reading Mary and Martha's anger into the text. I hesitate because I am still learning to recognize and honor Anger's voice. I hesitate because women have much to be angry about—with our sisters as well as our brothers—and precious little safe space in which to let our anger dance.

But here it is. This story may not be so much about Mary and Martha's anger as it is about mine and that of many women I know. And if Jesus' inaction in the face of his friends' pain doesn't make them angry, it does me.

The pain and anger I hear in the words of Martha, which Mary repeats, "Lord, if you had been here, my brother would not have died," echo the pain and anger I feel each time persons in power fail to respond to those who cry for help. Their words echo the pain and anger I feel when those who bear the power of life let suffering continue.

The question is never whether anger is right or wrong. Anger—like any other emotion—*is*, and it is always a sign of something deeper. Given appropriate expression, anger tells us about injustice, loss, grief, and damaged relationships. It tells us about ourselves. Given appropriate space, it opens a path toward change. And as Martha and Mary discovered, it leads to resurrection.

—— **MONDAY** ——

The taboos against our feeling and expressing anger are so powerful that even *knowing* when we are angry is not a simple matter. When a woman shows her anger, she is likely to be dismissed as irrational or worse. At a professional conference I attended recently, a young doctor presented a paper about battered women. She shared many new and exciting ideas and conveyed a deep and personal involvement in her subject. In the middle of her presentation, a well-known psychiatrist who was seated behind me got up to leave. As he stood, he turned to the man next to him and made his diagnostic pronouncement: "Now, *that* is a *very* angry woman." That was that! The fact that he detected—or thought he detected—an angry tone to her voice disqualified not only what she had to say but also who she was. Because the very possibility that we are angry often meets with rejection and disapproval from others, it is no wonder that it is hard for us to know, let alone admit, that we are angry.

—Harriet Goldhor Lerner in *The Dance of Anger*

Reflect

❖ Why does anger, real or perceived, prompt others to dismiss or ridicule us?

—— **TUESDAY** ——

When my younger brother killed himself, nobody talked about anger. We shared our shock, our grief, our despair. Numb, we sat together and wept together and agonized over the violence of his death. But we never spoke of anger—his, with its life-shattering power, or ours at his sudden leaving.

We never spoke of anger. And the anger never went away. Instead, it came back to us time and again, in a dozen clever, wretched forms.

The unspent anger disguised itself as sorrow and its hot tears scarred my mother's face. The unspoken anger disguised itself as hopelessness and my father, another victim, languishes in self-hate. The unacknowledged anger disguised itself as busyness and the workaholic hyperactivity finally ate away at my soul.

—Helen R. Neinast, from "Sacred Anger" in *Wellsprings: A Journal for United Methodist Clergywomen*

Reflect

❖ What disguises have you seen anger wear?

—— **WEDNESDAY** ——

It is not the anger of other women that will destroy us but our refusals to stand still, to listen to its rhythms, to learn within it, to move beyond the manner of presentation to the substance, to tap that anger as an important source of empowerment. . . .

For women raised to fear, too often anger threatens annihilation. In the male construct of brute force, we were taught that our lives depended upon the good will of patriarchal power. The anger of others was to be avoided at all costs because there was nothing to be learned from it but pain, a judgment that we had been bad girls, come up lacking, not done what we were supposed to do. And if we accept our powerlessness, then of course any anger can destroy us.

But the strength of women lies in recognizing differences between us as creative, and in standing to those distortions which we inherited without blame, but which are now ours to alter. The angers of women can transform difference through insight into power. For anger between peers births change, not destruction, and the discomfort and sense of loss it often causes is not fatal, but a sign of growth.

—Audre Lorde, from "The Uses of Anger: Women Responding to Racism" in *Sister Outsider*

Reflect

❖ How can anger be a clue to discovering and transforming our differences—with respect to race as well as other differences?

❖ How do you respond to the anger of other women? of men?

—— **THURSDAY** ——

It is my thesis that we Christians have come very close to killing love precisely because we have understood anger to be a deadly sin. Anger is not the opposite of love. It is better understood as a feeling-signal that all is not well in our relation to other persons or groups or to the world around us. Anger is a mode of connectedness to others and it is always a vivid form of caring. . . .

To grasp this point . . . is a critical first step in understanding the power of anger in the work of love. Where anger rises, there the energy to act is present.

—Beverly Wildung Harrison, from "The Power of Anger in the Work of Love" in *Making the Connections*

Reflect

❖ When has the recognition of your own anger given you the energy to act?

❖ How did this change you and/or the relationship that gave rise to the anger?

To a friend who angered me

I think your most valuable gift to me has been a space—a safe space—to share my voice. Through your willingness to hear, you have helped me to speak. I suspect that some days that may have felt like a mixed blessing to you—days when my voice spoke more pain and sadness and anger than I had ever been able to say and that erupted in ways that felt awfully sloppy and messy to me. There were times lately when I needed to say something just to say it without worrying whether you would hear it as pressure or as a desire for you to change. You heard me far more often than not, however. I remember being struck one time by how well you seemed to understand what I was saying. Then it hit me that your ability to hear so well seemed to coincide with the time that I started sharing more honestly and deeply. Funny how that works. . . .
—Jan L. Richardson, from a letter to a friend

Reflect
❖ When has someone's honest and caring listening enabled you to express and transform your anger?

—— **SATURDAY** ——

At a recent workshop on praying our anger, I invited participants to write their own psalms expressing anger, modeling them on some of the imprecatory psalms. Our purpose was to truly acknowledge the angry, vindictive feelings we had and then to offer them in prayer. We asked whether there were ways in which God was asking us to be part of the healing of the situation calling forth the anger. The following psalm is my own effort, based on Psalm 52:

> You oppressor, why do you practice tyranny
> against the poor year after year?
> You inflame hatred;
> your policies promote injustice,
> O wrecker of human families.
> You love segregation more than unity
> and bondage more than freedom.
> You cherish superiority
> O you twister of the truth.

Oh, that God would destroy your schemes,
thrust you out of your power structure
and incarcerate you on Robins Island
[a prison in which many South African dissidents are incarcerated].
The disenfranchised shall rise and rejoice,
they will dance and sing:
"This is the one who thought God was on his side,
who placed confidence in white supremacy
and relied on apartheid."
But I am like one whose dreams have come true;
I trust in the Gospel of freedom and life.
I will celebrate the wonder of God's compassion
and share liberty with my sisters and brothers for all time.

Often the original context of the psalm is lost to us but not its impact as we discover ourselves in its emotional milieu. I lived for a while in South Africa, and I agonize for those still so cruelly oppressed. At the same time I am called to pray. I pray for courageous leaders like Archbishop Desmond Tutu, for those who have lost their lives in the struggle for justice, and for those who remain incarcerated and silenced. As I pray for oppressor and oppressed, I am also challenged to search out my own collusion with oppressive ways of thinking and acting which so insidiously corrupt the environment in which I live.
—Elizabeth J. Canham, from "Sing a New Song" in *Weavings: A Journal of the Christian Spiritual Life*

Reflect
❖ How does it feel to bring your anger before God?

——— **SUNDAY** ———

"Anger and tenderness: my selves," Adrienne Rich writes in her poem "Integrity," which she records in her book *A Wild Patience Has Taken Me This Far.* She speaks of anger and tenderness as strands of the same web being spun and woven from the spider's body, "even from a broken web."

Mary and Martha know this web: the web of passionate feeling, of relationship, of creation from brokenness—the web that connects but does not entrap, that provides shelter but does not ensnare. Mary and Martha are websters, web-weavers. By their care and hospitality, they have established this web of relationship with Jesus.

This web enables each of them to speak out when Jesus finally arrives after Lazarus's death. It enables them to voice their anger, or at least their sharp disappointment, at his absence. In the face of Mary and Martha's pain, Jesus realizes that he has put lessons ahead of relationship. Perhaps Jesus wonders if God's glory can be displayed outside the context of care for his friends.

Mary and Martha's words free Jesus to rediscover his compassion, to remember the depth of their relationship and the strength of their web. In the real, immediate presence of their tears, Jesus realizes the depth of his own loss, a loss that spills beyond the borders of his well-intentioned plan. And he does not merely cry; he weeps. Within the web, within his circle of friends, the holy one's humanity runs down his face.

By their care and their words, Mary and Martha bear the strands of resurrection. With his compassion, with his tears, Jesus weaves them and fashions life anew.

—Jan L. Richardson

Reflect
* When has anger brought new life?
* What lies beyond your anger?

——— Meditation ———

Anger Is a Woman

Anger is a woman who has learned
that pleasantness
is not the way to peacefulness,
that silence
is not the way to strength.

Anger is a woman
who has learned
to breathe from her belly;
who waits at your door,
bringing you offerings;
who knows your true name
and gives it back to you.
She has lived on the streets.
She knows prisons
and alleys
and mud.

She has seen hungry children
and broken women
and desperate men
and spoken to them
in their own tongues.

They gave her a song.
She sings it to you.
—Jan L. Richardson

——— ❖ ———

Blessing: *Blessed are you who journey for a time with Anger, for you will know the resurrection that lies beyond.*

19 Stirring the Ashes
Elemental Blessings

Invocation: *God of fire, earth, wind, and water, embrace the elemental wounds we bear. God of grace and healing, help me return your embrace, that I may bring forth new blessings from the broken places.*

Text: Deuteronomy 30:19-20

Context: In Lent, we are laid bare. As we remember our pain, as we touch our wounds, as we journey toward the terror of the cross, we may find ourselves feeling vulnerable, sore, exposed. We may struggle against the way Lent strips us of pretense and beckons us to see what is basic to us. Yet the ashes of the first day of Lent affirm that we are elemental people. We who are fashioned of earth are also touched by fire, brought to life by the breath of God, and blessed by the birthing waters. Here, in the middle of the Lenten journey, we pause to reflect on the elements of which we are made, to consider not only the wounds that they sometimes harbor but also the possibilities they hold for blessing.

Several years ago I found myself on a Lenten journey that left me raw and intimate with brokenness. A friendship that had provided trust, safety, and delight gave way to alienation, insecurity, and anger. At the time I also was working as a facilitator of a group of emotionally and physically abused women. One night, in the midst of all this, I realized I couldn't take Communion. How could I share in the breaking of the body and the blessing of the cup after listening to the stories of women whose bodies had been broken and whose blood had been shed? And how could I share Communion with the friend who had led me to such brokenness, who had turned the cup of blessing bitter?

Friends who companioned me in the journey provided moments of communion when I couldn't share in the ritual of Communion. They shared blessings when I couldn't share the loaf and cup. Slowly, painfully, I came to understand Communion anew. Gathered around the table, we who are broken re-member the body of Christ. By our care for the broken of this world, we give birth to the Christ who wills blessing, not brokenness, for all.

That Lenten journey gave rise, much later, to the blessings contained in this week's readings. Written for the friend who had become a stranger, they became a cry of life and hope in the wake of pain and loss. Broken at an elemental level, I fashioned these blessings, and they bear witness to a keen memory that longed to re-member differently the elemental connections between us and within myself.

Excerpts from a letter that accompanied these blessings weave them together and provide the closing blessing. In the letter, I tried to give voice to the source of the blessings and to my understanding of blessing as an act of power in a seemingly powerless situation.

May this week's dance of blessing and reflection, lead you to your elemental places, the spaces within you that bear deep wounds as well as seeds of new birth. May God meet you in these depths, holding you as you remember.

 **MONDAY**

By Fire Be Blessed

May you dwell by the Sacred Fire.
May the flames of the Holy dance in your eyes:

> flame of wisdom
> flame of insight
> flame of longing
> flame of devotion
> flame of new vision
> flame of long memory
> flame of warmth-of-spirit
> flame of strength-of-body.

May the Sacred Fire dwell in you.
May you dance as flame in the eyes of the Holy.
—Jan L. Richardson

Reflect
❖ Remember the flames that have danced through your life . . . what are their names?
Light a candle as you remember them.

 **TUESDAY**

Blessings have become tremendously important to me. My quiet time has been deeply enriched by a collection of Gaelic hymns, incantations, prayers, and blessings. The Gaelic sense of the divine as permeating life, work, nature, relationships, *everything* is amazing. Last night I read a series of blessings for milking cows. Their (the Gaelic people's, not the cows'!) ability and desire to call forth the holy in all situations has fascinated me. I think that as I see more and more pain in the world, the ability to bless becomes an increasingly radical act—particularly on the part of those who have received the pain. One of the Gaelic blessings, a "Blessing of the Kindling," says in part, "God, kindle Thou in my heart within/A flame of love to my neighbour,/To my foe, to my friend, to my kindred all." Even "to my foe"!

—Jan L. Richardson

Reflect

❧   What and whom do you bless?

❧   When do you find it difficult to receive blessings—or to give them?

—— **WEDNESDAY** ——

By Earth Be Blessed

May you know the embrace of Earth.

May she teach you the wisdom of time:
    the unfolding of Spring
    the ripening of Summer
    the turning of Autumn
    the shedding of Winter.

May she teach you the wisdom of intimacy:
    seed embraced by warm, dark soil
    crevice traced by insistent stream
    raindrop clinging to new, soft leaf
    precious stones in hidden places.

May she teach you the wisdom of grace:
    flowers entwining fallen oak
    healing gifts of common "weeds"
    grain for bread, fruit for wine
    dancing stars through barren branches.

May you be known in Earth's embrace.

—Jan L. Richardson

Reflect

❖ What have you learned in Earth's embrace?

——— **THURSDAY** ———

I think being able to bless means that even in situations that aren't okay, one hasn't given up, hasn't lost power, hasn't cut off the parts of one's own spirit/self that were once intertwined with another. Remember those candlesticks I bought to match the chalice and paten I gave you? I got those because they symbolized a profound connection that I wanted a visible reminder of. A few other things occasionally elicited conflicting feelings when I remembered how they connected us—ocean waters, stars, particular songs. I didn't go around agonizing over these things constantly, but I did remember . . . and there were times when I wished I could turn some of the pain of those connections onto you.
—Jan L. Richardson

Reflect

❖ When have trusted connections brought a curse rather than a blessing?
❖ What does this experience do to your sense of power, to your ability to trust?

——— **FRIDAY** ———

By Wind Be Blessed

May you dance in the rushing wind.

May she blow open your door
    and wildly lead you across dawn-lit hills.
May she sing through the trees
    and beckon you to accompany her rhythms.
May she capture your breath,
    draw out the Spirit in you,
and run with it,
    laughing,
        under a star-drenched sky.

May the rushing wind dance in you.
—Jan L. Richardson

Reflect

❖   Where is the wind blowing through your life?

SATURDAY

These blessings for you come out of that pain, and they come out of those connections. They come out of a memory of how earth-embracing you are and how much I enjoyed the times I shared that with you . . . gazing at the stars through the barren branches of a tree that no longer stands . . . sharing the autumn wind that danced around us in the field of a Florida farm . . . partaking in the gifts of the earth in bread and wine (and a Thanksgiving meal, and a seafood feast, and a festive party with which you gifted me, and . . .) . . . witnessing your spirit as it danced to the very heartbeat of God. . . .

I'm reminded of the song you composed, "Out of Blessing We Give." Out of blessing we give, indeed, and out of pain and loss and sorrow and unnameable hope. Out of moments shared, dreams broken, trust scattered, and journeys intertwined. Out of trepidation we give, out of struggle, out of wonder, out of our very connectedness. Out of fire, earth, wind, water . . . the elemental, original blessings that form body and soul and which we share with all things. And which I now share with you.
—Jan L. Richardson

Reflect

❖   What blessings have you received?
❖   What blessings do you long to give?

SUNDAY

By Water Be Blessed

May you dwell with the spirits of many waters:

> May you befriend Creativity of the birthing waters.
> May Endurance accompany you in the raging rivers.
> May Pleasure embrace you beside moon-drawn oceans.
> May Sustenance lead you to her hidden springs.
> May Compassion bathe you in her healing waters.
> May you dance with Delight in the falling rain.

May the spirits of many waters dwell in you.
—Jan L. Richardson

Reflect
- ❖ What waters dwell within you?
- ❖ What blessings do you long to receive and enflesh?

—— **Meditation** ——

In Remembrance
   For Todd

This week laid me bare.
I came looking
   for rest
   for respite
   for relief
but I was led
   to remembering
the wounds
not only of others
but of myself,
my own elements
laid out on the table
I had unwittingly prepared.

I found myself
saying the words again
naming the wounds again
holding in my hands the bread
lifting to my lips the cup.

The aching of my body told me,
the longing in my blood reminded:
I have wrestled this blessing, yes,
but I have birthed it too.
—Jan L. Richardson

—— ❖ ——

Blessing: *By fire, by earth, by wind, by water be blessed. By all the things that have and do connect us may we both be blessed. By the God of journeys, of healing, of mystery, of hope may we continually be birthed.*

20 Bearing Witness
Etty Hillesum

Invocation: *God of history, you are present with all who suffer. In these words and in these times, O God, may I perceive the movement of your restless spirit.*

Text: Proverbs 14:5

Context: "If I have one duty in these times," wrote Etty Hillesum, "it is to bear witness." A Dutch Jew born in January of 1914, Etty witnessed one of the most terrifying times of this century. Just as the forces of Nazi oppression moved into Holland, Etty began to keep a journal. Into a series of eight exercise books filled during 1941 and 1942, Etty poured her soul. While deeply affected by the times, she passionately sought life, hope, and connection within herself and with her people.

A brilliant thinker and a graceful writer, Etty involved herself intimately in the lives of her friends and fellow Jews. When a roundup of Jews occurred in Amsterdam, Etty volunteered to go with them to Westerbork, a work camp considered to be the last stop before Auschwitz. By special arrangement, she traveled to Amsterdam from Westerbork many times, transporting letters, messages, and medicine to and from the outside. Although she had many opportunities to escape, Etty refused, even resisting an attempt by friends to kidnap her to safety. She considered her destiny to be bound with those who were suffering.

Reports from her companions at Westerbork confirm the luminous personality that her journals reveal. As the train that took Etty, her mother, her father, and her brother Mischa to Auschwitz left Westerbork on September 7, 1943, she threw a postcard from the window. On it she had written, "We have left the camp singing."

Etty died in Auschwitz on November 30, 1943. Her mother, father, and Mischa died there also; her other brother Jaap left the camp but died on his way back to Holland.

Etty left her journals with a friend in hopes they would one day be published. In 1983, J. G. Gaarlandt took an interest in them and published them in Holland. They have now been translated and published in nearly a dozen countries under the title *An Interrupted Life: The Diaries of Etty Hillesum*. The readings this week come from these diaries.

—— MONDAY ——

26 AUGUST [1941], TUESDAY EVENING. There is a really deep well inside me. And in it dwells God. Sometimes I am there too. But more often stones and grit block the well, and God is buried beneath. Then [God] must be dug out again.

I imagine that there are people who pray with their eyes turned heavenwards. They seek God outside themselves. And there are those who bow their head and bury it in their hands. I think that these seek God inside.

Reflect
Imagine a place within you where God lives.
❖ What does this place look like?

—— TUESDAY ——

FRIDAY MORNING [5 SEPTEMBER 1941], 9 O'CLOCK. One can't control everything with the brain; must allow one's emotions and intuitions free play as well. Knowledge is power, and that's probably why I accumulate knowledge, out of a desire to be important. I don't really know. But Lord, give me wisdom, not knowledge. Or rather the knowledge that leads to wisdom and true happiness and not the kind that leads to power. A little peace, a lot of kindness and a little wisdom—whenever I have these inside me I feel I am doing well.

Reflect
❖ How do knowledge and wisdom differ?

—— WEDNESDAY ——

MONDAY MORNING, 20 OCTOBER [1941]. There is a strange little melody inside me that sometimes cries out for words. But through inhibition, lack of self-confidence, laziness and goodness knows what else, that tune remains stifled, haunting me from within. Sometimes it wears me out completely. And then again it fills me with gentle, melancholy music.

Sometimes I want to flee with everything I possess into a few words, seek refuge in them. But there are still no words to shelter me. That is the real problem. I am in search of a haven, yet I must first build it for myself, stone by stone. Everyone seeks a home, a refuge. And I am always in search of a few words.

Reflect
Envision yourself with Etty.
- ❖ What words would you offer to Etty as shelter, as refuge?
- ❖ Where do you seek or create your refuge?

THURSDAY

27 FEBRUARY, FRIDAY MORNING, 10 O'CLOCK. [. . .] Something else about this morning: the perception, very strongly borne in, that despite all the suffering and injustice I cannot hate others. All the appalling things that happen are no mysterious threats from afar, but arise from fellow beings very close to us. That makes these happenings more familiar, then, and not so frightening. The terrifying thing is that systems grow too big for men and hold them in a satanic grip, the builders no less than the victims of the system, much as large edifices and spires, created by men's hands, tower high above us, dominate us, yet may collapse over our heads and bury us.

Reflect
- ❖ Which do you find more frightening, evil that comes from the familiar or from the unfamiliar? Why?

FRIDAY

SATURDAY MORNING, 7.30. [. . .] I went to bed early last night and from my bed I stared out through the large open window. And it was once more as if life with all its mysteries was close to me, as if I could touch it. I had the feeling that I was resting against the naked breast of life, and could feel her gentle and regular heartbeat. I felt safe and protected. And I thought: how strange. It is wartime. There are concentration camps. I can say of so many of the houses I pass: here the son has been thrown into prison, there the father has been taken hostage, and an 18-year-old boy in that house over there has been sentenced to death. And these streets and houses are all so close to my own. I know how very nervous people are, I know about the mounting human suffering. I know the persecution and oppression and despotism and the impotent fury and the terrible sadism. I know it all.

And yet—at unguarded moments, when left to myself, I suddenly lie against the naked breast of life and her arms round me are so gentle and so protective and my own heartbeat is difficult to describe: so slow and so regular and so soft, almost muffled, but so constant, as if it would never stop.

That is also my attitude to life and I believe that neither war nor any other senseless human atrocity will ever be able to change it.

Reflect

If you can, find a quiet place. Read these words of Etty aloud as you feel your own pulse.

- ❖ How do the words sound?
- ❖ How does your pulse feel?
- ❖ What is your "attitude to life"?

—— SATURDAY ——

[12 OCTOBER 1942] IN THE EVENING. And then again there are moments when life is dauntingly difficult. Then I am agitated and restless and tired all at once. Powerfully creative moments this afternoon, though. And now utter exhaustion.

All I can do is to lie motionless under my blankets and be patient until I shed my dejection and the feeling that I'm cracking up. When I felt like that in the past, I used to do silly things: go out drinking with friends, contemplate suicide or read right through the night, dozens of books at random.

One must also accept that one has "uncreative" moments. The more honestly one can accept that, the quicker these moments will pass. One must have the courage to call a halt, to feel empty and discouraged. Goodnight.

Reflect

- ❖ What do you do in your "uncreative" moments?
- ❖ How easy or difficult do you find it to give in to seeming uncreativity, to give yourself space for your creativity to emerge once again?

—— SUNDAY ——

[13 OCTOBER 1942] EARLY NEXT MORNING. *Vorwegnehmen.* To anticipate. I know no real Dutch equivalent. Ever since last night, I have been lying here trying to assimilate just a little of the terrible suffering that has to be endured all over the world. To accommodate just a little of the great sorrow the coming winter has in store. It could not be done. Today will be a hard day. I shall lie quietly and try to "anticipate" something of all the hard days that are to come.

When I suffer for the vulnerable is it not for my own vulnerability that I really suffer?

I have broken my body like bread and shared it out among men. And why not, they were hungry and had gone without for so long.

I always return to Rilke. It is strange to think that someone so frail and who did most of his writing within protective castle walls, would perhaps have been broken by the circumstances in which we now live. Is that not further testimony that life is finely balanced? Evidence that, in peaceful times and under favourable circumstances, sensitive artists may search for the purest and most fitting expression of their deepest insights so that, during more turbulent and debilitating times, others can turn to them for support and a ready response to their bewildered questions? A response they are unable to formulate for themselves since all their energies are taken up in looking after the bare necessities? Sadly, in difficult times we tend to shrug off the spiritual heritage of artists from an "easier" age, with "What use is that sort of thing to us now?"

It is an understandable but shortsighted reaction. And utterly impoverishing.

We should be willing to act as a balm for all wounds.

This was Etty's final journal entry.

Reflect

❖ How have Etty's words touched your wounds this week?

❖ To whom will you act as a balm this week?

—— Meditation ——

Bearing/Baring
    To Etty

In bearing witness
you bared the truth
the heart
the soul
of the times.

Forged in the depths
of a fire-filled heart,
your daily truths
were olives
pressed to oil,
grapes
crushed to wine.

The brutes laid you bare
to your very bones
but could not stave
the words you bore:
the balm for wounds
the cup of grace
poured out and mingling
for *tikkun olam*
for the healing of
these broken vessels.
—Jan L. Richardson

———— ❖ ————

Blessing: *Blessed are you who bear witness in these times, for from your words will flow a balm for all wounds.*

21 Loving Beyond the Boundaries
The Woman Who Anoints Jesus' Head

Invocation: *Compassionate God, you beckon us to touch and to heal. Move through us, so we may know the strength that comes from living with passion and compassion.*

Text: Mark 14:3-9

Context: In the Christian liturgical year, this week we remember Jesus' triumphal entry into Jerusalem (Mark 11:1-11). This familiar story, which has inspired songs, poetry, sermons, and paintings, tells of Jesus' sending two disciples ahead to prepare the way and of the crowd that greets him with hosannas. It constitutes a memorable, festive, dramatic moment in a perilous journey.

Yet others help prepare the way for Jesus in his final days; others accompany him in times of certain loneliness. We find one such companion in the woman who anoints Jesus' head as he sits at table in the house of Simon the leper. This woman emerges from beyond the boundaries of the table, a table most likely filled by men. She, of all those present, seems to know who Jesus is and what he needs. In her act of anointing, which is both a gift and a sign, she names Jesus as *Christos*, the Anointed One. In her touch, she reveals her awareness of his pain and her longing to heal it. She offers a prophetic act of beauty and grace. She both bears and becomes a balm for his wounds.

Jesus knows the depth of her gift and receives it with equal grace, delighting that one among them all possesses the heart to touch him. In his receiving he makes known his openness to those who possess the courage to touch, to love, and to heal beyond the boundaries that others set.

Jesus' gratitude is so deep that he promises that "wherever the gospel is proclaimed in the whole world, what she has done will be told in remembrance of her." Yet often we have forgotten her story and her grace-filled act, missing its vital message in our passage from Palm Sunday to Good Friday and beyond. As we live into this unnamed woman's story, we continue our Lenten journey. And we remember anew.

We see this transformation [of pain into passion] in the woman who anoints the head of her companion and friend, Jesus, in order to strengthen and empower him as he faced the possibility of death because of his actions on the boundaries. . . . She is a woman of wisdom who listens attentively and knows people and times. She does not deny her own pain, nor does she try to protect Jesus from his pain but she embraces pain with compassion. She anoints and the fragrance of pain-become-passion fills the room. And her story is told in memory of her and, in its telling, she gathers around her all those many women who have transformed their pain into passion which has reached out to become compassion. Many of you, I am sure, stand in her circle wanting to tell stories of other women whose healing hands must find voice to their memory. Many others, I am also sure, would want to tell your story, the story of your healing hands become a voice to your memory.

—Elaine Wainwright, from "Companions on the Journey" in *Women-Church*

Reflect

Consider your hands and think about how hands and healing go together.

❖ What stories do you remember of women's hands that have brought you healing, of your own hands that have brought healing to others?

Essential: of the essence. Basic. Fundamental. Necessary. Inherent. The woman who anoints Jesus knows what this means. She has sensed the need—the need of Jesus, her own need—and moves with grace to give what is perhaps costliest to her, perhaps the only thing she can give. In her hands she bears essence—perfume—but she also bears in her own flesh, in her own heart, her essence. That which is basic to her.

Her essence is a perfume pleasing to Jesus. The others at the table dismiss her beauty-infused act as frivolous. They miss the essence completely.

In defending her, Jesus does not intend to slight the poor or relieve the rest of us from our calling to be in community with them. Rather, he points out that acts of healing, of ministry, of hospitality can be beautiful. He honors the woman as a bearer of radical grace. In doing so, Jesus reminds us of what the woman already knows: that what is essential is the outpouring of ourselves, our essence, with as much grace as we can muster.

In reflecting on this woman, Helen Bruch Pearson in her book *Do*

What You Have the Power to Do notes that "song, dance, drama, poetry, painting, sculpture, art, movement, gesture—these are not luxuries. They are essentials to the Christian experience . . . they take us to God's heartbeat and the rhythms of all life." Heartfelt, grace-filled offerings are not frivolous. They are of the essence—of ourselves, of God.

—Jan L. Richardson

Reflect
- ❖ How can acts of ministry and justice be acts of art and grace, and vice versa?
- ❖ Where have you seen this happen?

―――― WEDNESDAY ――――

It was the woman, not Simon or the male guests and disciples, who was doing, acting, caring, touching, anointing, giving, and risking. And Jesus accepted her silent acts of intimacy and devotion with profound respect and reverent silence. Perhaps Jesus longed for the warmth and comfort of another's touch. Perhaps the cool ointment cascading from his head over his face and neck was like a baptism of sorts. Perhaps this tender act of mercy brought healing to his heavy heart. Perhaps, just once, it felt good to receive. To sit and be passive. To let someone minister to *him*. Perhaps to be cared for and loved was a balm to his soul. Perhaps this anointing was an act of emancipation for both Jesus and the woman. Jesus was not ashamed or embarrassed or defensive. He did not rebuke or resist or reject her. Rather, Jesus affirmed the woman for who she was and what she did.

—Helen Bruch Pearson in *Do What You Have the Power to Do*

Reflect
- ❖ How do you feel about receiving from others?

―――― THURSDAY ――――

Missing Betsey

I left her when I left Atlanta. I had scheduled one last massage with Betsey, but there was too much to do. I canceled. I wish I had gone. In the aching of those days, of that leaving, I wanted one more time to walk into her space. To stretch my body out on her table. To ease into the candle's light, the quiet music, the sure touch of her hands. To be once more with this friend I had known since before she became a massage therapist.

Early on, the easing into was not so easy. To allow myself the time, the space to be touched. To risk someone's learning her way around my body. Around me. To receive. But at Betsey's table I learned. We learned.

She knows the spiritedness of flesh. She is wise to the connections between body and spirit and teases out the boundaries. She understands geography; that the body is the spirit's landscape, which is not separate from it but both takes and gives it form.

She is a celebrant. She knows of broken bodies. Of communion. Of remembering. At her table. She knows of pouring out. Of grace. Of integrity. Of mercy. At her table. She knows of sacraments. Of oil. Of flame. Of touch. Of heart. At her table.

I miss her touch.

—Jan L. Richardson

Reflect

❖ Who touches you in ways that heal your body and spirit?

------ **FRIDAY** ------

From a letter to a friend with AIDS

Dear Edward,

There were no easy good-byes when I left Atlanta. But it was especially hard leaving you that last time we visited, especially difficult walking out of your hospital room filled with all the flowers and pictures and other gifts from the people who love you and who wish they could give you more. It was hard to hug you that last time while wondering how many more chances we'll have to do that. I pray there will be many—every day I pray for that. I know how strong you are—and I don't mean the kind of strength that people refer to when they say, in awed tones, "You're so *strong*" to people they perceive to be battling valiantly in the face of great adversity. I think that can be so distancing. It requires the other person to be so independent, so perfect, so superhuman. In you, I see strength in your connectedness, both within yourself and with others in your large and incredible community of friends. I see strength in your passion—for your music, your friends, your play, for the things and people you care about. I see strength in your creativity—your desire to write and paint and give shape to what is within you. I see strength in your willingness to let others share this journey with you—knowing that we can't quite feel your pain the same way you do or take it away but wanting to hold you and be held by you in the process. Marge Piercy writes about strength as something that is not intrinsic in us but rather moves us as wind moves a sail. I have seen strength move you. You live strongly. You love strongly. You create strongly. You touch strongly. And I pray that the strength that moves you and those you touch may sustain you in these days.

When I heard your voice yesterday, I ached over the distance between us. You—and Ray too—were significant in making Atlanta home for me, and I miss being at home with you, at least at a closer range! Your voice prompted an overwhelming longing for home—for the chance to touch the faces of my family there.

In working on my book lately, I've been living with the woman who anoints Jesus' head. I'm struck by the power of her gift, by the way she touches beyond the borders that her society considers acceptable, by Jesus' receptivity to her—how he allows himself to be cared for (strength moves him too!). And I wish I had an oil that would heal you, would prepare you for the days to come. I wish I were close enough to touch you, to hold you, to share a meal with you. I wish that, like the woman who touched Jesus, I had something powerful and precious to give you. And I pray that somewhere in these words may be found a bit of oil to heal some wounds, and that somewhere in our connectedness lies a touch that spans the present distance.

I love you, Edward.

—Jan L. Richardson

Reflect
- ❖ Whom do you touch, or long to?
- ❖ How do you touch across the distance?

—— **SATURDAY** ——

This God who does not leave us alone, who strengthens us, knows us, loves us, and claims us as God's own, this God guides us to places where our alabaster jar must be broken, where we do what we can do. She [the woman who anoints Jesus] has done what she could. On the surface this seems like very tepid tribute. Why praise a person for doing what she could? Because often that is the very thing denied. Doing what we can these days demands courage and a sense of freedom. It demands that we go with a God who has searched us and known us into a world that knows us not.

—Joanne Carlson Brown, from "The Unnamed Voice," sermon delivered in Cannon Chapel, Emory University, November 1990

Reflect
- ❖ Why are some touches, gifts, and offerings welcomed while others are not?
- ❖ Who decides which touches, gifts, and offerings are welcome ones?

—— **SUNDAY** ——

7:3 (excerpt)

love is believable.
keep that as a smooth stone, for sometimes you will be the
only one to love. for sometimes, you will be hated, & all the
love within reach will have to be your own, & what you can
tap from the spirits who fly to be with us at those moments,
& lend us their wings. who land on the lamps to give us comfort & courage, when we think we have nothing to say. when
we have nothing to say, perhaps it is time to listen.
to take dictation from the saints of
the past, without judgement can one say that, "saints," without judgement, can one love, can one seek out people who
make one feel good. without judgement, can one survive, buying food. without judgement. casting our pearls.

love is free, sometimes, & costly othertimes. we may only
have each other. our true touch. we may only have.
—Alta in *The Shameless Hussy, Essays and Poetry by Alta*

Reflect
- ❖ In what relationships have you found love to be free? to be costly?
- ❖ What is your true touch, and with whom?

—— **Meditation** ——

Sacred Worth
For Lesley, Linda, Nancy Lee, and all who love beyond the
boundaries

Your touch threatens
the way
they say

you must approach
the holy.

"Limits!"
they say,
"God lives
in these limits!"

But you dance beyond the boundaries
to the center of your selves,
your lives like vessels
filling up
and spilling over.

"Waste!"
they cry,
"Shameful gift!"

But the broken jar
belies the grace within.

And we laugh sometimes
at the beauty that emerges
and we weep sometimes
for the jagged edges
for those who do
what they have the power to do
and are mocked
by the powers that be
for those who miss
the meaning of the act:
that this is essence
that this is all.
—Jan L. Richardson

———— ❖ ————

Blessing: *Blessed are you who touch with integrity and grace, for you give flesh to the good news of Christ. May you be remembered.*

22 Passionate Companions
The Women of Holy Week and Easter

Invocation: *God of the shadows, you accompany us even in our most painful times. May I know the abiding passion you have for me; may I taste it, drink of it, feel it in the touch of those who journey with me.*

Text: See daily readings

Context: *Passion.* From the Latin *passio,* meaning "suffering." The term denotes the suffering of Christ from the night of the Last Supper through his crucifixion. But the women who have journeyed with Jesus know the meaning of passion too. They have seen Christ's pain—have held it, anointed it, felt it in themselves. And they know too the meaning of passion as devotion, as desire, as commitment, as love. Enflamed by his vision, healed by his touch, empowered by his friendship, the women who companion Jesus share his passion for wholeness, for salvation, for life. This shared passion prepares them for the Passion event. They do not leave Jesus alone during this time, not even at the cross.

In this week's readings, we encounter the passionate women who accompany Jesus in his Passion. With these women, strangers as well as intimate companions to Jesus, we move through the shadows of his final hours. With them we break bread, ask questions, and dream; with them we grieve, bear witness, and wait; with them we experience the joy of resurrection and the pain of our visions doubted. With them we pray for an end to suffering, for the healing of Christ's body.

—— **MONDAY** ——

Read Mark 14:22-25. See also Matthew 26:26-29; Luke 22:14-23; John 13:1-20.

In Remembrance

I wonder if they came to this table—those who fed him, those who followed him, those who provided for him, those who birthed him in flesh and spirit, those who touched him. Were any of them there?

When he washed
the feet of his friends,
did he remember
the one who anointed his flesh
essentially?

When he broke the bread,
did he remember the one
who opened her body
to bring him forth?

When he poured the wine,
did he remember the one
who poured out her blood
to give him life?

When he prayed for his friends
did he remember the women
who provided for him
out of their own resources?

When they sang the song,
did he remember the voice
of the one who rejoiced
with his family in the temple?

When they went out
did he remember the women
who had left everything behind
to journey with him?

Ah, I think the women feasted
here or somewhere,
bodies aching
as they broke the bread,
blood rising
as they shared the cup,
eating slowly
drinking deeply
for the days to come
for remembering.
—Jan L. Richardson

Reflect

Imagine that you are feasting with the women on this night.

❖ What memories, what stories do you share of Jesus, of journeying with him, of your companions?

—— TUESDAY ——

Read Matthew 26:69-72. See also Mark 14:66-69; Luke 22:56-57; John 18:15-17.

That Sort of Woman

> She is that sort of woman
> so annoying
> not content
> to let the shadows be
> not content
> to let the truth stay hidden.
> Dis-covering
> is her forte,
> revealing the masks
> that others choose,
> re-minding those
> who dwell near the holy
> fire will find them
> shadows will take form.
> —Jan L. Richardson

Reflect

❖ What do you think of this "sort of woman"?
❖ With whom do you most identify in this story?
❖ Why?

—— WEDNESDAY ——

Read Matthew 27:11-19.

The Dream

> Send to those
>   on the judgment seats.
> Tell them all

of visions
    of dreams.
Stand at their windows
    with songs of hope.
Beat down their doors
    with prayers for wisdom.
Cover their desks
    with charms for justice.
Surround their meeting-rooms
    with oracles of freedom.
Hurl prophecies of peace
    at their tallest buildings.
Weave banners of healing
    along their freeways.
Write this message
    in the smog-filled skies:
Say
    we have suffered much
    for the dreams we bear
    and washing your hands
    is not enough.
—Jan L. Richardson

Reflect

❖   How do you give expression to your visions and dreams?

─── **THURSDAY** ───

Read Luke 23:26-31.

The Daughters' Reply

We weep
that we may have the strength to live.
We wail
that we may have the power to speak
of these things
in the times to be.

Let not the days come
when we will mourn

for having given life
for having birthed
for having hoped.

Let not the days come
when we bid
the mountains fall
or the hills
to cover us.

Bid them, rather, to dance
for having loved so well.
Bid them, rather, to fly
for having dreamed so long.
—Jan L. Richardson

Reflect

❖ How do you give voice to grief?
❖ Where does your mourning lead you?

—— **FRIDAY** ——

Read Mark 15:40-41. See also Matthew 27:55-56; Luke 23:49; John
19:25.

The Women Muse

We bore wit-ness
we bared with-ness

living by our wits
living by our withs

wit to press beyond the lines
wit to improvise these lives

with our deepest selves
with integrity, with heart

Now we stand here
at wit's end,
with each other
and with him.

To wit: was it enough?
To with—did it suffice?
—Jan L. Richardson

Reflect

❖ What do you think?
❖ Standing with these women at the cross, what would you share?

—— **SATURDAY** ——

Read Luke 23:52-56. See also Matthew 27:57-61; Mark 15:42-47; John 19:38-42.

Shabbos

We had spices under our fingernails
as we baked the Sabbath bread.
The smell of ointment haunted us
as we lighted the Sabbath fires.

We tasted other wine as we breathed,
Baruch atah Adonai Elohenu melech ha-olam,
barah p'ri ha-gephen.
Blessed are you, O God, Ruler of the Universe,
who creates the fruit of the vine.

We tasted other suppers as we whispered,
Baruch atah Adonai Elohenu melech ha-olam,
ha-motsia lechem min ha-eretz.
Blessed are you, O God, Ruler of the Universe,
who brings forth bread from the earth.

But our cup of blessing lies poured out,
scarlet on the ground;
our sustenance lies broken,
still to return to earth.

We wait with one another
in this uneasy rest.
Creator, spread your arms;
draw us to your Sabbath breast.
—Jan L. Richardson

Reflect

Wait with these women. Sit with their grief, with their memories, with the unknown ahead. Tell the women of your own losses, your fears, your waiting.

—— **SUNDAY** ——

Read Luke 24:1-12. See also Matthew 28:1-10; Mark 16:1-11; John 20:1-18.

It seems that Easter always falls at a bad time for me; it seems to come consistently at the busiest time of the year. I haven't had time to prepare, to ponder, to live with the rhythm of the season. Often I try to cram it all into the time between Good Friday and Easter, and then I wonder why I don't feel elated on Easter morning. Although this habit still can elicit guilt in me, I'm beginning to learn that Easter is a season, not just a day. Resurrection is a process that I live into and live out of.

As I return to the stories of the women who accompanied Jesus in his final days, I wonder how much resurrection they felt on that Easter morning. They experience the joy of encountering the risen Christ, of seeing again the one who honored them, touched them, respected them, and took them seriously. But most of the disciples refuse to believe their "idle tale." And I find Mary Magdalene's story most poignant of all. She who had known Jesus intimately, had touched him, had loved and been loved by him, now is denied his touch. I wonder if she and the other women felt guilty on that Easter morning, caught between the joy of seeing their beloved companion and the disappointment of not receiving the responses they desired.

I think they too live into the resurrection. As these women continue to live with one another, as they reconstruct their lives, as they make new homes with one another, and as they remember their journeys with Jesus and plan for the journeys ahead, they learn what resurrection means. They learn that broken bodies and spirits can heal, that dry bones can dance, that the Spirit still can move. They learn that they who were intimate with Jesus-in-the-flesh now can become the birthers of Christ's new body as they learn to be the community, the body of Christ in the world.
—Jan L. Richardson

Reflect
- ❖ In your spiritual travels, where has this Lenten journey taken you?
- ❖ What do you see ahead?
- ❖ How do you begin to experience resurrection?

Turning/To the Women
    For D.L.D.

God hold you in this turning,
Christ warm you through this night,
Spirit breathe its ancient rhythm,
Peace give your sorrows flight.

Love robe you in her graces,
Faith offer rich repast,
Joy pour her healing wine
for ease, for cheer, for rest.
    —Jan L. Richardson

—— ❖ ——

Blessing: *Blessed are you who turn with passion, with strength, and with hope, for you will be filled with the God who is coming to life in you.*

Women in Community

The Season from Easter to Pentecost

AFTER JESUS' DEATH, RESURRECTION, AND ASCENSION, those who had lived, loved, and worked with him faced the challenge of creating community in his physical absence. With fear, hope, and divergent opinions about what it meant to be followers of Christ, those whom Jesus left behind began to struggle with what it meant to be the new body of Christ. Even in the days between the resurrection and Pentecost, the women and men of Christ began to create patterns that would shape the church to come as they met for prayer and broke bread together.

In our own journey from Easter to Pentecost, we will ponder the meaning of community and hear stories of several communities created by women. With one hand still touching the wounds of our Lenten journey and the other reaching forward to the day of Pentecost, we acknowledge that our communities are filled both with the pain of sin and the joy of healing as we learn to *understand* new languages as well as *speak* them.

Each community has a different rhythm, created by the movements of its comings and goings, work and play, meetings and partings. The rhythms of the community itself may change over time, depending on how it discerns its own identity in the midst of a changing world. We have our own individual rhythms within the community: some people thrive on contact while others prefer a more solitary life, and some devote their lives to the daily maintenance of the community while others breathe life into it through their art, music, and poetry. We may find ourselves in a radically altered relationship to the community as we move to its edges or outside it entirely for brief or lengthy periods of time.

We know that the rhythms of community can be both life-giving and stifling, liberating and oppressive. So in these days we listen to and follow the Spirit's own rhythms as it moves with us. Seeking to intuit its sacred movements, we listen to stories of other women in other communities. Praying for new language as well as new hearing, we gather at their table to listen, to learn, to commune. In our communion, may we better understand what it means to be a creative, spirited community of healing, of hope, of resistance, and of transformation.

A Prayer for the Beginning of Easter

————— ❖ —————

When the risen Christ appeared to the gathered disciples, he still bore the wounds of crucifixion. (See John 20:19-29.) As the living body of Christ in the world, we too bear wounds within our community. We continue to pray for vision, grace, and love not only to live as the risen body but also as the healing body of Christ, touching one another's wounds that we all may be whole.

You may light a candle.

God of community,
who calls us to be in relationship
with one another
and who has promised to dwell
wherever two or three are gathered,
hear this prayer:

By your Spirit you have graced each of us
with differing gifts.
To one you have given the speaking of wisdom,
to another, the utterance of knowledge,
to another, faith,
to another, gifts of healing,
to another, the working of miracles,
to another, prophecy,
to another, discernment of spirits,
to another, various kinds of tongues,
and to another, the interpretation of tongues. (1 Cor. 12:7-11)

For these and all gifts
by which you bless our communities,
I give you thanks.

And for any way in which I have shared
in deepening the wounds of the body of Christ,
I seek your love-filled forgiveness.

Open my eyes, O God, to perceive the gifts
you have placed within me

and to honor the differing gifts
which my sisters and brothers offer.
Bless our hands, our hearts, our vision
to work together for the bringing of your kindom,[*]
that in our differences, we may find grace;
in our laboring, we may find justice;
in our suffering, hope;
in our embracing, love;
and in our risking, transformation.

By these acts may we bring healing
to the tender, wounded, and strong
body of Christ,
rising in our midst.
—Jan L. Richardson

---

[*] *"Kindom" denotes a world in which we recognize that we are related, that we are "kin" in God, and work to build relationships of love, peace, and justice with all of creation.*

23 The Celebrants
Women of the Early Church

Invocation: *God of the feast, sustain me as I come to the table of memory. Fill me, Bread of Life, as I remember those who have shared the bread of their lives with me.*

Text: See daily readings

Context: I am pondering a picture that sits on my desk. Six women gaze back at me, beckoning me to remember that day. These women, holding guitars, fishing poles, and one another in the picture, have taught me much about community, about communion, about re-membering in the midst of brokenness and giving birth to blessings from struggle. Our community has dispersed as our visions and callings have led us to different places. Yet across the distance we remember that we have eaten of one loaf, and this memory sustains us.

The shadows in this picture hint at the forms of other women—women who also shaped and shared in this community as well as women who went before us. From the beginning of the earliest Christian communities, women knew intimately the joys and struggles of living and working together, of meeting and parting, of dwelling and of moving on as the Spirit led them into new communities. Yet wherever they went, they remembered breaking bread with old companions as they celebrated with new ones, rejoicing as they helped give birth to the new body of Christ.

Luke tells us that "Day by day, as they spent much time together in the temple, they broke bread from house to house and ate their food with glad and generous hearts, praising God and having the goodwill of all the people" (Acts 2:46-47). As my mind fills with memories of breaking bread with my own community, I begin to wonder about the breaking of bread among these early Christians. What words and prayers emerged as they broke bread with one another? What images, blessings, thanksgivings mingled with their tasting, with their smelling?

This week's readings invite you to break bread with some of these women who appear in the New Testament as leaders of the early Christian community. Drawing on the Jewish blessing of bread and on Christian liturgy for the Communion meal, these blessings recreate what these women might have said in the blessing of bread. Bread-bearers, bread-breakers, and celebrants of the body of Christ, they offer us the bread of their lives. May we be blessed.

—— **MONDAY** ——

Tabitha/Dorcas: The Bread of New Life—Read Acts 9:36-42.

> Blessed are you, O God,
> who brings forth the bread of new life
> from the earth.
> As you cause bread to rise
> fragrant
> and warm,
> so you call your people
> to rise,
> passionate
> and fire-formed.
>
> Bless to us
> this life-shaped bread,
> that we may rise
> into the newness of life in you.
> —Jan L. Richardson

Reflect

In this week, let us remember those who have shared the bread of their lives with us. Today I remember Betsey, whose touch brought new life to my body. I remember Ellen, who broke bread with me after I had gone without Communion for months.

❖ Who has borne the bread of resurrection, the bread of new life, to you?

—— **TUESDAY** ——

Mary and Rhoda: The Bread of Hospitality—Read Acts 12:12-16.

> Blessed are you, O God,
> who brings forth the bread of hospitality
> from the earth.

You made us to be
companions,
sharers of bread,
to gather
and to break
and to be astonished
by the flavor breaking forth.

Bless to us
this prayer-shaped bread,
that by its breaking
we too may gasp
at your Spirit's breaking forth
in us.
—Jan L. Richardson

Reflect
I remember Kary, with whom I have shared many fine tables; and Meinrad,
who offers amazing visions.

❖   Who has offered to you the bread of hospitality and wonder?

—— **WEDNESDAY** ——

Lois and Eunice: The Bread of Faith—Read Acts 16:1 and 2 Timothy 1:5.

Blessed are you, O God,
who brings forth the bread of faith
from the earth.
Like the yeast by which a bakerwoman
leavens the whole loaf,
our companionship with you
passes down from generation
to generation.
Like bread
shaped beneath a grandmother's palm
you sustain us,
filling and strong;
like a loaf broken
by a mother's familiar hand,
you nourish us,
tender and warm.

Bless to us
this faith-shaped loaf,
that the mothers may eat
and their children may live.
—Jan L. Richardson

Reflect

I remember my grandmothers, Geraldine and Flora; my great-aunt Dottye;
my mother Judy.

❖ Who has passed on to you the nourishing, filling, and strengthening bread of faith?

—— **THURSDAY** ——

Lydia: The Bread of Transformation—Read Acts 16:11-15.

Blessed are you, O God,
who brings forth the bread of transformation
from the earth.

As the baking of bread
begins with gathering the wheat,
so our transformation begins
with gathering our selves
with one another
with prayer.
Elemental offerings,
we give ourselves to you,
earth and fire and air and water
in these flesh and bones.
Shaped by your hand,
we rise,
we glow.

Bless to us
this circle-shaped loaf,
that it may sustain
our continual unfolding.
—Jan L. Richardson

Reflect

I remember Helen and Sue, whose prayers have transformed me.

❖ Who has blessed the bread of transformation with you?

—— **FRIDAY** ——

Priscilla (Prisca): The Bread of Partnership—Read Acts 18:1-3, 18, 24-26 and Romans 16:3-4.

Blessed are you, O God,
who brings forth the bread of partnership
from the earth.

This sustains us:
the daily sharing
the companioned breaking
the mutual blessing
the tender feeding.

Partnered with one another
and with you,
we partake of Mystery.
When the way is dangerous,
when our angers rise,
this tastes most sweet.

Bless to us
this companion-created loaf,
that its toughness may yield
your flavor-full joy.
—Jan L. Richardson

Reflect

I remember Brenda, who journeyed through seminary and beyond with me, and those who share in ministry at St. Luke's United Methodist Church.

❖ Who has shared the bread of partnership with you?

—— **SATURDAY** ——

Women in Ministry in Rome: The Bread of Community—Read Romans 16:1-16.

Blessed are you, O God,
who brings forth the bread of community
from the earth.

Often our bread comes from
hidden sources,
made by a way out of no way:
a handful of flour
a bit of yeast
a drop of oil
a touch of salt.

Fashioned by improvisation,
blessed by Mystery,
it is sufficient,
and we are filled.

Bless to us
this Wisdom-formed loaf,
that we may be whole
and wholly joined.
—Jan L. Richardson

Reflect

I remember Linda, Lesley, Dorri, Sandra, Carol, Leslee, Nancy Lee, Carolyn, Lori, Laura, Jeanne, Karin, Tonya, and Elizabeth, who have fashioned and broken and shared the bread of community with me.

❖ Who has broken the bread of community with you?

—— **SUNDAY** ——

Euodia and Syntyche: The Bread of Struggle—Read Philippians 4:2-3.

Blessed are you, O God,
who brings forth the bread of struggle
from the earth.

The laboring of ministry
has worn us
like wheat against a stone.
We search for sweetness
for flavor

for salt
in the struggle.
By this may we know
that even those of different minds
may share one loaf.

Bless to us
this struggle-shaped loaf,
that we may be surprised
at the sweetness
of feeding one another.
—Jan L. Richardson

Reflect
I remember Nancy, who holds a broken loaf with me.
❖ Who has tasted the bread of struggle with you?

——— **Meditation** ———

Saying Grace

God is gracious,
God is good,
let us give thanks
for our food.

Through these hands
may all be fed;
make us, God,
your daily bread.
Amen.
—Jan L. Richardson

——— ❖ ———

Blessing: *Go in peace, blessed by the bread of new life and of hospitality. Go in strength, filled by the bread of faith and of transformation. Go in solidarity, joined by the bread of partnership and of community. Go in hope, challenged by the bread of struggle.*

24 "We're All Women Together"
The Mothers of the Plaza de Mayo

Invocation: *I cry out to you, O God; God, hear my prayer. Giver of Life, who yearns for the lost with a compassionate heart, hold us all in your arms.*

Text: Jeremiah 31:15-17

Context: They gathered slowly, quietly, by ones, by twos. Never too many together, not at first. But it didn't take long for the women gathering in the Plaza de Mayo to draw attention. Across from the Government House in Buenos Aires, Argentina, the Plaza de Mayo became the place of meeting and then of transformation for hundreds of women whose children had been "disappeared"—kidnapped, imprisoned, sometimes raped, often murdered following the coup in 1976. In the eight years of military rule that followed the ousting of President Isabel Peron, an estimated 30,000 people became *desaparecidos*, "disappeared ones." Any persons attempting to protest, organize, or speak out risked being labeled a subversive and subsequently arrested, their location and the charges against them often unknown or unavailable to their families.

As the mothers visited the prisons, police stations, military offices, and government buildings in search of their disappeared children, they became aware of one another. As their efforts were stymied and their questions began to endanger them, they decided to band together. In April 1977, Azucena Villaflor de Vicenti said, as recorded in *Mothers of the Disappeared*, "Let's go to Plaza de Mayo and when there's enough of us"—she envisioned a thousand—"we'll go together to Government House and demand an answer."

The women who gathered in ones and twos began to gather in fives and tens. Each Thursday afternoon at half past three they gathered, recognizing one another by the pictures they carried of their disappeared loved ones and by the white kerchiefs they later adopted, decorated with the words *aparacion con vida*—"reappearance with life." In August 1979, they registered themselves under the name *Asociación Civil Madres de Plaza de Mayo*—Mothers of the Plaza de Mayo.

Others began to notice the gathering women, and the government tried to silence them. Many received threats, others "disappeared" themselves, and a few were killed. Yet the resurrection had begun, and nothing could stop it.

In their demand for *aparacion con vida*, the mothers knew that not all the children would be returned alive. Indeed, for many of the mothers the search ended with the discovery of a body in a mass grave. Yet the life they demanded was not only for their children; it was for a resurrection of life itself, of freedom, of hope.

The quest of the mothers has brought life to others as thousands have been "disappeared" and/or murdered across Central and South America. In El Salvador, Guatemala, and elsewhere, mothers and grandmothers have joined together not only to heal the bodies that have been broken but ultimately to make possible the resurrection of the spirit—of their people, of their land, of the holy.

————— **MONDAY** —————

In the Ministry of the Interior I met another mother looking for her child. When I left the building she was waiting for me outside and she called me over. She asked me if they'd taken my child too. I told her what had happened. She said, "Come to the square on Thursday and join the Mothers. We meet every Thursday." I said yes, that I'd already heard something about the Mothers. She said, "Come, they won't ask you any questions. We're all women together." Within a few days of my son's disappearance I was in Plaza de Mayo.

The first Thursday I got off the bus and just stood there in the street. I saw some women but I didn't know what to do. There was one here, two there. They weren't allowed to be in a group so they were all dispersed around the square. I asked myself, "Is that a Mother? Is she a Mother?" I felt afraid, like you always do when you do something for the first time. Then I saw the woman who had waited for me outside the Ministry of the Interior. What luck she was there! I walked straight towards her, without looking to either side, without looking at the police. At first you feel afraid, but when I got to the Mothers they all seemed so strong . . . and how can you feel afraid when you are fighting for a just cause? I cried a lot, but they were tears of relief. I felt like another person. Because looking at the faces of other mothers who had experienced the same as me gave me the strength to fight.

—Aída de Suárez in *Mothers of the Disappeared* by Jo Fisher

Reflect

Come to the Plaza de Mayo.

❧   What must you risk in order to be there?

❧   Whom do you see as you arrive?

—— TUESDAY ——

They started to call us *las locas* [the madwomen]. When the foreign embassies began to ask questions about the disappearances, because they didn't only take Argentines they took all nationalities, and the foreign journalists began to ask about us, they used to say "Don't take any notice of those old women, they're all mad." Of course they called us mad. How could the armed forces admit they were worried by a group of middle-aged women? And anyway we were mad. When everyone was terrorized we didn't stay at home crying—we went to the streets to confront them directly. We were mad but it was the only way to stay sane.

—Aída de Suárez in *Mothers of the Disappeared*

Reflect

Listen to the madwomen.

❧   What are they mad for?

❧   What would you reply if they asked you what in your life you were *loco* for?

—— WEDNESDAY ——

I remember that night [after escaping arrest for handing out leaflets outside a cathedral; on the leaflets were Pope Paul VI's words, "If you want peace, defend life."] I didn't want to go home and I sent my daughters to stay with a friend and I went to my sister's house. Her husband didn't want me to sleep in their house because he thought it would endanger his family. I went to my sister-in-law's but she wasn't at home and in the end I knocked on the door of a Jewish friend of mine. I asked if I could stay because the police were looking for me. She let me in and said, "We Jews understand what this means." That's how she replied. She didn't ask for any explanation.

—Marina de Curia in *Mothers of the Disappeared*

Reflect

Marina knocks at your door.

❧   What history would she find behind it?

❖ Is there anything that would connect you with her?

—— THURSDAY ——

I began to read everything I could find so that I could understand what they were doing, everything, how they were torturing them, where. It was the only way to get the strength to fight them. And then you realize that it's not just your own sons that matter, but all the *desaparecidos*. All these were stages, sudden shocks. In a few years a world had opened up before me that I'd never seen before, that no one had ever shown me, a world that I'd never believed was also my own. My life had been the life of a house-wife—washing, ironing, cooking and bringing up my children, just like you're always taught to do, believing that everything else was nothing to do with me. Then I realized that that wasn't everything, that I had another world too. You realize you're in a world where you have to do a lot of things.

—Hebe de Bonafini in *Mothers of the Disappeared*

Reflect
    ❖ What things must you do in your world?
    ❖ Who is in your world?
    ❖ What would you tell Hebe about your world?

—— FRIDAY ——

We are fighting so that it won't be forgotten, because to forget the past, to have no memory, is a danger for the country, because what happened will happen again. The Mothers have this memory, this pain, and we are working for the future so that the new generations won't live through what we've lived through, so people won't disappear, aren't tortured or kidnapped. We are working so that what our children wanted will become a reality. Our children wanted every family to have a decent home, enough food and clothing, and they wanted every child to have the opportunity to go to school. Because our country can give all this and has to give this. Our children worked in the *villas* as doctors, building homes, teaching. When people understand why they were taken, what they wanted, they are going to understand us and we'll have something better.

—Juanita de Pargament in *Mothers of the Disappeared*

Reflect

❖ What memory would you be willing to risk your life for so that it would be passed down?

—— **SATURDAY** ——

I have four children, including Ana Maria, the *desaparecida*. . . . My daughter was concerned about injustice, like all the *desaparecidos*. Like all of them she used to give her clothes to people who needed them more than her. She couldn't imagine this world of other people or why they had to live this life with no help. She liked to help people. She helped in times of floods and disasters. She couldn't understand why the government did nothing to help the people, to alleviate their suffering, why children were living without enough food or clothes. All the *desaparecidos* were like this. She used to write a lot. When she disappeared I found a letter among her things and it gives me strength when I read what she wrote in that letter. She did what she had to do.

—Marta de Baravalle in *Mothers of the Disappeared*

Reflect

On your doorstep, miles away, you have found Ana Maria's letter.

❖ What does it say?
❖ What will you do with it?

—— **SUNDAY** ——

Here we are, Jews and Catholics, all religions and all classes and we all work together as one. We all respect each other and this is something wonderful. Recently we were saying what could be better than to be together like this. A family celebration can't give us more than we have here every day. Because we each have the same pain, we each understand how the other feels, we can understand each other's problems. When one weakens or gets disheartened there's always someone standing by her side to give her strength. A Mother who comes to the House can find the strength to continue the struggle. It's the one who stays at home, who only comes occasionally to the square, who give[s] up. Here in this House there's always work to be done, always a reason to be on our toes. Together we give each other a strength which I think is unique in the world. . . .

This is a permanent struggle. We believe that when we're all dead, the young people who work here with us and our children will continue with our demands. The *desaparecidos* can never be allowed to be forgotten. What happened to our children must never be allowed to happen to another generation of young people.

—Elisa de Landin in *Mothers of the Disappeared*

Reflect

You walk into their House. The Mothers greet you and ask why you have come.

❖ What do you tell them?

❖ What questions do you ask of one another?

❖ What will you each have when you leave?

——— Meditation ———

Escribo Nuevo / Writing Anew

Here
in this land,
they write their history
across your body,
a tale of terror
winding scarlet
and cutting deep
into your precious flesh.

Franco (outspoken)
they stitch across your lips,
as they seek to bind them closed.

Traidore (traitor)
they carve into your hands
as they plot to cut them off.

Subversivo (subversive)
they shoot into your heart
as they scheme to still its thunder.

But here
in this plaza
we rewrite your history,
speaking *esperanza*
to see your face again,

singing *memoria*
to touch your hands again,
dancing *justicia*
to hold your heart again.

We are writing *resurrección*
in this land,
to give you *vida,*
to give you life again.
—Jan L. Richardson

—— ❖ ——

Blessing: *May the God who dwells with those called outspoken, traitors, and subversive dwell also with you, writing peace across your soul. Go with God, speaking hope, singing memory, and dancing justice in your land.*

25 Souls on Fire
The Beguines

Invocation: *God of new visions, visit me with your fiery presence. Open me to hear your new word, to receive your new touch, and to delight in your new insight.*

Text: Jeremiah 20:9

Context: Toward the end of the twelfth century, women across Europe began to search for new ways to live out their spirituality. These women wanted to embrace a life of simplicity, chastity, and religious devotion, while resisting the cloistered life of the Catholic convent and the authority of the Catholic hierarchy. Women who had pursued independent religious lives began to organize themselves into groups that focused on shared spiritual disciplines and work. As the groups evolved into the thirteenth century, many of the communities took on physical dimensions as the women, who became known as Beguines, acquired houses and other buildings. At the height of the movement, one such community, the Great Beguinage at Ghent, included "two churches, eighteen convents, over a hundred houses, a brewery, and an infirmary," according to Elizabeth Petroff's *Medieval Women's Visionary Literature.*

Centering primarily in the Low Countries, Northern France, and Germany, the beguinages offered hundreds, and perhaps thousands, of women the opportunity to live in autonomous communities that respected and encouraged their own religious experiences. Surviving accounts of those experiences reveal a passionate spirituality, sometimes characterized by visions, an intimate relationship with God, deep concern for all souls, and a desire to give voice to the intricacy and power of God's love in human lives.

We know little about Mechthild of Magdeburg, a German Beguine born around 1207 to a well-born, possibly noble, family. She received a profound call from God at the age of ten and related that she saw "all things in God and God in all things." When she was about twenty-two, that call led her to Magdeburg, where she lived as a Beguine. There she began to write her book *The Flowing Light of the Godhead*, a combination of visions, poetry, and theological reflections. She completed the book after moving around 1270 to Helfta, the site of a great Cistercian convent that was an influential center of women's spirituality during the Middle Ages. Mechthild probably died in 1282.

Hadewijch of Brabant, a Flemish Beguine who also lived in the thirteenth century, either founded or joined a group of Beguines and became its leader. In time, however, her leadership met with opposition, and it seems she was evicted from her community. As the translator Mother Columba Hart notes in *Hadewijch: The Complete Works*, the eviction may have come about "because of her doctrine that one must live Love." Mother Columba conjectures that after Hadewijch became homeless, "she offered her services to a leprosarium or hospital for the poor, where she could nurse those who suffered and sleep at least part of the night in some corner, with access to the church or chapel always attached to such establishments in her time." Although we know little about Hadewijch's formal education, Mother Columba notes that her surviving writings—poetry, visions, and letters—reflect familiarity with Latin, the rules of rhetoric, numerology, Ptolemaic astronomy, music theory, and French.

In time, the autonomous nature of the beguinages and the independent lives of the Beguines aroused suspicion and many accusations of heresy. Many beguinages came under the authority of the Catholic church; others disbanded in the wake of persecution or other stresses. By the end of the Middle Ages, few communities remained.

—— MONDAY ——

"Can the Son of God not comfort thee?" [the creatures ask of the Bride]
Yea! I ask Him when we shall go
Into the flowery meadows of heavenly knowledge
And pray Him fervently,
That He unlock for me
The swirling flood which plays about the Holy Trinity,
For the soul lives on that alone.
   If I am to be comforted
According to the merit to which God has raised me,
Then [God's] breath must draw me effortlessly into [God]self.
For the sun which plays upon the living Godhead
Irradiates the clear waters of a joyful humanity;
And the sweet desire of the Holy Spirit
Comes to us from both. . . .

Nothing can satisfy me save God alone,
Without [God] I am as dead.
Yet would I gladly sacrifice the joy of [God's] presence
Could [God] be greatly honoured thereby.
For if I, unworthy, cannot praise God with all my might,
Then I send all creatures to the Court of Heaven
And bid them praise God for me,
With all their wisdom, their love,
Their beauty; all their desires,
As they were created, sinless by God,
To sing with all the sweetness of their voices
As they now sing.
Could I but witness this praise
I would sorrow no more.
—Mechthild of Magdeburg in *The Flowing Light of the Godhead*

Reflect

"Where there is no vision, the people perish" (Proverbs 29:18, King James Version). We are challenged to envision and re-vision as the people of God. To re-vision involves taking visions of the past and dreaming them into the future with new eyes in a new context.

❖ What visions and re-visions do the words of this foremother, written hundreds of years ago, spark in you?

❖ How do you re-vision this song of praise, one that encompasses even the animals, into a world where the creatures of God often live in danger at our hands?

—— TUESDAY ——

Therefore shalt thou [a Prior, Prioress, or other Superior] speak thus to each Brother or Sister with the deep humility of thy pure heart:—

Beloved! I, unworthy
Of merit, am thy servant;
I am not thy master
Power is made for service!
Go forth in God's true love.
Suffer? I too suffer!
Wound? And I have wounded!
Merit God's praise? I sing!

Now I send thee forward
In God's name, as Jesus
Went out seeking lost sheep
Till He died of loving.
Love of God teach thee too
To be kind and useful,
Take with thee my prayers,
Take my soul's desire,
Take my sinful tears,
God in mercy home thee
Brimmed with love and goodness
Home thee safe to me. AMEN.

Thus shalt thou comfort thy brethren
As they go forth, and rejoice with them
When they return.

—Mechthild of Magdeburg in *The Flowing Light of the Godhead*

Reflect

❖ How do you re-vision this vision of power as service, love, prayer, desire, and tears into a world that bases power on economics, gender, race, and other measures of status?

—————— **WEDNESDAY** ——————

An unworthy creature thought simply about the nobility of God. Then God showed him in his senses and the eyes of his soul, a Fire which burned ceaselessly in the heights above all things. It had burned without beginning and would burn without end. This Fire is the everlasting God Who has retained in [God's self] Eternal Life from which all things proceed. The sparks which have blown away from the Fire are the holy angels. The beams of the Fire are the saints of God for their lives cast many lovely lights on Christianity. The coals of the Fire still glow; they are the just who here burn in heavenly love and enlighten by their good example: as they were chilled by sin they now warm themselves at the glowing coals. The crackling sparks which are reduced to ashes and come to nothing are the bodies of the blessed, who in the grave still await their heavenly reward. The Lord of the Fire is still to come, Jesus Christ to whom [God] entrusted the first Redemption and the last Judgment. On the Last Day He shall make a glorious chalice for the heavenly [Creator] out of the sparks of the Fire; from this chalice [God] will on the day of [God's] Eternal Marriage drink all the holiness which, with [God's] Beloved Son, [God] has poured into our souls and our human senses.

> Yea! I shall drink from thee
> And Thou shalt drink from me
> All the good God has preserved in us.
> Blessed is he who is so firmly established here
> That he may never spill out
> What God has poured into him.

The smoke of the Fire is made of all earthly things which [we use] with wrongful delight. However beautiful to our eyes, however pleasant to our hearts, they yet carry in them much hidden bitterness. For they disappear as smoke and blind the eyes of the highest, till the tears run.

The comfort of the Fire is the joy our souls receive inwardly from God, with such holy warmth from the Divine Fire, that we too burn with it and are so sustained by virtues that we are not extinguished. The bitterness of the Fire is the word God shall speak on the Last Day, *Depart from Me ye cursed into everlasting fire!* (St. Matthew, xxv. 41). The radiance of the Fire is the glowing aspect of the Divine countenance of the Holy Trinity, which shall so illumine our souls and bodies that we may then see and recognize the marvellous blessedness we cannot even name here.

These things have come out of the Fire and flow into it again according to God's ordinance in everlasting praise.

> Wouldst thou know my meaning?
> Lie down in the Fire
> See and taste the Flowing
> Godhead through thy being;
> Feel the Holy Spirit
> Moving and compelling
> Thee with the Flowing
> Fire and Light of God.

—Mechthild of Magdeburg in *The Flowing Light of the Godhead*

Reflect

❖ How do you re-vision this vision of the fiery dynamism of God and community into a world that often narrowly defines God and community?

—— THURSDAY ——

Now understand the deepest essence of your soul, what "soul" is. Soul is a being that can be beheld by God and by which, again, God can be beheld. Soul is also a being that wishes to content God; it maintains a worthy state of being as long as it has not fallen beneath anything that is alien to it and less than the soul's own dignity. If it maintains this worthy state, the soul is a bottomless abyss in which God suffices to [Godself]; and [God's] own self-sufficiency ever finds fruition to the full in this soul, as the soul, for its part, ever does in [God]. Soul is a way for the passage of God from [God's] depths into [God's] liberty, that is, into [God's] inmost depths, which cannot be touched except by the soul's abyss. And as long as God does not belong to the soul in [God's] totality, [God] does not truly satisfy it.

—Hadewijch of Brabant in *Hadewijch: The Complete Works*

Reflect

❖ How do you re-vision this vision of the soul in partnership and contentment with God into a world frayed by discontent?

—— FRIDAY ——

On a certain Pentecost Sunday I had a vision at dawn. Matins were being sung in the church, and I was present. My heart and my veins and all my limbs trembled and quivered with eager desire and, as often occurred with me, such madness and fear beset my mind that it seemed to me I did not content my Beloved, and that my Beloved did not fulfill my desire, so that dying I must go mad, and going mad I must die. On that day my mind was beset so fearfully and so painfully by desirous love that all my separate limbs threatened to break, and all my separate veins were in travail. The longing in which I then was cannot be expressed by any language or any person I know; and everything I could say about it would be unheard-of to all those who never apprehended Love as something to work for with desire, and whom Love had never acknowledged as hers. I can say this about it: I desired to have full fruition of my Beloved, and to understand and taste him to the full. I desired that his Humanity should to the fullest extent be one in fruition with my humanity, and that mine then should hold its stand and be strong enough to enter into perfection until I content him, who is perfection itself, by purity and unity, and in all things to content him fully in every virtue. To that end I wished he might content me interiorly with his Godhead, in one spirit, and that for me he should be all that he is, without withholding anything from me. For above all the gifts that I ever longed for, I chose this gift: that I should give satisfaction in all great sufferings. For that is the most perfect satisfaction: to grow up in order to be God with God.

—Hadewijch of Brabant in *Hadewijch: The Complete Works*

Reflect

❖ How do you re-vision this vision of intimacy with God into a world wounded by separatism and division?

——— SATURDAY ———

(Continued from the previous vision)

Then he came from the altar, showing himself as a Child, and that Child was in the same form as he was in his first three years. He turned toward me, in his right hand took from the ciborium his Body, and in his left hand took a chalice, which seemed to come from the altar, but I do not know where it came from.

With that he came in the form and clothing of a Man, as he was on the day when he gave us his Body for the first time; looking like a Human Being and a Man, wonderful, and beautiful, and with glorious face, he came to me as humbly as anyone who wholly belongs to another. Then he gave himself to me in the shape of the Sacrament, in its outward form, as the custom is; and then he gave me to drink from the chalice, in form and taste, as the custom is. After that he came himself to me, took me entirely in his arms, and pressed me to him; and all my members felt his in full felicity, in accordance with the desire of my heart and my humanity. So I was outwardly satisfied and fully transported. Also then, for a short while, I had the strength to bear this; but soon, after a short time, I lost that manly beauty outwardly in the sight of his form. I saw him completely come to nought and so fade and all at once dissolve that I could no longer recognize or perceive him outside me, and I could no longer distinguish him within me. Then it was to me as if we were one without difference. It was thus: outwardly, to see, taste, and feel, as one can outwardly taste, see, and feel in the reception of the outward Sacrament. So can the Beloved, with the loved one, each wholly receive the other in all full satisfaction of the sight, the hearing, and the passing away of the one in the other.

After that I remained in a passing away in my Beloved, so that I wholly melted away in him and nothing any longer remained to me of myself; and I was changed and taken up in the spirit, and there it was shown me concerning such hours.

—Hadewijch of Brabant in *Hadewijch: The Complete Works*

Reflect

❖ How do you re-vision this vision of communion with the holy into a world that draws sharp distinctions between clean and unclean, sacred and profane?

❖ How does the sensual imagery used by Hadewijch and Mechthild challenge, stretch, or affirm your understanding of God?

—— **SUNDAY** ——

I know well that if Love wanted to,
She would be able to console my sad mind.
Alas! Did she think any harm of me,
Thus to send me to wrack and ruin?
She holds me with great woe,
    Wholly without success, desperate.
    Unless she quickly has mercy on me
    And lets me become wiser in her,
    She will come to me perhaps too late.

However painfully I stray in Love's path—
And for me, experience of her has been delayed too long—
However deep I wade in her dangerous waters,
I will always give her thanks.
For I depend wholly on her,
    If I shall ever ascend clear to her summit.
    Whatever else I did,
    My hunger would remain as strong as ever:
    Did she not give me full satisfaction in her.

So I remain on Love's side,
Whatever may happen to me after that:
The pain of hunger for her, the joy of satisfaction in her,
    No to desires, or yes to delight.

—Hadewijch of Brabant in *Hadewijch: The Complete Works*

Reflect

❖ How do you re-vision this vision of union with Love into a world where much is unlovely?

────── **Meditation** ──────

Mystic Fires

The night is late, all souls are sleeping,
but still I move across the floor,
and while the moon and stars are passing
I light a flame, and then one more.

One for Hadewijch,
one for Mechthild;
Sisters! Bless you
in this hour
for words of flame
for sight unveiled
for flowing light
and fire-formed power.

How you burned!
but weren't consumed
except by passion,
except by thirst
to drink of Love's
transforming cup,
to deeply taste
Her healing words.
—Jan L. Richardson

────── ❖ ──────

Blessing: *May the Fire of God consume you. May the Burning of wisdom renew you. May the Flame of Love transform you and bring new vision to your soul.*

26 Voices from the Edge
Homeless Women

Invocation: *Companion in solitude, Protector in exile, you inhabit the shadows of our communities. Grant me new eyes, O God, to see how you break bread with all who live on the edge.*

Text: Isaiah 58:6-9a

Context: Community looks different to those who, for a little or a long while, live outside of it. Contemplating this, I mused to a friend recently, "I think there is a difference between solitude and exile. I'm just not sure where the borderline is." Women across time have chosen or found themselves living with various kinds of aloneness, both physical and spiritual.

It seems easy to say that choices determine the difference between solitude and exile and that solitude is aloneness we choose, while exile is aloneness forced upon us. This explanation holds partial truth, yet the threads of providence, choice, and circumstance woven through our lives make the truth less clear.

The stories of homeless women lay bare the complexity of the truth. While usually living within the physical bounds of a community, homeless women often live in exile within it. With little or no access to money, shelter, political or economic power, homeless women risk being swallowed by invisibility as the larger community accommodates their presence but not their needs. At the same time, some homeless women value the solitude and relative autonomy their lives necessitate. Failing to find support in "the system," they have constructed alternative systems and even communities based on improvisation and living by their wits.

These voices challenge us to contemplate our own movements through solitude and exile as well as how—and with whom—we create our own communities.

—— MONDAY ——

[After losing a job and attempting suicide] I was taken to Roosevelt Emergency and then to intensive care. I was unconscious for four days.

When a psychiatrist came to see me, he asked me if I would be willing to go to Central Islip Hospital. Of course I was so upset at being alive I said I didn't give a damn where I went, so I went out there voluntarily because I didn't give a damn. Nothing mattered. I was furious to still be alive. I still am. It's a terrible thing to say to yourself. I have no home. No place that is mine where I can go and close the door.

I arrived that first time at Central Islip on my fortieth birthday. Quite ironic, they say life begins at forty. Since then I've had a great many admissions out there. I work for a year then I get this terrible depression and I have to go back. I just stop functioning. I just sit. I know I should take a shower, wash my hands, eat. But I don't do any of this. I just reach the point where I can pack my bags and I go. I reach my desperation and I need help.

After I went in the hospital I lost my apartment. My friend put the things I wanted into storage but I couldn't keep paying the rent so I had to tell them to get rid of everything. Clothes, my books which hurt more than anything, all my mother's beautiful silver and dishes. They even charged me twenty dollars to get rid of them. I've never put down roots again.

—Mary Lou Prentiss in *Shopping Bag Ladies* by Ann Marie Rousseau

Reflect
Ponder your empty hands. Try to hold Mary Lou's words, her story in them.
❖ How would her hands look next to yours?

──── **TUESDAY** ────

I use them churches just like Jesus would want everyone else to. If God meant for churches to be built, He meant for them to be used. So why shouldn't I? The ones who keep saying they're so religious don't go except on a Sunday when someone makes them go. I got a mat that I put down on a pew to make it more comfortable, and I can take a snooze or sit in peace and read or knit or write in my book. Poetry. That's what I write. . . .

I got this good relationship with St. Anne. I tell her what I feel and she listens real good. She has to. She's stone. But every once in a while I feel like she's staring at me—when I'm not sitting where she should be staring at me. Maybe her spirit and what's left of mine get together in those empty halls and mix it up. I don't want you thinking I'm nuts, but I get these times when I hear us both talking to each other. . . . It's just the nerves playing tricks on an old woman. . . . This is Hell, you know. . . . Hell is here.

—Ruthie in *Shadow Women: Homeless Women's Survival Stories* by Marjorie Bard

Reflect

You have slipped into the church late one afternoon and notice Ruthie talking.

- ❖ What might she and Saint Anne say to each other?
- ❖ What are you thinking as this conversation between Ruthie and Saint Anne takes place?

—— **WEDNESDAY** ——

When I was in the chips, my favorite day was Sunday. After church we ladies got together in the big hall for a potluck lunch that lasted all afternoon. The men always said we got together to gossip, but while we were getting our tables set up properly and arranged by salads, sandwiches, casseroles, fruits, and then desserts, we were exchanging the important news of the week. Then we made a great fuss about filling our plates with first one type of food and then another, and commenting on how wonderful everything looked so that everyone was feeling proud about their platters....

If I could be in a church again, I'd like to see the Sunday brunches back again, and this time I'd make sure that we focused on doing some social good. I mean really important good, like sponsoring a place for women like me—and I see a lot of us wandering around the malls and stores all day and in movies most nights. We could even be responsible for making the churches the places for nighttime slumber palaces. There they are, just empty houses of God, and there could be cots put up at night ... and all those unused rooms would be signals to God that people care.

It wouldn't take much more than a couple of Sunday potlucks to solve the traffic and parking problems that the council people keep arguing about. And what would be even better would be to have every second Sunday set aside for a group-church potluck day. Then we ladies could tackle the really big issues. If all the women who belong to churches get others who don't come to regular potluck meetings, why we could set up a network of church-sponsored houses across the country and take care of all the women who need everything from food to housing.

Oh, to be arranging platters of ham, potato salads and cole slaw between the pretty green and red aspics, and smelling the warm desserts at the end of the table, wondering how much you could save aside before anyone noticed.

—Clare in *Shadow Women*

Reflect

- ❖ What would it take for such a feast to happen?

I came here [to The Shearers and Spinners, a cooperative store in Pennsylvania created by homeless women and men in which they make and sell clothing from sheepskins and wool] one day completely disoriented from not eating or sleeping regularly. About all I could do was to ask for some food. The next thing I knew I was sitting in a warm barn drinking hot, thick soup and eating cornbread. Every once in a while someone came by and asked if I needed a blanket or more soup. I think I slept for two days straight. . . .

They were an odd bunch, but they had more in common than not, and by putting together their abilities and desire not to perish, they started with just sheer hope—no pun intended—and hard work. I have been part of their sharing now for almost eight months, and I'm in charge of the antiques shop. My husband and I were dealers for years, and when he left me for another woman I sort of went downhill, drinking and taking drugs and such. But now I'm going to make it, and I'm going to stay with these terrific people, all of them who began over again like I have. If I hadn't been able to share my story with them, I would have just kept it bottled up and drowned myself in its slop. When I started to talk about all of my misadventures, I found that they all had similar problems, and this is like a giant support group. You know, not so much in size, but like a little church of some kind.
—Anonymous in *Shadow Women*

Reflect
This woman has woven a blanket out of her desire not to perish, and she wraps it around your shoulders.

❖   How do you respond?

—— **FRIDAY** ——

I have been alone for so long, just dwelling on this matter so much and going nearly nuts in the process, that when I was in the group [a support group meeting at a church] with the other women and heard my own story, well, I just couldn't have been happier. I wasn't alone anymore. I didn't even have to hear the whole stories; I could fill in the middle and ending with my own experiences. . . .

If only I had had this opportunity three years ago. I wouldn't have been so miserable, thinking that I was probably the only one going through this. Maybe if we could have talked about these things then I wouldn't have ended up on the street. Just think, June doesn't have to run away and try to change her identity. We've all shared how it just isn't possible. . . .

Did anyone here not interrupt poor June? She never really did get to finish! Let's give her a chance to get it all out. Okay? Then we'll all jump in again and see how all of these things come from the same problems in the legal system. It seems that we all have come up with a better scheme than the City Attorney's Office has!

—Amy in *Shadow Women*

Reflect

There is a silence so strong that its breaking shatters worlds.

❖ What worlds are being born in their place?

❖ How are these women midwives in the process, helping to bring new worlds into being?

<hr/>

—— **SATURDAY** ——

I want to get on welfare now so I can at least get on my feet, build a foundation. Then I can get a job. I'll be independent again, have my own apartment, pay my own bills, buy my own food, my clothes. But I don't need anyone to hurt me anymore. I need someone to love me and help me. I want a nice man to fall in love with me and I know I could fall in love with him eventually. He could work and I could work and we could build a life together.

Maybe you will go home tonight and say, "I met a girl today. Her name is Ellie Fredricks. We had a long conversation. It was very fascinating." This is what you will be thinking to yourself and good feeling will come out of it. I guess I can leave a good impression on people. I want to make people smile, make people happy.

—Ellie Fredricks in *Shopping Bag Ladies*

Reflect

Maybe you will close this book and think, *I met many women this week. I heard their words. It was very fascinating.*

❖ What will you do with their words?

<hr/>

—— **SUNDAY** ——

The doctors and physicians know how to cut and control the brain because brains is power. But I keep fighting them. They're pulling the veins in my heart. They're pulling the heart strings but I'm a doctor too. I have this medicine to stop the pain. I just put it on the skin and it helps. It's Anacin, Bayer Aspirin, and Tylenol all stomped on and mixed together in cold cream and two different kinds of lotion.

When I get the pain, that's okay because I get a dollar and I get dimes and keep calling. I keep calling randomly. I dial the numbers, any numbers and talk to who I get. It doesn't matter. It's better to call that way, to dial out into the universe and see what you get. That way you know you get what you should.

—Darian Moore in *Shopping Bag Ladies*

Reflect

In this way Darian finds contact, presence, and community.

- ❖ How do you find contact, presence, and community?
- ❖ Do you find contact, presence, and community randomly, or with an orderly plan?

—————— **Meditation** ——————

Dialing Out

It's not so far
from the edge of here
to out into the universe
and I wonder
what the voices answer,
whether they
bridge the gap a little
or whether you stretch them enough
so that they come back around
another way
toward home.
—Jan L. Richardson

—————— ❖ ——————

Blessing: *In solitude, in exile; in the center of community, on its edge; and in all the shadows that lie between, may God dwell with you.*

27 The Extra Room
Ellen Anthony

Invocation: *Bless the spaces of home and heart, O God, that my life may be a place of welcome.*

Text: 2 Kings 4:8-37

Context: How do we prepare ourselves to be in community? How do we welcome community into our lives? How does the shape we give to our inner and outer spaces—the space of our souls and the space of our homes—give shape to our community?

In her poetic essay "The Extra Room," Ellen Anthony draws on the story of the Shunammite woman who prepared an extra room in her home for the prophet Elisha. With her words, Ellen gives life and breath to what the Shunammite woman also must have known: that extending one's hospitality is a sacred act requiring intention and care. True hospitality links the space of our home—whatever or wherever our home may be—with the space of our soul. And community begins when we open up those places within ourselves, within our homes, to the holy.

Ellen challenges us to ponder how our hospitality extends beyond our immediate community to include a wider community: those who live at a distance, those who come from beyond our usual borders, and those who forever change us as they pass in and out of our lives.

—— **MONDAY** ——

Let us make a small roof chamber with walls, and put there for him a bed, a table, a chair, and a lamp, so that whenever he comes to us, he can go in there.

—2 Kings 4:10, RSV

I

A long time ago
someone in Shunem
built an extra room

on the roof of her house
for the holy one.

That's what I want to do.
I want to go up
to the roof of my house
where the sky starts
and make this room in case the holy one
needs a place to stay.

A table, a chair,
a bed and a candle.
I'll work on it
when I can,
weekends maybe
or before breakfast.

II

It's coming along.
I go up there,
work with what I have.
Some wood, some stone.
The chair and table
aren't hard to make
and I got a candle
from a friend.

But the bed is still stone.
And I know that isn't comfortable.

It's grey
and looks billowy from far off,
like a feather comforter,
but it's stone.

I put my hands on it,
on the faces of the stone.
Questions come up
all about work and what my life is for.
I answer what I can.

We're both getting softer, I think,

but not yet a bed.

Reflect

> ❖ Where and with what do you start in preparing a space?
> ❖ What do you want from your home?

—— **TUESDAY** ——

III

One day the holy one
stays overnight, asks
What can I do for you?
Nothing, I say. I can't
think of anything I need.
You will have new life,
says the holy one leaving.
Don't lie to me.
Don't lie to me
is what I answer back.
I sit down right there
in the kitchen thinking
What new life?

And why do I think it is a lie
that I will have new life?

IV

Someone is waiting there
in that room upstairs.

Someone is dying.

Someone is holding the river
in their hands.
Someone is letting it go.

Someone is crying.

Someone is getting ready.

Someone wants to be
softer than stone.

Who is waiting for me
in the extra room?

Reflect

❖   For whom do you prepare your space?

———— **WEDNESDAY** ————

V

I go up,
open the door.

It's pretty much done.
The room.
All I can do anyway.

I sit in the chair.
Plain square chair.

Look at the table.
Flat relaxed wood.

Strike a match
to the wick of the candle,
see the light
pulling the walls into the glow,
corners going blurry.

Holy chair?
Holy table?
Holy candle, holy walls?
or just extra ones?
I sit in the extra chair
watching the extra walls
wondering if we're holy.

Over there
the stone is taking a long time
becoming a bed.

So am I.

We wait here together.

VI

I wonder what the Shunammite
went through.
Whether hospitality
came easy to her
and the furniture
knew itself right off.

I know that after the holy one
came to her extra room
the Shunammite conceived
and bore a son.

I wonder what my extra room
is for. Who will come
and whether it is holy
the way it is, empty.

Reflect

❖ In your home, in your soul, what spaces have come with difficulty?

❖ What questions arise in working on your space?

—— **THURSDAY** ——

VII

Lots of time passes.
Time, time, time.
Life goes on downstairs.

Busy one day
I'm in the kitchen

when the phone rings.
Not thinking I go upstairs.
Why? There's no phone
in the extra room.
But I open the door
and there all over the place

is the sky. Sky, sky, sky.
No edges to it. No sign
of roof ending or sky beginning.
As if Sky is the answer
to this phone call.
All seeing, all hearing.

I want to cry
but it is beyond crying.
This is some phone call.

Lots of time passes differently.
Inside time, I don't know how much.
At some point I go downstairs again.

VIII

I pinch my skin
down in the kitchen.
Testing what's real.
Did that really happen?

What kind of phone call
is all sky on the other end?

What kind of answer holds your feet up,
surrounds your shoulders,
and moves through your hair
leaving you nothing at all
to say?

What if here in the kitchen
I could listen that well?
Pull the sky down
into all my conversations.

I want to do it.
That's the next thing
I want to do.

Reflect

❖ When has your space surprised you?
❖ What does your space open onto, give way to?

IX

Well, now I go up there all the time
to the extra room that is definitely holy
waiting for the phone to ring,
wishing the sky would answer me
over and over again without edges.

But it doesn't work that way.

I go up there some days
and all the furniture is dead.
Even the wooden stuff
gone to stone on me.

I want to cry and I do cry
and the bed is no comfort to me.
Why? Why did the table and chair
come so easy and the bed so hard?
Is it about working and resting?
Easy to work but hard to rest?
The in-between times,
when nothing is happening,
can I rest in those?

I touch the old faces
of the stone. Someone is dying,
someone is crying, someone is trying
to become softer than stone.

Trying. Why am I trying?
Is the chair trying?
Is the table trying?
Is the sky trying?
Am I the only one around here
who keeps trying?

Please, phone. Ring again.

Reflect
❖   What happens when even your own space offers little solace?

❖ Why do you keep trying?
❖ The in-between times, when nothing is happening—how do you rest in those?

— **SATURDAY** —

X

In the old story
the woman loses her son,
loses her new life.
And she tears off after the holy one
and grabs those feet, Didn't I say
don't lie to me?

And the holy one goes back
to the room where the son lies dead
and stretches out on that boy,
mouth on his mouth, eyes on his eyes,
hands on his hands. Twice.
And the boy comes back to life.

I want to know what that means,
to lie on someone dead,
to get on top of them
mouth on their mouth, eyes on their eyes,
hands on their hands and lie there
stretched out touching our full lengths
breathing into the dead.

How can I match the dead one
that close, like lovers?
Loving the dead one,
is that what that means?

And could I, just as I am,
climb on top and put my
mouth to their mouth,
eyes to their eyes,
hands to their hands
and believe over and over again
in new life

especially when it is dead?

Who is the dead one?
Is it me?
Is it the room itself
or that stone bed?
Is it someone I know
who has gone dead inside?
Someone I am avoiding
loving dead?

XI

I don't know.
I usually don't know.

I touch the stone bed, kneeling,
and say I don't know
who is waiting or what will happen
from day to day in this extra room.
What my new life is
or when it will die on me.

But I have this extra room,
and I just know that I believe in it.
I believe in the extra room,
in making an extra room,
in the possibility of the holy one's coming,
in making new life, in its sometime dying,
and in constantly watching what sleeps there
as if I were ready for the sky
to come in over and over again without edges.

This place, this extra room,
is where I'm becoming
hollow and ample at the same time.

Reflect

❖ What hospitality do you extend to your own self?
❖ When have you experienced becoming hollow and ample at the same time?

XII

I won't ask
what your extra room is like.
Or what went on
inside the Shunammite lady.
It's not for me
to know other people's
private stuff.

But I want you to know
that when I say my extra room
is for the holy one,
it means you.
It means whoever
needs an extra room that night.
I can't guarantee
there won't be dead furniture
in there from time to time.
Or that the bed will be comfortable.
But if you ever need
an extra room to stay in,
a place where seeing and hearing
have no edges,
I have this place inside me now,
and you are welcome there.

Reflect

❖ How do the comings and goings in your space change your space
and your self?

——— **Meditation** ———

The Studio

From the time I moved in I knew that this would be
    the room most mine.
That this would be the space that would make me feel at home.
Yet it has been the longest in taking shape. I did not know
all the things I would have to do for it to become mine.

Months after the move I told her that it felt like something in my soul
was shaking loose. She asked me what that looked like
and I said I didn't know. But the next time I saw her
I brought her the cards I'd been making.
The cards I'd begun to create after a year of no images,
of fearful wondering if I would ever do that again.
I brought her the cards, so much less precise now,
with their rough edges and torn shapes.
The ones that told the truth about my life.
The ones I'd made for you.
This, I told her, is the shape of my soul shaking loose.

The rough edges told me they needed a place to stay
and so I gave them this space that now takes the shape
of drafting table   of chair
of shelves spilling with the textured   the colored papers
and of the wall draped with the designs
of Lenten light   the vigil candles
the indigo evening   the story blanket

Oh these are the things of an artist
and I laugh when I enter this room and realize
this is who I finally am and you have helped reveal
this name to me, you who have never seen this room
but who breathe in it daily.

This is the shape of a soul coming home
and now I know I will always have this space
for certain in different places
and perhaps with different people
but in these edges, these breaths, oh blessed home.
—Jan L. Richardson

———— ❖ ————

Blessing: *In each act of making welcome, in each search for a hospitable space, may God give grace and a place to stretch out your soul.*

28 The Community of Two
Kary Kublin and Gehan Shehata

Invocation: *In the beginning was the Word. And the Word became flesh and dwelt among us, full of grace and truth. Be with us, Word of Life, as we taste and share words; by them may we give birth to community and give flesh to communion.*

Text: Ecclesiastes 4:9-12

Context: Community. Communion. Communication. Common. The same Latin root, *communis*, links them, meaning "to share gifts or service, to hold with one another." The words also hearken back to *koinonia*, the Greek word for close mutual relationship, partnership, and intimate community. Such community begins with the sharing of two. In this week, Kary Kublin and Gehan Shehata remind us of this.

Brought together by their passion for communication, Kary and Gehan met at a speech/language clinic in Toronto, Canada, in 1991. A doctoral student in speech/language pathology at Florida State University, Kary had moved to Toronto to spend part of the year working at the clinic. There she met Gehan, a native of Egypt who emigrated to Canada with her family in 1988 after living briefly in Saudi Arabia. Their shared professional interest in communication gave way to communion as together, across a span of cultures and a nineteen-year age difference, they broke the bread of words, struggles, experiences, and lives.

Kary has returned to Florida, where she now devotes herself to her cats, her dissertation, and her quest for new adventures. Gehan remains in Toronto, weaving together her work at the clinic and life with her husband and sons. Together Kary and Gehan continue to create community with each other across the physical distance, sharing passionate letters, phone calls, and occasional visits.

Excerpts from their letters invite us to share their community, to be warmed and challenged by their communion as we ponder our own friendships, near and far, and the community we create within them.

19 September 1992

Dearest Kary,

Many happy returns of the day. Yes, we are getting older every day but I do not know if we are getting wiser. The days go by and we seem like we are not getting what we would like for ourselves. When will our wishes come true, I have no ideas but that will be the day.

I do thank you for the beautiful days spent in Montreal. Right now I think I feel homesick to the extent that nothing can satisfy my need to be with my people. I cannot complain for work and home, children and husband as well as friends are at their best but I seem to be restless.

I am suffocating as I have been for too long trying to be careful and sensitive to the needs of others. I need to feel carefree and more trusting. But I do not feel that the time has come yet for me to let go and allow myself. I am too scared.

Reflect

❖ Dear friend, who offers you the communion/community of friendship?

❖ In what forms does that communion take place?

28 September 1992

My dear Gehan,

When do you feel safe and satisfied? Do you remember a time? For me Montreal held many precious moments of such a feeling. My only longing was that it would continue until I could get my fill. . . .

What is joyful about the struggle? Only that which I see in reflection after a difficult time has passed. I am happy to have come this far. . . .

I wish you Fall
    and Colours,
the chance to display your Brightness,
    to show that which burns within you.

DROP YOUR LEAVES!
    the risk of spite or laughter.

What will it take to share this drama?

You have already known barrenness,
    exposed to the elements.

Not again.

I want the warmth to fill your cup,
    sky and wind to welcome your Presence,
shouting for joy the Glorious Pageant,
    gifts given,
        returned,
        full circle 'round.

Reflect
- ❖ Dear friend, what are words to you?
- ❖ How do you play with them, shower them onto other people?
- ❖ What does it feel like to put words on paper, to offer them to others?

——— WEDNESDAY ———

10 October 1992
Kary my dearest,

I do sometimes . . . in my life feel safe and satisfied and it only happens when I stop for a moment to look around me and contemplate my existence. No one provides it; in a sense, I have to let go and allow it.

January 30, 1993
My dear Kary,

What have I done in the past to address those things I long for and how long can one wait?

There are many things I longed for and I have never been able to achieve or even reach. A few, as I grow older, have been sublimated; others most probably were forgotten as they were, most probably, not that important after all. But there are a few that still linger in my mind. . . .

Events in life unfold by themselves. . . . They must take their rightful course in life. I am experiencing difficulty, the need; I am suffering and many others are and it cannot go on forever. There is always an end to misery, to everything in life, even to us living creatures.

What is helping me to sustain my fate is that I firmly believe that I am doing what I believe is right for me, for my lovely husband and children.

Reflect

❖ Dear friend, what words do you use to describe your life, your past, your longing, your community?

❖ What longings have you released or set aside?

—— **THURSDAY** ——

March 6, 1993
(after a phone conversation)
Gehan,

You visit me
a Springtime of warmth and sun
upon my face

And when I ask for the moon
you bring it to me
tempered by the understanding
we create

Your years and experience serve to
emphasize to me
how beautiful you are
for I have seen the face of God

At times
it's all futility—
absurd efforts at creating New World

But together we hope
and it takes two
applauding the effort

two hands
one yours, one mine.

Reflect

❖ Dear friend, how do your relationships call forth your words and thoughts?

❖ How freely do you share your words with others?

❖ How do your words give life to your relationships with other persons?

March 17, 1993
(after receiving the March 6 letter)
My lovely Kary,

My years of experience and me, my self, have no meaning but those you, Kary, hold. I am in tears, for when you allow me to share your vision of me, I feel empowered. I can get to see finally what I have always wanted to find out. I can get to see, for myself, my self. I love you.

Reflect

❖ Dear friend, how does it feel when someone hears your words?

❖ In what ways is that experience an empowering one for you?

—— **SATURDAY** ——

10 April 1993
Dearest Gehan,

You asked me about how one can set up opportunities for oneself that may provide *choices*. For me it goes back to feelings of control and whether I have the chance to be proactive in a situation or whether I am forced to react to circumstances and events. I cannot believe in the idea of God having one ultimate plan or path for me to follow. If I did believe that, then it would mean to me that I could only be in one of two states: inside or outside the will of God.

I see myself as co-creating this life I am part of by the choices I make and the questions I ask. Like you, the questioning and seeking are an integral part of my knowing what is good and right for me. For it is within this reflection that I am aware of the potential. Answers are only the reminiscence of a specific opportunity realized as such after the fact. These opportunities and choices are only (relatively) clear to me *after* the decisions have been made.

In new environments I have so much to learn about the variables which come into play. I try to decide what is me and what is not me (what I can control and what I cannot control) and what part lies somewhere in between the two and can be co-created. Gehan, *you are doing this!* . . .

Reflect

❖ Dear friend, what are your words creating?

❖ Where are your words taking you?

(Continued from previous letter to Gehan)

We are spending our lives studying, trying to understand *communication*, fascinated by the wondrous ways children acquire it and wanting to help those for whom it is difficult. We know the cultural importance and significance of communication. Yet we are also aware of the ways our lives, personally, are shaped by relationships. There is resonance between us—you and I that first night we stayed late at work finding the beginning of our connections. Later, your taking me home to share a meal with your family was the invitation to communion—wine and bread, bodies broken, grace given and received.

Dissonance too we find as together we consider the worlds around us. Those who speak and hurt with words. Those who hear but cannot listen. I become so angry when they are not open to a new or different voice. What makes the difference? I am *thrilled* by your words; they challenge me to open my mind and heart to new possibilities. I am free to raise my voice with the passion that is subdued when I am with others. You bring me the fire. I know I am alive.

I am envious of the languages you have access to, the possibilities. To hear you speak is to recognize the choices created as windows to your soul. The words, they are your history, your story being told even now. . . .

Gehan, dear friend, may the angels watch over you and bring you peace.

Reflect

❖ Dear friend, what worlds are your words opening within you, between you and others?

――― **Meditation** ―――

I am in search of a haven, yet I must first build it for myself, stone by stone. Everyone seeks a home, a refuge. And I am always in search of a few words.

—Etty Hillesum, *An Interrupted Life*

Writing Home

In search of a few words
I come to you,
my pen across the page
a knock on your door.

I knock hungry

I knock thirsty
I knock longing
I knock lonely

You take me in
you write bread
you write wine
you write rest
you write stay

And together
we are writing home:

in the kitchen
we are writing home,
savoring words

in the dining room
we are writing home,
tasting words

in the hallway
we are writing home,
tossing words

in the bedrooms
we are writing home,
dreaming words

and with words
dripping from my hands
I am bidding you
welcome home,
dear friend,
welcome home.
—Jan L. Richardson

———— ❖ ————

Blessing: *May you give birth to words of healing, challenge, and power. Stirred, savored, tossed, and dreamed, may the words you create with one another give way to revelation, to community, to home.*

29 Bearers of New Wine
Women of Spirit

Invocation: *Blessed are you, O God, who creates new wine for us. Thirsting for the Spirit to move through us, we come to your table, seeking the cup of blessing you offer.*

Text: Acts 2:1-13

Context: Acts 1:14 tells us that, following Jesus' ascension, the disciples "were constantly devoting themselves to prayer, together with certain women, including Mary the mother of Jesus, as well as his brothers." Certainly the women were also there on the day of Pentecost, the fiftieth day after the second day of the Jewish festival of Passover. The Holy Spirit descended on the women as well as on the men; the gift of speaking in other languages came to the women as well as to the men; accusations of being drunk on new wine were hurled against the women as well as against the men.

No wine had touched their lips that day, as Peter goes on to explain; rather, he says, this was a fulfillment of what the prophet Joel had spoken: "I will pour out my Spirit upon all flesh, and your sons and your daughters shall prophesy" (Acts 2:17). Filled with the Spirit, the women as well as the men remembered the new wine offered by Jesus—the new wine of his life poured out among them; the new wine of healing brought to those who lived in sickness and on the margins; the new wine of justice for women, men, and children; the wine of shared, life-giving power. The new wine that had satisfied their thirst without touching their lips was Spirit-stirred and tasted anew on the day of Pentecost. Touched by wind and by flame, the women as well as the men realized again their power as vessels of the wind, fire, and new wine of the living God.

In this week of Pentecost, we remember these and other Spirit-filled women who poured out the wine of their lives, their dreams, their prayers, and their struggle to find a new language. We remember women whose lives were stirred and transformed by the wind of the Spirit, women who became bearers of hope, healing, justice, and peace. From many ages and lands we gather at their table, knowing their journeys made a way for our own. We call their names, we remember their stories, we taste the new wine they bear, and we invoke the Spirit who stirred their lives. In so doing, may we be blessed.

—— **MONDAY** ——

We bless *Beruriah*,
> who lived in second-century Jerusalem;
> who intimately knew the Torah;
> who is remembered in the Talmud for her great scholarship
> > and wise teaching;
>
> who, when her husband Rabbi Meir prayed for the death of robbers
> > who had plagued the town, told him to pray instead that their sin
> > would die, that they might thus repent, and they did.

Come, Spirit of Wisdom!
> and bless this cup;

stir its depths
> and feast with us.

Thirsting for wisdom,
> we call Beruriah's name;

fill us, O Wind,
> transform us, O Flame!

—Jan L. Richardson

Reflect

❖ In a world where knowledge is a commodity and education a privilege, to whom will you bear the cup of Wisdom?

—— **TUESDAY** ——

We remember *Saint Brigid*,
> who was born in fifth-century Ireland;
> whose arrival at sunrise was marked by a flame that stretched from
> > the top of her head to the heavens;
>
> who established a religious community at Kildare and became its first
> > abbess;
>
> who was revered for her wisdom;
> whose healing wells brought new life to the inhabitants of the
> > countryside;

whose fire was tended by priestesses and later by Catholic sisters
until a bishop declared it pagan
and had the fire extinguished in 1220.

Come, Spirit of Healing
and be our guest;
by words of passion
this cup be blessed.

Thirsting for healing,
we cry Brigid's name;
fill us, O Wind,
transform us, O Flame!
—Jan L. Richardson

Reflect

❖ In a world that often forgets its capacity to imagine, to whom will
you bear the cup of healing?

—— **WEDNESDAY** ——

We remember *Saint Gertrude the Great*,
who came to the convent of Helfta in Germany
in 1261 at the age of four or five;
who had a passion for study, for speech, and for writing;
who, at age twenty-five, began to have visions of Christ, who
promised she would "drink from the torrents"
of his delights;
whose visions of the sacred heart of Christ sparked a tradition
of religious devotion that still continues;
who became abbess of the convent that educated women in
grammar, rhetoric,
logic, arithmetic, geometry,
astronomy, music, and theology.

Come, Spirit of Vision!
Give shape to our sight,
that we may perceive you
and drink your delights.

Thirsting for vision,
we call Gertrude's name;

fill us, O Wind,
    transform us, O Flame!
—Jan L. Richardson

Reflect

    ❖   In a world often comfortable with its familiar patterns of seeing, to whom will you bear the cup of vision?

—— **THURSDAY** ——

We remember *Phoebe Worall Palmer*,
    who lived in New York City in the nineteenth century;
    who became a leader of the Holiness movement;
    who believed that the baptism of the Pentecostal Spirit
        was available to all believers;
    who helped pave the way for Wesleyan Methodists, Free Methodists,
        the Church of the Nazarene, the Salvation Army, and Pentecostal
        and charismatic movements in the United States;
    whose work as a writer and as a revivalist in the United States,
        Canada, and the British Isles helped ignite the Great Awakening
        that brought over two million people into the church;
    who promoted ministries by and for women;
    who brought social reform to the slums of New York City.

Come, Spirit of Holiness,
    and blow through us;
sanctify to its depths
    this blessing-cup.

Thirsting for the holy,
    we call Phoebe's name;
fill us, O Wind,
    transform us, O Flame!
—Jan L. Richardson

Reflect

    ❖   In a world broken by sin, to whom will you bear the cup of holiness?

—— **FRIDAY** ——

We remember *Harriet Tubman*,

who escaped enslavement in nineteenth-century Maryland;
who returned as a conductor on the Underground Railroad;
who, in nineteen trips, saved over 300 enslaved people,
> including her father, who had taught her how to survive
> in the woods as a child;
> her mother, who had taught her nursing skills as she grew;
> and all her brothers and sisters

who never lost a passenger
> as she led them to the "Promised Land" of Canada;

who wove messages and signals into her songs;
who had bounties on her head of up to $40,000;
who served the Union Army in the Civil War as a nurse, spy,
> and commander of intelligence operations;

who, near her death, dreamed of flying to freedom,
> helped by women dressed in white.

Come, Spirit of Freedom!
> and make this cup sweet
to give strength to our hands
> and speed to our feet.

Thirsting for freedom,
> we call Harriet's name;
fill us, O Wind,
> transform us, O Flame!
—Jan L. Richardson

Reflect
❖ In a world that is home to people still seeking liberation, to whom
will you bear the cup of freedom?

—— **SATURDAY** ——

We remember *America Sosa*,
> who struggles today for justice for her people of El Salvador;
> whose fourteen-year-old son Juan was captured by soldiers and
> tortured for ten months;
> whose son Joaquin was imprisoned for ten months
> and went into exile in Mexico;
> whose husband, who had not shared in her struggle against injustice,
> was captured and died as a result of injuries from his torture;

who fled to the United States in 1985 and received sanctuary
in Dumbarton United Methodist Church in Washington, D.C.;
who is the United States representative of COMADRES
(the Committee of Mothers of Political Prisoners, Disappeared
and Assassinated of El Salvador);
who was arrested in 1989 by Immigration and Naturalization Services
at the COMADRES office for illegal entry;
who received political asylum following her trial.

Come, Spirit of Justice!
and bless our hands
to pour out your cup
and give life to all lands.

Thirsting for justice,
we call America's name;
fill us, O Wind,
transform us, O Flame!
—Jan L. Richardson

Reflect

❖ In a world where daughters disappear and sons die, to whom shall
you bear the cup of justice?

────── **SUNDAY** ──────

We remember *unnamed women*,
who wove the threads of history;
who gave to the world
their music, their labor,
their children, their struggle,
their art, their visions,
their laughter, their wisdom,
their words, their lives;
who survived in wars;
who died in death camps;
who told the stories;
who made a way out of no way;
who gave life to women
who do so still:
who minister as priests in the underground church in the former Soviet

Union—whose ordination is not recognized by the Catholic Church;
who fight for freedom in South Africa;
who pray for their missing children in El Salvador, Argentina,
    Chile, Guatemala;
who live with AIDS and other illnesses;
who work as healers, teachers, mothers,
    laborers, community organizers;
who bear the cup of life;
who poured it out to heal the ground on which you stand;
who bid you taste and see
    how good it is.

Come, Spirit of Memory,
    and stir up in us
remembrance of all
    who passed us this cup.

Thirsting for memory,
    we cry out their names;
fill us, O Wind,
    transform us, O Flame!
—Jan L. Richardson

Reflect

    ❖   In a world that often forgets its past, to whom will you bear the
cup of memory?

—— Meditation ——

On the Day of Pentecost

the wine came to us
on the winds,
defiant sweetness
soaking the air
and settling into
our flesh.

We had thirsted
for this
for so long.

It soaked our hands
our hearts
our lips
and, stunned by its sweetness,
we cried in new languages
and heard with new ears:

These are our bodies
vessels
made whole in you

this is our blood
rising
to bring life to you.

O taste and see;
we have thirsted
for this
for so long.
—Jan L. Richardson

———— ❖ ————

Blessing: *Filled with the Spirit, may you taste and know the sweetness*
of new language, the sustenance of new hearing, and the power of bearing
the cup of blessing to one another.

Living the Rhythms

Ordinary Time

THE CHURCH HAS STRUGGLED with what to call the long season between the feast of Pentecost and the beginning of Advent. Spanning nearly half the year, these months contain no major holy days that give a defining theme to the season. Whitsuntide, Kingdomtide, the season after Pentecost—these are some of the names that the church has attached to these days. Some denominations, giving up on any attempt to infuse an identity into this season, simply call it "Ordinary Time."

Although it eludes easy definition, this long stretch of the year called Ordinary Time ought to be cause for celebration. It invites us to contemplate the rhythms that sustain us between the feast-times and the fast-times of our lives. Ordinary Time reminds us that while we have times and rhythms of predictability, we spend much of our lives dealing with the day-to-day, often unpredictable, happenings. The "stuff" of these days shapes our lives. We find who we are in these in-between times through improvising meaning out of the different rhythms of these days.

And so this section of the book mirrors the ordinary times, the ordinary rhythms of our lives. In these pages you will find a feast of different women, stories, themes, and insights. In this unfolding season you will encounter women crafting holiness out of chaos and fashioning extraordinary lives out of ordinary days. Like these women, we are called to find the patterns in this season ahead.

"This is just life I'm writing about, after all," Nancy Mairs writes in her book *Ordinary Time*, "and life outside the seasons of fast and feast—Advent and Christmas, Lent and Easter—at that: ordinary time." With wisdom may we journey through these ordinary days, rejoicing in the rhythms they offer us.

A Prayer for the Beginning of Ordinary Time

❖

In this season, we remember that God dwells even in the ordinary times and places. We never know when the divine presence may show forth as we go about our daily work. I was standing in the kitchen with Lesley Brogan, watching her dry dishes, when she began to tell me about a ritual she shared at Common Ground, a space designed to help men with HIV and AIDS reflect on their spiritual journeys. She uses this ritual as one of remembrance for members who have died. I think it speaks powerfully of how we dwell in time. If you are celebrating the beginning of Ordinary Time alone, you may wish to gather around yourself memories of those who have dwelt in time with you.

You may light a candle.

This is the candle of the present.
This is where we are together.
Our time and our energy
are gathered into this space.
Here we recognize one another,
we know one another,
and we are known.

You may light a second candle.

This is the candle of the past.
This is the time before any of us
know one another,
the time when we are in
our mother's womb
and she is in
her mother's womb,
and all that is to be
is contained in the
very being of God.

You may light a third candle.

This is the candle of the future.
I light this candle

because I believe in the past
and I believe in the present.
Because I have touched
these times,
I know there is energy
that goes on ahead of us.
Because there is tangibleness,
because we have marked these times,
I have hope for the future.

Bless to me, O God, these times
of present
and past
and future.
May these flames
of dwelling
and of memory
and of hope
become an endless ring of blessing
to you.
—Jan L. Richardson

30 Mystery at Every Turn
The Daily Trinity

Invocation: *Divine Mystery, blessed be you in all your forms! Widen my imagination, that I may glimpse you in the hidden places.*

Text: Psalm 139:1-12

Context: The Trinity tickles the mind: Three-in-one, one-in-three; three "persons" yet not divisible. We usually resort to everyday symbols to approach its meaning: shamrocks, fleur-de-lis, three interlocking circles.

Such symbols point us toward two notions that lie at the heart of the Trinity. First, the Trinity suggests that God, in God's very being, dwells in community. God's own nature is relational, and God seeks to draw us into that divine community. Second, our doctrines of the Trinity still fall short of completely naming or explaining God. As one author notes in the *Handbook of the Christian Year*, Trinity Sunday is a day in which we celebrate "the infinitely complex and unfathomable mystery of God's being." And in doing so, we turn most often to the basic symbols and images.

The week in which we celebrate Trinity Sunday offers an opportune transition from the season of Easter to the season of Ordinary Time. As we who have journeyed with different communities during the weeks following Easter begin to ponder the ways in which God dwells in ordinary days and spaces, Trinity Sunday captures images of both: the God who is communal by nature showing forth in the dailiness of life.

—— **MONDAY** ——

earth, sky, sea

The holy writ says that, in the end,
all will be gathered together:
all that dwell above the earth
and all that dwell upon the earth
and all that dwell below the earth.

And we who touch the wounds

that line creation's body
and we who search through darkening air
to see the blessedness of sky
and we who taste with trepidation
the waters running with pollution
will cry,

"Blessed be the God of the universe,
restorer of creation,
who makes all things new!"
—Jan L. Richardson

Reflect
- ❖ Earth, sky, sea—what are your earliest memories of them?
- ❖ What do they reveal to you?

—— TUESDAY ——

morning, noon, night

Up from the dark waters of night
the great God comes,
hands dripping with the dreams
of the slumbering creatures.

Dancing with dawn,
the bearer of sun
takes a world-sized step,
gasps,
and goes back down again.
—Jan L. Richardson

Reflect
- ❖ What are the rhythms of your day?

—— WEDNESDAY ——

eye, ear, hand

In all her newness
I watch her discover each part
and pray that eye

and ear
and hand may always be open
to know the one who fashioned them.

Babies:
God's way of retracing
the shape of incarnation.
—Jan L. Richardson

Reflect
- ❖ Where do you experience moments of discovery and wonder?
- ❖ With sight, sound, and touch, where do you sense God's spirit showing forth?

—— **THURSDAY** ——

silence, sound, space

We are at the altar and with
hands and lips I am
trying to tell her that
she doesn't need ears
to hear God's voice,
that she has heard it
through those who have
surrounded her in these days.

Anne ponders this. Then,
tracing the air with her hands,
she tells me,
"Now I understand
that deafness is not
the opposite of hearing;
it is silence
filled with sound."

"Oh," I signed.
"Yes!"
And for the first time
we heard.
—Jan L. Richardson

Reflect

- ❖ What dwells in your silences and what do you learn from them?
- ❖ What kind of space does silence create in your life?

—— FRIDAY ——

work, rest, celebration

I heard him tell the story of a colleague,
a woman working for justice
for peace
in Guatemala
or El Salvador
or Nicaragua.
All day long she worked.
All night long she worked.
There was so much to be done.

Finally one of the people
came to her
and asked her,
"Why do you always work?
Why do you not sit with us
outside our homes?
Why do you not join
in our celebrations?"

"But there is so much
to be done,"
she replied.

"Ah," the people said.
"You are one of those
who are only with us
a short time.
You will grow tired,
and you will go.
The ones who stay,
they are the ones
who have learned

to sit with us
and to come
to our parties."

I think
she is there still.
　—Jan L. Richardson

Reflect

❖ What are the rhythms of work, rest, and celebration in your life?

❖ How does your spirit become restored?

 **SATURDAY**

justice, kindness, humility

[God] has told you, O mortal, what is good;
　and what does the LORD require of you
but to do justice, and to love kindness,
　and to walk humbly with your God?
　—Micah 6:8

Reflect

❖ Justice, kindness, humility . . . what meaning do these qualities
have for you?

❖ What place do these qualities have in your life?

SUNDAY

salt, light, power

It is not might
that will finally save us.

It is power
like salt,
giving ourselves over
to the flavor of the holy;
like light indiscriminate,
caressing each face
it happens to meet.
　—Jan L. Richardson

Reflect

- ❖ The holy showing forth in the ordinary: where else do you perceive it?
- ❖ What other images and relationships reveal the presence of God in your life?

────── **Meditation** ──────

Names

To the One
who laughingly gave us
language
and absconded
with its limits:

I smile
to think of all
your names
I may never know.
—Jan L. Richardson

────── ❖ ──────

Blessing: *May the God who dwells beyond us*
and the God who dwells among us
and the God who calls us to dwell together
bless you now
and always.

31 Ordinary Time and Space
The Shape of Dwelling

Invocation: *Praised be you, who have made your dwelling among us!*
Let me linger in this time with you, O God, as I trace the lines of my living.

Text: Psalm 90:1-2

Context: *Dwelling.* The word evokes images of habitation, of space, of
home. More than a physical place, our dwelling is formed in the intersection
of time and space, created as our daily living gives shape to our surroundings and to ourselves.

We do not dwell alone. The Bible stories continually remind us that
God has established a dwelling among us. The movement of God in our lives
and the stories of generations of faithful people shape our dwelling, even
when we may live alone.

Along the journey, God calls us to times of tarrying, of being attentive
to time as it unfolds in a particular place. For those of us who are intensely
future-oriented, paying attention to the now presents a challenge.

Learning to dwell means learning to look at time not simply as something that happens on our way to somewhere else but rather as something
that unfolds in space, space that we shape and craft by our daily routines,
rituals, movements, interactions. It means lingering with God, with creation,
with one another, and with ourselves in *this* time, in *this* space.

—— **MONDAY** ——

Greeting the Day

Mornings I am sullen. A child of the night, it is there I dwell best. Each day
I have to reacquaint myself with morning. Only the routines and rituals keep
us on speaking terms.

I open the shades, squinting. Flashes of red in the neighbor's yard
slowly take the shape of hibiscus under my gaze. I reach for the book
Changing Light: The Eternal Cycle of Night and Day (it is hard to find my
own words at this hour).

O God, who broughtst me from the rest of last night
Unto the joyous light of this day,
Be Thou bringing me from the new light of this day
Unto the guiding light of eternity.
   Oh! from the new light of this day
Unto the guiding light of eternity.

And the day has begun.
—Jan L. Richardson

Reflect

- ❖ How do you greet the day?
- ❖ What rituals, practices, or habits carry you through the day?

—— **TUESDAY** ——

Blessing the Meal

Living alone, I eat many meals in solitude. Yet each morning I open a book of graces and whisper a mealtime blessing from its pages. Today I read from *One Hundred Graces*,

> Lord, bless our ears with your word.
> Bless our bodies with Your bounties.
> Bless our lives with Your love.

I know that somewhere, someone also lifts up this prayer. We break bread and eat together.
—Jan L. Richardson

Reflect

- ❖ How and where do your meals usually take place?
- ❖ How does eating alone differ from eating with others?
- ❖ What is it like for you to eat alone?

—— **WEDNESDAY** ——

Midday

An exhausting day. I lie down to rest, but my mind won't let go of the worries, the things undone, the loneliness of this day, the emptiness of this house that has crept up on me again. Then, suddenly, the women come. I can almost feel their touch as in my mind's eye they lay their hands on me. So many who, in presence or in memory, have shared my journey—grandmothers, teachers, friends, women I know only through the stories I have lived with over the last two years. Their simple touch of love unspoken moves into those fearful, tender places.

These women dwell with me too.

I talk with Helen that night. She offers almost an identical image. I can't tell her of my own vision of the women without weeping harder. "Rest in them," she tells me. "Rest."

—Jan L. Richardson

Reflect

❖ When has creating a place of dwelling been a struggle?

❖ What memories, images, or visions have helped you?

—— THURSDAY ——

Early Evening

I discovered her one day, resting on her web—a magnificent multilevel creation unlike any other I'd seen. It stretched between my patio door and the rose bush just beyond. She appeared when I'd been devoting much time to working on my home, setting up a studio in one of the spare rooms, unpacking boxes that had waited for months. For days I continued to watch her, fancying her a companion as we each engaged in this tenuous, intricate, mysterious process of creating a dwelling.

I came home one day to a trimmed rose bush. And no web. For days I kept looking in the same place, hoping she'd rebuild.

Sitting on the porch this evening, writing and thinking about dwelling, I hear a rustle in the greenery outside the patio. I walk over to investigate. Searching, my eyes settle on a lizard in the underbrush. As I draw back, I realize I've nearly stuck my nose in a web being built in the corner. I recognize the tiny inhabitant, the flash of gold on her green body. "Hello," I murmur. "I've been waiting for you!"

Home isn't always where we look for it.

—Jan L. Richardson

Reflect

❖ What unexpected moments have blessed your dwelling?

——— FRIDAY ———

Twilight

This is my favorite time of day, when the sun has set and blue begins to drape itself across the land. I sit on the porch and watch the trees, the grass, the sky as they change and deepen.

Night to night declares knowledge . . . their voice goes out through all the earth (Psalm 19:2b, 4).

I want to capture this scene, to share it. I go into the house, grab the box of papers, take it to the porch, and rifle through it for the colors, the textures of this twilight. I fold a card and across its whiteness lay down shreds of blue, of purple, of the gold of emerging stars. The sky is dark by the time I finish.

I take the card inside, look at the scene once more before opening to the inside to tell my friend of this indigo evening. "This is my favorite time of day," I write, "when the sun has set and blue begins to drape itself across the land . . . "
—Jan L. Richardson

Reflect
❖ What is your favorite time of day?
❖ What time do you take to ponder the space that extends beyond your physical dwelling?

——— SATURDAY ———

Night

Each night since before I lived in this place I lighted a lamp for them before going to bed. "Bless Edward and Ray," I prayed as I struck the match, "with life and health and peace in abundance." Once I moved here, this evening lighting and blessing became even more important; it became a plea for connection over the distance and for comfort in the face of AIDS.

Returning from a trip to Atlanta for Edward's memorial service, I light the lamp. I don't know what to pray. Edward was never in this house, but it feels different now. I gaze at the flame, feeling almost betrayed by it.

"God bless Edward and Ray," I pray. I can't change the words completely. I realize how these words, this ritual have shaped my dwelling in this year of change. "God bless us all. May we learn what it means to be at home with one another. In peace."
—Jan L. Richardson

Reflect

❖ How do you close your day—at whatever time it ends?

❖ When your dwelling has changed, what rituals, objects, or habits have helped to make the space more familiar and comfortable?

—— SUNDAY ——

Before Dawn

It is the morning after my brother's wedding. I stayed in town longer than planned, wanting to squeeze in as much time as possible with those who had gathered from far-flung places to share in the celebration. I drag myself out of bed early, too early, to make the trip back to Orlando in time for church.

The interstate would be quickest, but I take the highway instead. South of Micanopy I make the turn toward Evinston, silencing the radio and rolling down my window. I hear crickets; a sliver of a crescent moon hangs over the land as I pass the house where I grew up, the pastures, Freddie's pond, Mount Olive A.M.E. Church. The places are familiar, but I have not seen them at this time of night in years. I marvel at the stillness of the homes I pass; these are the dwellings of the people who grew me up—the Glissons, Aunt Nancy, Aunt Lois, the Deadericks. I turn the corner and pass the farm, the land where my great-grandfather and my grandfather and his brothers poured out their lives, the house across the way in which my grandmother and grandfather lived and died. There's a new baby in that house now, born last week to my cousin and his wife who have moved in and made the house their own.

Time unfolds, and generations continue. The sky grows lighter; I roll up the window, turn onto the highway, and head toward home.

—Jan L. Richardson

Reflect

❖ What memories of other dwellings now inhabit and give shape to your own home?

—— Meditation ——

Shortly after I moved to Orlando, I received an invitation to a home blessing that two friends were having. I couldn't be there, but weaving a blessing for their home enlarged my own understanding of dwelling and how it happens, even for those who live alone.

Turning Home

This is the tale
  of the house turning home.

By sparking sparkling fire closely sitting
  it is turning home.
By starry evening companioned dreaming
  it is turning home.
By early morning together waking
  it is turning home.
By hurry friends are coming cleaning
  it is turning home.
By smiling welcome come-in greeting
  it is turning home.
By hold you when you're hurting loving
  it is turning home.
By warm bread strongly sharing breaking
  it is turning home.
By good drink deeply sweetly tasting
  it is turning home.
By spirit-flinging with abandon dancing
  it is turning home.
By side-splitting stop I'm dying laughing
  it is turning home.
By my lonely missing long to be there wishing
  it is turning home.
By tender wholly love-filled blessing
  it is turning home.

This is the tale
  of the house turning home.
—Jan L. Richardson

Blessing: *Go in peace, knowing yourself to be at home.*

32 Stalking the Holy
Annie Dillard

Invocation: *God of mystery, who inhabits the silences and the spaces, who knows and is known by the creation you have fashioned, grant me courage to seek you in the wild, hidden places. Fill my vision with your wisdom, that I may perceive your holy dwellings.*

Text: Psalm 104

Context: "When everything else has gone from my brain," Annie Dillard writes in the prologue to her autobiographical *An American Childhood*, "—the President's name, the state capitals, the neighborhoods where I lived, and then my own name and what it was on earth I sought, and then at length the faces of my friends, and finally the faces of my family—when all this has dissolved, what will be left, I believe, is topology: the dreaming memory of the land as it lay this way and that."

Author and poet Annie Dillard writes out of this "dreaming memory of the land." From the hills, mountain valleys, and rivers of her hometown to the land surrounding her Waldenesque Tinker Creek, Annie unravels her sacred landscape and weaves it into reflections on beauty, terror, mystery, and the holy. In the eyes of a weasel she has stalked along Tinker Creek, in sunlight slamming down a hill in Washington State during an eclipse of the sun, in a moth become a flaming wick atop a candle, she probes the glory as well as the shadow side of God with a unique sense of sight.

The readings this week invite us to see anew the landscapes that surround us and lie within us. Annie reminds us that the contours of the land and of our lives tell out the glory of the holy. To perceive the sacred requires both focused pursuit and a radical openness to the unexpected.

—— **MONDAY** ——

In summer, I stalk. Summer leaves obscure, heat dazzles, and creatures hide from the red-eyed sun, and me. I have to seek things out. The creatures I seek have several senses and free will; it becomes apparent that they do not wish to be seen. I can stalk them in either of two ways. The first is not what you think of as true stalking, but it is the *Via negativa*, and as fruitful as actual pursuit. When I stalk this way I take my stand on a bridge and wait, emptied. I put myself in the way of the creature's passage, like spring Eskimos at a seal's breathing hole. Something might come; something might go. I am Newton under the apple tree, Buddha under the bo. Stalking the other way, I forge my own passage seeking the creature. I wander the banks; what I find, I follow, doggedly, like Eskimos haunting the caribou herds. I am Wilson squinting after the traces of electrons in a cloud chamber; I am Jacob at Peniel wrestling with the angel.

—From *Pilgrim at Tinker Creek*

Reflect

❖   What do you seek in your life?

❖   How do you discern when to wait for and when to pursue that which you seek?

—— **TUESDAY** ——

When her doctor took her bandages off and led her into the garden, the girl who was no longer blind saw "the tree with the lights in it." It was for this tree I searched through the peach orchards of summer, in the forests of fall and down winter and spring for years. Then one day I was walking along Tinker Creek thinking of nothing at all and I saw the tree with the lights in it. I saw the backyard cedar where the mourning doves roost charged and transfigured, each cell buzzing with flame. I stood on the grass with the lights in it, grass that was wholly fire, utterly focused and utterly dreamed. It was less like seeing than like being for the first time seen, knocked breathless by a powerful glance. The flood of fire abated, but I'm still spending the power. Gradually the lights went out in the cedar, the colors died, the cells unflamed and disappeared. I was still ringing. I had been my whole life a bell, and never knew it until at that moment I was lifted and struck. I have since only very rarely seen the tree with the lights in it. The vision comes and goes, mostly goes, but I live for it, for the moment when the mountains open and a new light roars in spate through the crack, and the mountains slam.

—From *Pilgrim at Tinker Creek*

Reflect

Recall a time when something in the landscape of your life suddenly shifted.

❖ What poured in through the cracks?

----- **WEDNESDAY** -----

Several months later, walking past the farm on the way to a volleyball game, I remarked to a friend, by way of information, "There are angels in those fields." Angels! That silence so grave and so stricken, that choked and unbearable green! I have rarely been so surprised at something I've said. Angels! What are angels? I had never thought of angels, in any way at all.

From that time on I began to think of angels. I considered that sights such as I had seen of the silence must have been shared by the people who said they saw angels. I began to review the thing I had seen that morning. My impression now of those fields is of thousands of spirits—spirits trapped, perhaps, by my refusal to call them more fully, or by the paralysis of my own spirit at that time—thousands of spirits, angels in fact, almost discernible to the eye, and whirling. If pressed I would say they were three or four feet from the ground. Only their motion was clear (clockwise, if you insist); that, and their beauty unspeakable.

There are angels in those fields, and, I presume, in all fields, and everywhere else. I would go to the lions for this conviction, to witness this fact. What all this means about perception, or language, or angels, or my own sanity, I have no idea.

—From *Teaching a Stone to Talk*

Reflect
❖ What do you think of angels?
❖ What landscapes have offered images of holiness to you?

----- **THURSDAY** -----

That it's rough out there and chancy is no surprise. Every live thing is a survivor on a kind of extended emergency bivouac. But at the same time we are also created. In the Koran, Allah asks, "The heaven and the earth and all in between, thinkest thou I made them *in jest*?" It's a good question. What do we think of the created universe, spanning an unthinkable void with an unthinkable profusion of forms? Or what do we think of nothingness, those sickening reaches of time in either direction? If the giant water bug was not made in jest, was it then made in earnest? Pascal uses a nice term to describe the notion of the creator's, once having called forth the universe, turning his back to it: *Deus Absconditus*. Is this what we think happened? Was the sense of it there, and God absconded with it, ate it, like a wolf who disappears round the edge of the house with the Thanksgiving turkey? "God is subtle," Einstein said, "but not malicious." Again, Einstein said that "nature conceals her mystery by means of her essential grandeur, not by her cunning." It could be that God has not absconded but spread, as our vision and understanding of the universe have spread, to a fabric of spirit and sense so grand and subtle, so powerful in a new way, that we can only feel blindly of its hem. In making the thick darkness a swaddling band for the sea, God "set bars and doors" and said, "Hitherto shalt thou come, but no further." But have we come even that far? Have we rowed out to the thick darkness, or are we all playing pinochle in the bottom of the boat?

—From *Pilgrim at Tinker Creek*

Reflect

❖ What do you think of the created universe? of nothingness?

❖ Where do you find yourself more comfortable—rowing into the thick darkness of the questions or playing pinochle in the bottom of the boat?

——— **FRIDAY** ———

Cruelty is a mystery, and the waste of pain. But if we describe a world to compass these things, a world that is a long, brute game, then we bump against another mystery: the inrush of power and light, the canary that sings on the skull. Unless all ages and races of men have been deluded by the same mass hypnotist (who?), there seems to be such a thing as beauty, a grace wholly gratuitous. About five years ago I saw a mockingbird make a straight vertical descent from the roof gutter of a four-story building. It was an act as careless and spontaneous as the curl of a stem or the kindling of a star.

The mockingbird took a single step into the air and dropped. His wings were still folded against his sides as though he were singing from a limb and not falling, accelerating thirty-two feet per second per second, through empty air. Just a breath before he would have been dashed to the ground, he unfurled his wings with exact, deliberate care, revealing the broad bars of white, spread his elegant, white-banded tail, and so floated onto the grass. I had just rounded a corner when his insouciant step caught my eye; there was no one else in sight. The fact of his free fall was like the old philosophical conundrum about the tree that falls in the forest. The answer must be, I think, that beauty and grace are performed whether or not we will or sense

them. The least we can do is try to be there.
—From *Pilgrim at Tinker Creek*

Reflect
- ❖ Where do you encounter beauty and grace in your life?
- ❖ How could you be more present to such moments?

——— **SATURDAY** ———

I am drinking boiled coffee and watching the bay from the window. Almost all of the people who reef net have hauled their gears for the winter; the salmon runs are over, days are short. Still, boats come and go on the water—tankers, tugs and barges, rowboats and sails. There are killer whales if you're lucky, rafts of harlequin ducks if you're lucky, and every day the scoter and the solitary grebes. How many tons of sky can I see from the window? It is morning: morning! and the water clobbered with light. Yes, in fact, we do. We do need reminding, not of what God can do, but of what [God] cannot do, or will not, which is to catch time in its free fall and stick a nickel's worth of sense into our days. And we need reminding of what time can do, must only do; churn out enormity and beat it, with God's blessing, into our heads: that we are created, *created*, sojourners in a land we did not make, a land with no meaning of itself and no meaning we can make for it alone. Who are we to demand explanations of God? (And what monsters of perfection should we be if we did not?) We forget ourselves, picnicking; we forget where we are. There is no such thing as a freak accident. "God is at home," says Meister Eckhart, "We are in the far country."

We are most deeply asleep at the switch when we fancy we control any switches at all. We sleep to time's hurdy-gurdy; we wake, if we ever wake, to the silence of God. And then, when we wake to the deep shores of light uncreated, then when the dazzling dark breaks over the far slopes of time, then it's time to toss things, like our reason, and our will; then it's time to break our necks for home.
—From *Holy the Firm*

Reflect
- ❖ What calls you home?
- ❖ How do you know it's time to go there?
- ❖ What do you toss aside in order to get there?

Thomas Merton wrote, "There is always a temptation to diddle around in the contemplative life, making itsy-bitsy statues." There is always an enormous temptation in all of life to diddle around making itsy-bitsy friends and meals and journeys for itsy-bitsy years on end. It is so self-conscious, so apparently moral, simply to step aside from the gaps where the creeks and winds pour down, saying, I never merited this grace, quite rightly, and then to sulk along the rest of your days on the edge of rage. I won't have it. The world is wilder than that in all directions, more dangerous and bitter, more extravagant and bright. We are making hay when we should be making whoopee; we are raising tomatoes when we should be raising Cain, or Lazarus.

Ezekiel excoriates false prophets as those who have not "gone up into the gaps." The gaps are the thing. The gaps are the spirit's one home, the altitudes and latitudes so dazzlingly spare and clean that the spirit can discover itself for the first time like a once-blind man unbound. The gaps are the clifts in the rock where you cower to see the back parts of God; they are the fissures between mountains and cells the wind lances through, the icy narrowing fiords splitting the cliffs of mystery. Go up into the gaps. If you can find them; they shift and vanish, too. Stalk the gaps. Squeak into a gap in the soil, turn, and unlock—more than a maple—a universe. This is how you spend this afternoon, and tomorrow morning, and tomorrow afternoon. *Spend* the afternoon. You can't take it with you.

—From *Pilgrim at Tinker Creek*

Reflect

❖ What are you making or raising with your life?
❖ How are you spending your time?
❖ What gaps are you stalking, squeaking your way into, unlocking?

—— **Meditation** ——

From the dream-filled land,
   cry!
What shall I cry?
That all earth
   is sacred ground,
the dwelling-place
   of God.

From the rushing wave,
   cry!
What shall I cry?
That earth
   is drenched with mystery
dancing over
   the face of the deep.

From the restless wind,
   cry!
What shall I cry?
That the Spirit
   rushes through
the one placed
   in Her path.

From the burning flame,
   cry!
What shall I cry?
That creation is ablaze
   with the holy;
to see
   is to be consumed.
—Jan L. Richardson

———— ❖ ————

Blessing: *By earth and water bless me, Creator God; with wind and flame inhabit my spirit. Bless my sight to perceive the holy and my hands to heal your sacred earth.*

33 Grandmother Tales
Sue Joiner

Invocation: *God of the dance, bless the rhythms of my remembering. Illuminate the shadowed and sacred stories that have graced my life.*

Text: Hebrews 12:1-2

Context: This story is one of celebration, of remembrance, of calling, of two lives connected across time. When Sue told me of the time leading to her ordination and how it was graced by the gifts and visions of her grandmother, I asked if she would write some of the story down.

The narrative emerged in pieces, recollections like candles illuminating the story of Sue's grandmother and lending light to moments along the way. In these words we find not only the memory of a life but a vision too, born of the spirit her grandmother passed on.

Sue has taught me much about different ways of prayer. Along our journey she has sustained me with her reminders of the candle she lights for me. During this week, I invite you to light a candle each day to illumine your prayers and to remember those who have graced your spirit with theirs.

You may not remember your grandmothers, or you may not have good memories of them. If you have other elders who have been wise companions in your life, then remember and celebrate them. If you don't have these either, then light a candle and say a prayer for the one you are becoming.

—— MONDAY ——

Her name was Mary Elizabeth. She loved the color purple so much that she drove a purple car. She read the newspaper from cover to cover to stay in touch with the world from several perspectives, including that of the Dallas Cowboys. She did not have children of her own. She married my grandfather when his children were (mostly) grown, and she had invested most of her childbearing years in her work, which she valued very much. She was a woman who valued wisdom, compassion, and generosity.

Reflect
Light a candle and remember grandmothers or others . . . their work, their family, their passions.

—— TUESDAY ——

She chose me. She needed someone to mentor, to teach what she had learned. Without knowing I had been chosen, I eagerly embraced all that she offered me: honest conversation, learning to care for those in trouble, laughter and joy in the creatures that share this planet, and fierce anger at injustice. She loved me enough to tell me the truth, even when it was painful for us both. She gave generously to others to improve their quality of life.

Reflect
Light a candle and remember grandmothers or others . . . who chose you, who taught you, who gave you the truth.

—— WEDNESDAY ——

She loved the church. She had served on a church staff and appreciated being able to give herself to the institution that meant so much to her. She was proud of my call to ministry. She died a year before I was ordained. As I looked back on those people and events that have shaped me, I knew that her influence was profound. My response to her presence in my life is one of gratitude for the privilege of being loved by one of God's human saints.

Reflect
Light a candle and remember grandmothers or others . . . who shared their faith, who passed on their traditions, who shared in God's call on your life.

—— THURSDAY ——

A guided meditation, and the leader is saying, "Invite the Christ to come with you." Suddenly I am filled with an empty void. No Christ figure appears. Each day the leader issues the same invitation, and each day I encounter the same void. Where is the Christ?

The last day. The leader says, "Enter the upper room." I walk into a room full of women sitting around a large table. It is a holy place, and I know that I belong in that space. "The Christ enters the room," the leader says. I look up and there she is—the Christ is my grandmother. She is not sick and frail as she was in her last days. She is dancing with delight.

Reflect
Light a candle and remember grandmothers or others . . . who showed you the face of Christ, who shared their sacred spaces with you.

—— **FRIDAY** ——

The meditation continues. My grandmother's laughter fills the room and her pale green eyes are sparkling. She surrounds me with her joyful movement. She is waving two purple scarves. She invites me to join the dance with her. I am awed and comforted by her presence. She is celebrating my upcoming ordination. As she prepares to leave, she lovingly places one of the scarves over my shoulders. Yes! She is passing the mantle on to me. Her life and ministry will live on in me. She will be with me, empowering me to carry on the call of God.

Reflect
Light a candle and remember grandmothers or others . . . who celebrated with you, who revealed God's power within you.

—— **SATURDAY** ——

Ordination. The day is here. Twelve years ago I heard God's call and now the day of public celebration and worship has arrived. I am in Boise, Idaho, far from many of my family and friends. But I am not alone. Many have promised to remember me on this day. Colleen is lighting a purple candle in honor of this day in North Carolina. Rebecca gave me a purple candle to remember my grandmother as I prepare for the service this evening.

I light the candle and close my eyes. I see my grandmother as she appeared to me in the upper room meditation. I see her pride. Her love for me has prepared me for this day, enabling me to passionately follow the God who has called me. I am ready.

Reflect
Light a candle and remember grandmothers or others . . . who prepared you, who strengthened you for your journey.

—— **SUNDAY** ——

The service of worship begins. It is time. I stand before the bishop. The congregation sings the hymn by Dan Schutte, "Here I am, Lord. Is it I, Lord? I have heard you calling in the night. I will go, Lord, if you lead me. I will hold your people in my heart."

I am still, taking it all in. Suddenly she appears. She has come to be with me, and she is dancing with great joy. As hands are laid on my head, I am surrounded with the company of saints, all who have faithfully responded to God's call. I feel the power of her presence beckoning me to continue the work she began; I follow, rejoicing.

Reflect

Light a candle and remember grandmothers or others . . . who journey with you still.

—— Meditation ——

Anchorage

For my grandmothers Flora Yon Richardson
and Geraldine Bruster Scott

The candle flickers in this nighttime upper room.
Wind howls as I have rarely heard before,
and looking out over these mountains
I remember those who came too as visitors here,
journeying with their husbands, my grandfathers,
to this place where my parents began their marriage.

Blowing out the flame
I will lie down with the wind tonight
and pretend its moaning doesn't unsettle me
so much as it calls to me
with the grandmothers' cries of memory
their greeting long-missed daughter and son
their exclamation over this landscape of reunion
their blessing for
this sacred journey.
—Jan L. Richardson

—— ❖ ——

Blessing: *Remember. Rejoice. Rest.*

34 To Be the Sun Again
Chung Hyun Kyung

Invocation: *Dwell with us in new places, God of grace, that we may witness your Word's being birthed anew.*

Text: Isaiah 30:26

Context: In the beginning of her book *Struggle to Be the Sun Again: Introducing Asian Women's Theology*, Chung Hyun Kyung writes of the Japanese poet Hiratsuka Raicho's poem "The Hidden Sun," in which the poet claims that "originally, woman was the sun. She was an authentic person. But now woman is the moon." The struggle of women, Hyun Kyung asserts, is to be the sun again—to relearn how to shine with our own light rather than reflecting the light of others.

A native of Korea who earned theological degrees in the United States, Hyun Kyung has struggled to integrate the experiences of her people with her Western education. Now a professor of systematic theology at Ewha Women's University in Seoul, she claims and draws on stories, songs, traditions, and prayers that formed her as she grew. A Christian who was influenced by the Buddhism, Confucianism, Shintoism, and Taoism of her culture, Hyun Kyung places the Korean concept of *han* at the center of her theology. "*Han*," she writes, "is the most prevalent feeling among Korean people, who have been violated throughout their history by the surrounding powerful countries." Becoming free of the pain, oppression, and powerlessness of *han* lies at the heart of the struggle to become the sun again.

Hyun Kyung writes out of the deep awareness that our Christianity emerges out of many influences, including geography, culture, family history, national and ethnic heritage, gender, and class. In this week's journey, let us recall the stories, traditions, and history that have influenced our own faith.

—— **MONDAY** ——

The following two readings come from Chung Hyun Kyung's address to the Seventh World Council of Churches Assembly in Canberra, Australia, in 1991. After entering the Assembly with Korean and Australian Aboriginal dancers and drummers, Hyun Kyung invited those present to take off their shoes to honor the holy ground that they shared. She then called on the spirits, the memories, of those who have shaped our history but whose stories we have often forgotten or ignored. As we enter this week, let us share in this invocation with her, pondering the holy ground on which we stand and the memories of those who journeyed here before us.

For many Asian and Pacific people, taking off our shoes is the first act of humbling ourselves to encounter the Spirit of God. Also in our Judeo-Christian tradition God called Moses to take his shoes off in front of the burning bush to get on the Holy Ground—so he did. Do you think you can do that too? I would like to invite all of you to get on the Holy Ground with me by taking off your shoes while we are dancing to prepare the way of the Spirit. With humble heart and body, let us listen to the cries of creation and the cries of the Spirit within it.

Come. The spirit of Hagar, Egyptian, black slave woman exploited and abandoned by Abraham and Sarah, the ancestors of our faith. (Gen. 16–21)

Come. The spirit of Uriah, loyal soldier sent and killed on the battlefield by the great King David out of the king's greed for Uriah's wife, Bathsheba. (2 Sam. 11:1-27)

Come. The spirit of Jephthah's daughter, the victim of her father's faith, burnt to death for her father's promise to God if he were to win the war. (Judges 11:29-40)

Come. The spirit of male babies killed by the soldiers of King Herod upon Jesus' birth.

Come. The spirit of Joan of Arc and of the many other women burnt at the "witch trials" throughout the medieval era.

Come. The spirit of the people who died during the Crusades.

Come. The spirit of indigenous people of the Earth, victims of genocide during the time of colonialism and the period of great Christian mission to the pagan world.

Come. The spirit of Jewish people killed in the gas chambers during the Holocaust.

Come. The spirit of people killed in Hiroshima and Nagasaki by atomic bombs.

Come. The spirit of Korean women in the Japanese "prostitution army" during World War II, used and torn by violence-hungry soldiers.

Come. The spirit of Vietnamese people killed by Napalm, Agent Orange or hunger on the drifting boats.

Come. The spirit of Mahatma Ghandi, Steve Biko, Martin Luther King, Jr., Malcolm X, Victor Jara, Oscar Romero and many unnamed women freedom fighters who died in the struggle for liberation of their people.

Come. The Spirit of people killed in Bophal and Chernobyl and the spirit of jelly babies from the Pacific nuclear test zone.

Come. The spirit of people smashed by tanks in Kwangju, Tiananmen Square and Lithuania.

Come. The spirit of the Amazon rain forest now being murdered every day.

Come. The spirit of Earth, Air and Water, raped, tortured and exploited by human greed for money.

Come. The spirit of soldiers, civilians and sea creatures now dying in the bloody war in the Gulf.

Come. The spirit of the Liberator, our brother Jesus, tortured and killed on the cross.
—From speech to the Seventh WCC Assembly in Canberra, Australia

Reflect
Come. Take off your shoes this week and be attentive to the holy ground on which you stand.

❖ What spirits and memories stand with you?

——— TUESDAY ———

I came from Korea, the land of spirits full of *Han*. *Han* is anger. *Han* is resentment. *Han* is broken-heartedness and the raw energy for struggle for liberation. In my tradition people who were killed or died unjustly became wandering spirits, the *Han*-ridden spirits. They are all over the place seeking the chance to make the wrong right. Therefore the living people's responsibility is to listen to the voices of the *Han*-ridden spirits and to participate in the spirits' work of making the [wrong right]. These *Han*-ridden spirits in our people's history have been agents through whom the Holy Spirit has spoken her compassion and wisdom for life. Without hearing the cries of these spirits we cannot hear the voice of the Holy Spirit. I hope the presence of all our ancestors' spirits here with us shall not make you uncomfortable. For us they are the icons of the Holy Spirit who became tangible and visible to us. Because of them we can feel, touch and taste the concrete bodily historical presence of the Holy Spirit in our midst.

—From speech to the Seventh WCC Assembly in Canberra, Australia

Reflect

❖ Whose spirits call you to participate in righting the wrongs?

❖ Who has been an icon in your life, helping make the Holy Spirit tangible and visible to you?

―――― **WEDNESDAY** ――――

Three years after my mother's death, I returned to Korea. There I heard about the existence of my other mother from my cousin-sister. She told me that I had a birth mother besides my late mother. I could not believe it.

If it were true, how could it be that I had never heard about her? If it were true, it would mean that my late parents had totally deceived me. Even in their last words, my father and mother did not mention her to me. If I really did have another mother, a birth mother, then this woman had been erased from my family history, totally erased for the entire thirty years of my life.

My cousin-sister took me to meet my other mother. With confused emotions, I silently followed her until we came to the door of my other mother's home just outside the city of Seoul. I had brought a dozen red roses with me to give to my other mother. I stood at her doorway, holding the roses, and timidly reached for the doorbell.

An old woman opened the door. When she saw me her eyes filled with tears. She took my hands in her own and asked, "Is this Hyun Kyung?" I said, "Yes." Then she began to sob. She told me, "Finally I have met you! I thought I would die without seeing you. Now I can leave this world without holding my *han*."

I did not even know how I felt. I felt numb. Without knowing how to respond, I listened to her story.

—From "Following Naked Dancing and Long Dreaming" in *Inheriting Our Mothers' Gardens: Feminist Theology in Third World Perspective*

Reflect

❖ What stories lay hidden in your childhood?

❖ What have you encountered in the journey to uncover them?

—— **THURSDAY** ——

When I first went to meet my birth mother and listened to the stories of her hard life's journey, I felt that something in my deepest being was broken open. It was like the experience of baptism: something was washed away and I felt truly free. Through this ill, seventy-two-year-old woman, my mother, I felt that I was encountering the power of the despised in my people's history. "Hyun Kyung," I said to myself, "you have studied theology for more than eleven years. For whom have you done your theology? Why did you want to do theology? You always thought you studied theology in order to empower the oppressed people in your country. But face it! Have you really paid attention to the culture and history of the poor in the development of your theology? Have you been willing to learn from them? With whom have you spent most of the time in order to formulate your theology—the poor or the intellectuals in academia? You have tried so hard, consciously and unconsciously, to prove yourself, your intelligence, to the dominant theological groups using the language of those very groups."

I felt ashamed of myself, of my hidden desire to be better than the dominant theologians of Europe and North America. I felt an inner, powerful spirit turning me from my wish to do theology like Europeans and toward the open arms of my mother, where I could rest safely in her bosom. There was no turning back, and I felt a strong existential urge to cross and then destroy the bridge called theological higher education, which stood between "them" and "me." Then I looked at my mother. My sobbing mother looked like an icon of God through which I could clearly see what God was telling me about my mission.

—From *Struggle to Be the Sun Again*

Reflect

❖ To whom do you listen as you form your understanding of God?

❖ Who has helped clarify what God is telling you about your mission?

—— **FRIDAY** ——

Their [Asian women's] theology. . . . is also their vision quest. . . .

For Asian women, theology is a language of hope, dreams, and poetry.

It is firmly based on concrete, historical reality but points to the mystery and vision that calls Asian women from the future and the depth of all that is. The power of this vision and mystery carries Asian women through their *han* and impasse. It enables them to keep moving, flowing with the rhythm of the universe even when the heartbeat of the universe seems to be destroyed by human greed and hatred. Theology as a language of hope, dreams and poetry is not a luxury for Asian women. It is an active healing power in the midst of despair. Theology as vision quest is not an escapist, otherworldly addiction of the oppressed. It is remembering the original wholeness of creation and activating the dangerous memory of the future.

—From *Struggle to Be the Sun Again*

Reflect

❖ What does theology mean to you?

❖ What images, stories, dreams, experiences, and visions help define your theology?

❖ How does theology help you to keep moving through the greed, hatred, and despair of the world?

─── **SATURDAY** ───

Who are the theologians in emerging Asian women's theology? If Asian women's theology is people's theology and popular theology, then every Asian woman who believes in and reflects upon the meaning of the goodness of creation, the radical egalitarian values of Jesus Christ, and the coming of God's justice in her midst—and tries to live out that reality—is a theologian. Asian women have expressed their theology through their prayers, songs, dances, devotional rituals, drawings, and the way they live in the community. They are the theologians who are carving out oral theology and non-verbal theology from body languages. The majority of such women have not received formal theological training from traditional educational institutions.

—From *Struggle to Be the Sun Again*

Reflect

❖ What does it mean to you to claim the title of theologian for yourself?

❖ How do you express your theology?

[Korean women's theology] starts with women's *storytelling*. Women from various backgrounds gather and listen to one another's stories of victimization and liberation. Educated middle-class women theologians are committed to inviting or visiting poor farmers, factory workers, slum-dwellers, dowry victims, and prostitutes and listening to their life stories. Storytelling has been women's way of inheriting truth in many Asian countries because the written, literary world has belonged to privileged males. Until the turn of the century many Asian families did not teach girls how to read and write. Women sustained their truth, which was distorted by the definitions of the male literary world, by telling stories mouth to mouth. The power of storytelling lies in its *embodied truth*. Women talked about their concrete, historical life experience and not about abstract, metaphysical concepts. Women's truth was generated by their *epistemology from the broken body*. Women's bodies are the most sensitive receiver for historical reality. Their bodies record what has happened in their lives. Their bodies remember what it is like to be a *no-body* and what it is like to be a *some-body*. . . .

When women hear other women's stories, they cry, experience anger, and console one another. The boundaries between storyteller and listener become softened. Listeners feel the oppressed women's pain deeply; their hearts are touched and transformed when other hearts reach out for healing on the personal and political level.

—From *Struggle to Be the Sun Again*

Reflect

Think about your mother's body, your friends' bodies, your own body.

❖ What life stories do these bodies record and tell?

❖ How do these bodies, these stories, inform and transform you?

——— **Meditation** ———

In one address to a women's conference, Chung Hyun Kyung spoke about asking women in Asia what kind of church they would like to create. One group responded that it wanted a "church of the risen woman" in which women could have a ritual of biting into apples to symbolize their power to make choices for themselves.

In the Church of the Risen Woman

In the Church of the Risen Woman

the apples are very sweet,
for the trees from which they come
have been watered for thousands of years
by streams of hope,
and the roots have grown in the soil
of millions of dreams,
and the leaves have danced
with the spirits
of generations of prayers.
And in the Church of the Risen Woman
the people who come to pick the apples
wash them with their tears
and this makes them very sweet too;
and there is enough for everybody,
for the women
and the children
and the men also.

And they smile as they bite into their apples,
and they laugh as they chew
and tell their stories,
and the taste of freedom on their tongues
is very sweet
in the Church of the Risen Woman.
—Jan L. Richardson

———— ❖ ————

Blessing: *Arise, beloved of God, and taste the sweetness of hope that is shared!*

35 Midwives of Freedom
Shiphrah and Puah

Invocation: *God of life, you labor with all creation to bring forth the holy. Be with me, breathe through me as I ponder the life I am fashioning.*

Text: Exodus 1:8-22

Context: The Exodus was born in the hearts of women. Before Moses ever encountered the burning bush, even before he could walk, women already had begun to enflesh their visions of freedom. In the first chapter of the Book of Exodus, we meet the amazing array of women who, in their passion for life, set in motion the exodus of the Hebrew people from their oppressors.

Shiphrah and Puah, the midwives to the Hebrew people, inaugurate the journey with their crafty defiance of Pharaoh. Their daring ingenuity saves the life not only of Moses but of countless other Hebrew children, and it sets the stage for other clever women who enable the story of the Exodus to unfold: Jochebed, Miriam, Pharaoh's daughter, Zipporah, and others.

Midwife literally means "with-woman." Shiphrah and Puah embody this "withness" in their solidarity with each other, with God, and with the Hebrew people. Their creative partnership offers one model of the way in which women together challenge the people and systems that limit our choices, dreams, and lives. Working together, Shiphrah and Puah speak to us of the necessity to draw strength from one another as we give birth to new visions, to different ways of living, to one another, and even to ourselves.

—— **MONDAY** ——

Pharaoh had no idea what he was asking. How does a midwife, whose very vocation is grounded on the hope of assisting in birthing life, drop the vocation with a stab wound of death in the birthing room?

Pharaoh had no idea what he was asking. All he could see was his precious and imagined threat to Egyptian national security. All he could see were two ordinary women who had no power, whom he considered weak, and who would certainly obey him.

But Shiphrah and Puah knew who they were. They knew their vocation meant assisting in life, not death. They knew they had no power before Pharaoh. So they let Pharaoh go—to think his own thoughts—to go his own way—while they followed their own way assisting in life. . . .

Who are our pharaohs? They are slavemasters who want to convince us that there are no hungry in this land, only the lazy and irresponsible. . . .

They are national pharaohs who want to convince us that being held hostage in the greatest terrorist act in human history, with the whole human family targeted for destruction, is for our security. . . .

[They are] any institution or any person who rules or controls our lives. Anyone or anything that stands in our way of claiming our high calling from God.

—Nancy Hastings Sehested, from "Let Pharaoh Go" in *And Blessed Is She: Sermons by Women*

Reflect

❖ Who or what are your pharaohs?

❖ What would it take for you to let them go?

—— **TUESDAY** ——

Imagine. Imagine them, Shiphrah and Puah, walking out of Pharaoh's presence. Running down the hallways of power. Bursting through the gates of oppression into the open air. Breathless. Laughing. Stunned, perhaps, at their own boldness. Their cunning. Their craftiness. Holding on to each other, around the corner, in the shadows, catching their breath. Alone, could either have done it? But they were not alone.

And the tale goes out, whispered by mothers to one another as they gather to draw their water. Passed on even by the fathers, uttered as the bricks are pounded. Traced in the dirt with a piece of hay.

They told Pharaoh no. They did it. We can do it. The day is coming. . . .

Shiphrah and Puah are the mothers, the sisters of those who resist—who stand on the side of freedom. They are the midwives, the with-women—with those who dream; with those who labor, groaning; with those who risk their lives for lives not their own, knowing that truly they are.

—Jan L. Richardson

Reflect

❖ How do you imagine Shiphrah and Puah?

- ❖ How did they come to work together, to labor with each other and the Hebrew women, to possess the wits to defy Pharaoh?
- ❖ What do you think they said to each other as they left Pharaoh?

—— WEDNESDAY ——

Every birth is Holy. I think a midwife must be religious, because the energy she is dealing with is Holy. She needs to know that other people's energy is sacred.

Spiritual midwifery recognizes that each and every birth is the birth of the Christ child. The midwife's job is to do her best to bring both the mother and child through their passage alive and well and to see that the sacrament of birth is kept Holy. The Vow of the Midwife has to be that she will put out one hundred percent of her energy to the mother and the child that she is delivering until she is certain that they have safely made the passage. This means that she must put the welfare of the mother and child first, before that of herself and her own family, if she has to make a choice of that kind.

A spiritual midwife has an obligation to put out the same love to all children in her care, regardless of size, shape, color, or parentage. We are all One.

The kid in front of you is just the same as your kid. We are all One.

By religious, I mean that compassion must be a way of life for her. Her religion has to come forth in her practice, in the way she makes her day-to-day, her moment-to-moment decisions. It cannot be just theory. Truly caring for people cannot be a part-time job.

—Ina May Gaskin in *Spiritual Midwifery*

Reflect
- ❖ How do the words of this midwife apply to what you are creating?

—— THURSDAY ——

The truth is that Pharaohs, in some form or fashion, always will exist. And as Shiphrah and Puah faced the Pharaoh of their day, so we must face ours. We must face with courage and power those who want to take freedom because we, today, still are called to bring liberation into being, to be co-creators with God in the continual re-creation of the world. We may not be midwives in the literal sense, but each of us has a calling to bring to birth that which is in us and each other which, left to its own, likely will die. The God we worship is a God of liberation, one who gives and frees and makes new. Our task, our calling, is to stand on the side of life and freedom and new beginnings.

And it is our sisters, the two Hebrew midwives of so many years ago, who teach us *how* to stand on the side of freedom. How were these two women able to make their choice for liberation? . . . How did they find the courage to be defiant, to choose civil disobedience over compliance, safety, and the gratitude of the pharaoh? Even as they loved and feared God, and knew that they were agents of healing and not death, how did they make their stand so boldly?

Together. It was *together* that these two women were able to choose freedom. Pharaoh tried to impose his power on them. But instead, these two claimed the power that already belonged to them, a power which brought blessing and hope. Together, strengthened by one another, they rejected the slavemaster who sought to control them, and they claimed their high calling by God to enable the growth and nurture of God's people.

And as it was with them, so it is with us. Shiphrah and Puah acted in community, in concert with each other, giving one another strength and courage and power. And our power, our ability to face the ones who threaten our lives—this power and this ability come from our willingness to act *together. We need each other* to be able to face our Pharaohs, to be able to choose freedom in the face of those who command captivity. Our lives—*if we really are to live*—are bound together.

—Dorri Sherrill, from "The Power to Choose," sermon delivered at First United Methodist Church, Trussville, Alabama

Reflect

❖ What images, thoughts, and feelings do Dorri's words evoke?

——— FRIDAY ———

Women who are exploited and oppressed daily cannot afford to relinquish the belief that they exercise some measure of control, however relative, over their lives. They cannot afford to see themselves solely as "victims" because their survival depends on continued exercise of whatever personal powers they possess. It would be psychologically demoralizing for these women to bond with other women on the basis of shared victimization. They bond with other women on the basis of shared strengths and resources. This is the woman bonding feminist movement should encourage. It is this type of bonding that is the essence of Sisterhood.

—bell hooks in *Feminist Theory: From Margin to Center*

Reflect

Ponder the bonds that connect you with other women.

- ❖ What do these bonds look like?
- ❖ Which relationships give you a greater sense of control in your life than do other relationships?
- ❖ What makes the difference between these relationships?

—— **SATURDAY** ——

With-craft *n* 1. The art of organizing/structuring one's life/resources around a commitment to be with a person, group, organization, cause, etc., particularly when being with them calls for great cleverness, ingenuity, and improvisation in the face of divisive outside forces. 2. The art of being mutual. Not characterized by obsessiveness but by the extent to which the withness brings life to the relationship and all that it touches. *Note:* Being with does not mean being without conflict, without struggle, without pain. When conflict, struggle, and pain arise, it means moving through them *with integrity, with one another, with something deeper*; i.e. *with passion, with feeling, with hope, with desire, with dreams, with imagination, with wisdom, with memory, with awareness, with strength, with grace, with compassion, with love.*

—Jan L. Richardson

Reflect

Play around as you ponder your "with-ness."

- ❖ What does your "withcraft" look like?
- ❖ What, who, how are you with?
- ❖ Why?

—— **SUNDAY** ——

We are midwives in the between-times: The creation that is the cosmos, and each of us who feel lost on its threshold of becoming, need the midwife's powerful intent to pull us through. We need the midwife who lives in each of our souls to coach the birthing of an ever-new and renewing womanself. We need to be midwife to others, lending our energy to their heroic attempts to break through barriers of the lifeless into new life. Together we need to midwife the world.

The midwife enters the lost places with her who will give birth. The midwife is the woman-between: the liminal woman, the threshold woman.

She focuses her energy upon the process of coming through. Coming through birth. Coming through disease. Coming through death. She keeps us breathing, keeps us one with the universal rhythm of creation. She sings the song of breath, turning our fear and the frenetic struggle resulting from it into an intricate dance of becoming. "Behold, the Holy One makes all things new," she reminds. "She dances the New Year in; she dances in your soul; she *is* the dance of your soul bringing you through, making you new." . . .

The midwife calls us by name, measures time by our breath, and sings of home. When we dance to her song, stepping through the emptiness of the between-space, we arrive, finally, in the promised place. She is the dreamer who envisions what is possible, and we, by believing, give birth to the dream in ourselves.

—Christin Lore Weber in *Blessings: A WomanChrist Reflection on the Beatitudes*

Reflect

Find a quiet place, if you can. Focus on your breathing: its rhythm, its sound. Imagine your breath, coming in, passing through, leaving your body.

❖ What do you hear?
❖ What do you feel?
❖ What does your breath pass over, flow through?

―――― **Meditation** ――――

In Hebrew, the name Puah derives from words that mean "cried out." According to one Jewish legend recorded in Tractate Sotah, *the midwife Puah was so named because she uttered a charm in the mother's ear to bring the child out. What might she have spoken to Moses as she and his mother brought him through the passage of birth?*

With Hope

This is a charm for not forgetting
    the mother who bore you
    the midwives who birthed you
    the sister who rocked you
    the stranger who saved you

This is a charm for not forgetting
    the wellsprings that formed you
    the waters that birthed you

the tears that cleansed you
the river that held you

This is a charm for not forgetting
this is a charm for deep remembering
this is a charm for breaking silence
this is a charm for truthful telling.
—Jan L. Richardson

——— ❖ ———

Blessing: *Go with peace, with hope, with faith, with love. Go with dreams of freedom, with strength for the labor, with hands to hold you in the birthing. Go with God.*

36 Imagining Peace
Saint Elizabeth of Portugal

Invocation: *Blow across the landscape of my soul, O God, that I may be wise this day to the things that make for peace.*

Text: Isaiah 2:2-4

Context: In 1271, the king and queen of Aragon gave birth to a daughter. They named her Elizabeth after her distant relative, Saint Elizabeth of Hungary. At age twelve, Elizabeth married King Denis of Portugal, who was a good ruler but a poor husband. Elizabeth gave birth to two children and crafted a life of prayer and devotion. Her good works included establishing hospitals, orphanages, and homes for "fallen women."

The Oxford Dictionary of Saints records that Elizabeth was a "peacemaker all her life," bringing reconciliation between her husband and son and preventing a war between Portugal and Castile near the end of her life. Following the death of her husband, she continued to live a life of simplicity and peacemaking. Her last peace effort exhausted her so much that she died at Estremoz on July 4. Reports of miracles followed her burial at the Poor Clares' convent in Coimbra, and she was named a saint in 1626.

Saint Elizabeth's feast day falls on a day when many in the United States celebrate independence and freedom. Yet we know in our world and in our very midst, people and places torn by oppression, by hunger, by violence, and by war. More than six hundred years after Elizabeth's peacemaking efforts, we still dream of peace. In this week that surrounds her feast day, I am imagining Elizabeth and longing to tell her stories of women in this time who share her dream of peace. And so I write.

—— **MONDAY** ——

Dear Elizabeth,

I have struggled deeply with this week. I knew somehow I wanted to honor you in this week in which we in the U.S. celebrate the signing of the Declaration of Independence. So many will celebrate freedom this week, yet so many within the U.S. and beyond it live without freedom, without independence, and with limited choices as to how they may pursue life, liberty, and happiness.

More than six hundred years after your death, I wonder how honored you would be to know of the wars that still rage on all levels—from our psyches to our nations. More than six hundred years after you sought to journey with peace, I wonder how honored you would be to know of the days when it seems we have not journeyed as far as the time between you and me might suggest.

Perhaps because of these things, Elizabeth, I have had a difficult time finding words for you. Lamenting to a friend that I couldn't find my passion for this week, she asked me if I knew someone who might. And I thought of Janet, and of her passion for peace, and I called her. And she came back with words, hers and a friend's, born of their passionate commitment to walk in the ways of peace.

More than six hundred years later, Elizabeth, we still have so far to go. But oh, Elizabeth, I want you to know there are many still on the journey, and I want you to hear some of their words. I'm sending them back to you, and I'm sending them on.

—Jan

Reflect
- ❖ What does peace mean to you?
- ❖ What struggles do you encounter as you search for it?

—— **TUESDAY** ——

Birth Pains
(Based on passages from Mark 13)

I travelled to Iraq after the war. The bridges in the south were flattened and twisted and looked like pictures I had seen of the bridges in San Francisco after the earthquake, except that these bridges looked worse. The hospitals were full of dying children and virtually empty of necessary medicines. The water was unclean and meat was priced far above the means of most people.

In Basrah, a woman with a tear-streaked face approached me with a dying baby under her arm. She handed me a note scribbled in Arabic; I could not read it. I turned to my Iraqi taxi driver who said the baby needed blood. The hospital said that it did not have any. The taxi driver offered his blood. He and the baby were both type A-positive. I am type A-positive too, but I just stood by, unsure if the malaria medication I was taking would make my blood dangerous for the baby.

I doubt the baby lived. I will never forget the desperate look on her mother's face. Jesus said that in the days before the final coming that it would be dreadful for pregnant women and nursing mothers. But he also said that these terrible times of suffering would be the beginning of birth pains and that the time of suffering would be shortened for the sake of the faithful.

I think the days of suffering have been too long, and the labor pains have been too intense. Whatever life there may be beyond the labor is not a certainty. If we are giving birth to anything it often appears to be a monster.

But then a baby cries, or a taxi driver gives his blood. A poor family offers me tea and stale biscuits; and for the moment, it is enough. Enough to keep me in labor, hoping that the new birth will come quickly, hoping that the signs of new life on the way can be seen even in the present age.

—Janet Horman

Reflect
- ❖ What visions, images, and meetings keep you going in the laboring?

——— WEDNESDAY ———

During the Persian Gulf War as we heard the news and saw the terrible devastation and loss of life, I, like many others, experienced a deep sense of loss and sadness. I remember going out into the yard in the spring of that year and digging, digging. My hands turned over the warm earth and tears flowed as the soil slipped through my fingers. As I dug I reflected on the mysterious, hidden properties of our earth and its wonderful life/death/life cycle. In a deep sense of reverence, I planted tomatoes.

At the time I wasn't aware of what was beginning to happen to me, but since then I have often reflected not only on Earth's life-giving properties but also on its powers of healing. Earth had helped me get in touch with my pain, and healing tears had come.

—Martina W. Linnehan

Reflect
- ❖ What places bring you a sense of peace and connect you with the broken parts of your spirit and your world?

─── THURSDAY ───

On January 15, 1989, Kings Bay Naval Base received its first Trident submarine. Janet was there, and she entered the water after making a statement to the press. An excerpt follows.

In the name of the one true God, and in the spirit of love, I act to reclaim the seas for life. As the U.S.S. Tennessee enters the channel, I will enter the water as an act of reclamation . . . .

I swim into the channel to choose life. The Trident is not a tool of the God who made the waters for life. It is a tool of a false god. The sea-god Neptune carries a three-pronged spear, called a trident, from which this deadly submarine gets its name. But Neptune is not the true God. And a submarine that has the destructive capacity of 7,296 Hiroshima bombs is no tool of the God who made the waters to bring forth life.

I swim into the channel to reclaim these seas for life. I swim in the spirit of love, in the spirit of the one Christ who taught us to love. As the United Methodist bishops in their document about the nuclear crisis called upon United Methodists to act in defense of creation, and as they themselves wrote in defense of creation, I now swim in defense of creation.

And on this day of Martin Luther King, Jr.'s birth, I swim in the hope that his belief in the power of nonviolent love will transform our hearts and move us to act for the sake of the sea, the children, and the world.
—Janet Horman

Reflect
- ❖ How far are you willing to go in the pursuit of peace—what measures or actions are you willing to take?
- ❖ What waters will you trouble in the hope of a more just world?

─── FRIDAY ───

This morning I was hurriedly eating my breakfast as John came through the kitchen. I had just finished a grueling hour of basic exercises, trying to get this old body back into condition after months of radiation and chemotherapy which has left me without much energy. I was feeling pressure to get to my desk and made the comment to John about how long it had taken me to get through my exercises and how I was feeling "late for work." As I said this to John, it struck both of us at the same time, I've been working for a few hours already. Our meditation, our reading, and our exercise are all part of our real work to be whole, balanced, and healthy in body, mind, and spirit. It's such a simple idea, one that my body and spirit have been trying to tell my head for a long time. But sometimes, like this morning, I slip back into old habits of thinking and acting and begin to neglect the body and spirit for what I've always understood as the real work of peace and justice—organizing!

Though I fall back into old patterns like today and berate myself for things not done, I'm beginning to understand the importance of tuning in to myself—my body, my spirit, listening to that inner voice that may say, "Yes, you're on the right track," or "Hey, wait a minute, you need to take some reflection time or just 'be' for a while."

—Martina W. Linnehan

Reflect

Listen to your body, your spirit in this moment.

❖ What rhythms have you been keeping?

❖ What is your inner voice telling you?

—— **SATURDAY** ——

Written when I first began longing to tell Elizabeth . . .

Dear Elizabeth,

It's nighttime in New England, and I'm on vacation. In the next room, my sister nurses my three-month-old niece Caroline, and on the other side of this wall my three-year-old nephew Scott lies sleeping. The cabin, filled earlier in the day with laughter and occasional ear-splitting wailing, is quiet.

It is these children who live closest to my heart, Elizabeth, and they have changed my perspective on a great many things. They lead me to my lighter side, to a place where I think again about what is really vital in this life.

I know you had children, Elizabeth, a boy and a girl, and that you longed for peace in their lives. I wonder what songs you sang to them, what stories you told them, whether you had the same dreams for them as I do for Caroline and Scott. I wonder if it will take six hundred more years to realize those dreams.

Sally has just brought my full and content niece into the room. As Caroline gazes at me through peace-filled eyes, I pray it will be far sooner than that. For her. For Scott. For us all.

—Jan

Reflect

❖ For whom do you long to create a more peaceful world?

❖ What will you give to them that will bring us closer to that world?

Dear Elizabeth,

It's nighttime once again, and I am on vacation again, only this time it's a year later and I am in Alaska. In this place, the nighttime is still bright with the sun's light. From where I sit, I can see Mt. Susitna, "The Sleeping Lady." Legend tells us that she will sleep until peace comes again.

I remember pictures of Susitna from when my parents lived here years ago. I was fascinated by her, by how like a woman she looked as she lay across the land. When I laid eyes on her for the first time, just days ago, I was startled. I did not know, or had not remembered, the snow-filled crevices that line her body like rivers. They are a bit unsettling, and I am uncertain whether they seem to be tears for all her years of waiting or evidence that new life and motion and change persist even in a landscape that appears stagnant. Perhaps they are both.

I gaze out on Susitna tonight and wonder what the sleeping lady imagines for us. Perhaps she imagines a peace that we have barely begun to make, barely begun to lean into. Perhaps she dreams of rising, of shaking off her sleep, of striding across the land, of dancing under the sky.

Tonight I think that her crevices-like-rivers stream with gladness and relief for those who have begun to make peace . . . gladness for Janet, for Martina, for women and men of courage around the world who have dared to imagine . . . for you, Elizabeth. May we imagine and make peace together.

In peace,

Jan

Reflect

❖ What stories, what struggles, what imaginings, what lives would you share with Elizabeth?

❖ What will you take from this week to sustain you for the journey ahead?

—— **Meditation** ——

In The Vigil *Wendy Wright comments, "Peace has to do with the fullness of things, with lion and lamb lying down together, not a world without lions."*

On the eve of the Gulf War, I wrote this lullaby for my nephew Scott, then six months old. The day the war ended, Kary set it to music.

Lion and Lamb

Lion and lamb will sleep tonight,
lying together with no more fright;
stars and moon will bless their slumber,
wind will sing with awe and wonder
to all who breathe in every land:
"Behold the lion, behold the lamb!"

Lion and lamb will rest tonight,
sorrow and trouble be put to flight.
See how peaceful they look in sleep,
as angels flying from heaven's keep
whisper across the wounded land:
"Behold the lion, behold the lamb!"

Lion and lamb will dream tonight
of a world that will greet the dawn with delight,
where all will sit and share one feast,
and all will dream and dwell in peace,
and children will come from every land
to hold the lion, to hold the lamb.
—Jan L. Richardson

—— ❖ ——

Blessing: *Go in peace. Peace in your body, peace in your soul, peace in your spirit, peace to be whole. Go in peace.*

 **The Storied Life**
Madeleine L'Engle

Invocation: *Creator of the stars, you fill me with wonder. How blessed you are, who dwells in mystery and delights in the universe!*

Text: Psalm 78:2-4

Context: "When I am asked why I write at least half my books for children," comments Madeleine L'Engle in *Twentieth-Century Children's Writers*, "I answer, truthfully, that when I have something to say which I think is going to be too difficult for adults, I write it in a book for children." Having greatly enjoyed her books as a child, I was surprised as an adult to receive her book *A Circle of Quiet* from a friend. This gift led to the delightful discovery of a dazzling array of Madeleine's books for children and adults—many of which blur the assumed distinctions between children and adults.

As an only child, born in New York City in 1918, Madeleine devoured books in her solitude. When she ran out of books to read, she began to write her own. More than forty books of fiction, nonfiction, and poetry later, Madeleine continues to write, beckoning us to enter the worlds of wonder that stories offer to us.

 **MONDAY**

Once I'm over the stone wall, the terrain changes. I step into a large field full of rocks left from glacial deposits; there are many ancient apple trees which, this summer, are laden with fruit. From the stone wall to the brook takes two balls of twine. Unreliable eyes make my vision variable, and there are days when my string path is extremely helpful, although, as my husband remarks, "All anybody who wants to find your secret hide-out needs to do is climb the stone wall and follow the string."

That's all right. All secret places need to be shared occasionally. So the string guides me across a high ridge where there are large outcroppings of glacial stone, including our special star-watching rock. Then the path becomes full of tussocks and hummocks; my legs are etched by the thorns of

blackberry brambles and wild roses. Earlier this summer the laurel burst from snow into fire, and a few weeks later we found a field of sweet wild strawberries. And then there are blueberry bushes, not very many, but a few, taller than I am and, to me, infinitely beautiful.
—From *A Circle of Quiet*

Reflect
- ❖ Where are your secret places, those spaces that invite you to stay present to the moment, to dwell in the now?
- ❖ Whom do you trust enough to share those spaces?

—— **TUESDAY** ——

Chronology, the time which changes things, makes them grow older, wears them out, and manages to dispose of them, chronologically, forever.

Thank God there is kairos, too: again the Greeks were wiser than we are. They had two words for time: *chronos* and *kairos*.

Kairos is not measurable. Kairos is ontological. In kairos we *are*, we are fully in isness, not negatively, as Sartre saw the isness of the oak tree, but fully, wholly, positively. Kairos can sometimes enter, penetrate, break through chronos: the child at play, the painter at his easel, Serkin playing the *Appassionata*, are in kairos. The saint at prayer, friends around the dinner table, the mother reaching out her arms for her newborn baby, are in kairos. The bush, the burning bush, is in kairos, not any burning bush, but the very particular burning bush before which Moses removed his shoes; the bush I pass on my way to the brook. In kairos that part of us which is not consumed in the burning is wholly awake.
—From *A Circle of Quiet*

Reflect
Call forth a time when you were fully awake, fully in "isness."
- ❖ What did you see and know, touch and hear, taste and smell?

—— **WEDNESDAY** ——

One time, when I was little more than a baby, I was taken to visit my grandmother, who was living in a cottage on a nearly uninhabited stretch of beach in northern Florida. All I remember of this visit is being picked up from my crib in what seemed the middle of the night and carried from my bedroom and out of doors, where I had my first look at the stars.

It must have been an unusually clear and beautiful night for someone to have said, "Let's wake the baby and show her the stars." The night sky, the constant rolling of breakers against the shore, the stupendous light of the stars, all made an indelible impression on me. I was intuitively aware not only of a beauty I had never seen before but also that the world was far greater than the protected limits of the small child's world which was all that I had known thus far. I had a total, if not very conscious, moment of revelation; I saw creation bursting the bounds of daily restriction, and stretching out from dimension to dimension, beyond any human comprehension.

—From *The Irrational Season*

Reflect

❖ What do you remember of your first look at the stars, at the ocean, at the mountains?

❖ What is your earliest memory, your first revelation, your initial awareness of something beyond you, of creation's bursting its bounds?

—— **THURSDAY** ——

The birth of my own babies (every woman's Christmas) shows me that the power which staggers with its splendor is a power of love, particular love. Surely it takes no more creative concentration to make a galaxy than a baby. And surely the greatest strength of all is this loving willingness to be weak, to share, to give utterly.

—From *The Irrational Season*

Reflect

❖ Creative concentration . . . from whence does it come?

❖ What is it bringing to birth in your own life?

—— **FRIDAY** ——

One night after a small dinner party at a friend's house, I wrote for him:

Sitting around your table
as· we did, able
to laugh, argue, share
bread and wine and companionship, care
about what someone else was saying, even

if we disagreed passionately: Heaven,
we're told, is not unlike this, the banquet celestial,
eternal convivium. So the praegustum terrestrium
partakes—for me, at least—of sacrament.
(Whereas the devil, ever intent
on competition, invented the cocktail party where
one becomes un-named, un-manned, de-personned.) Dare
we come together, then, vulnerable, open, free?
Yes! Around your table we
knew the Holy Spirit, come to bless
the food, the host, the hour, the willing guest.
—From *The Irrational Season*

Reflect

❖ Laughter, passionate words of agreement or disagreement, conviviality, companionship . . . at what tables have you tasted this,
feasted on this?

❖ How intentional are you about seeking or creating such feasts?

——— SATURDAY ———

I wrote stories because I was a solitary, only child in New York City, with
no easily available library where I could get books. So when I had read all
the stories in my book case, the only way for me to get more stories to read
was to write them.

And I knew, as a child, that it was through story that I was able to
make some small sense of the confusions and complications of life. The
sound of coughing from my father's gas-burned lungs was a constant
reminder of war and its terror. At school I read a book about the Belgian
babies impaled on bayonets like small, slaughtered animals. I saw pictures
of villages ravaged by the *Bôches*. The thought that there could ever be
another war was a source of deep fear. I would implore my parents, "There
won't be another war, will there?" My parents never lied to me. They tried
to prepare me for this century of war, not to frighten me.

But I was frightened, and I tried to heal my fear with stories, stories
which gave me courage, stories which affirmed that ultimately love is
stronger than hate. If love is stronger than hate, then war is not all there is. I
wrote, and I illustrated my stories. At bedtime, my mother told me more
stories. And so story helped me to learn to live. Story was in no way an
evasion of life, but a way of living life creatively instead of fearfully.

It was a shock when one day in school one of the teachers accused me of "telling a story." She was not complimenting me on my fertile imagination. She was making the deadly accusation that I was telling a lie.

If I learned anything from that teacher, it was that lie and story are incompatible. If it holds no truth, then it cannot truly be story. And so I knew that it was in story that I found flashes of that truth which makes us free.

—From *Walking on Water: Reflections on Faith and Art*

Reflect

❖ Who told you stories when you were younger?

❖ What stories do you remember or tell that help you to live out of creativity rather than fear?

—— **SUNDAY** ——

Meg speaks with Proginoskes, a cherubim who has befriended her.

Proginoskes waved several wings slowly back and forth in thought, which would have felt very pleasant on a hot day, but which, on a cold morning, made Meg turn up the collar of her jacket. The cherubim did not notice; he continued waving and thinking. Then she could feel his words moving slowly, tentatively, within her mind. "If you've been assigned to me, I suppose you must be some kind of a Namer, too, even if a primitive one."

"A what?"

"A Namer. For instance, the last time I was with a Teacher—or at school, as you call it—my assignment was to memorize the names of the stars."

"Which stars?"

"All of them."

"You mean *all* the stars, in *all* the galaxies?"

"Yes. If he calls for one of them, someone has to know which one he means. Anyhow, they like it; there aren't many who know them all by name, and if your name isn't known, then it's a very lonely feeling."

"Am I supposed to learn the names of all the stars, too?" It was an appalling thought.

"Good galaxy, no!"

"Then what *am* I supposed to do?"

Proginoskes waved several wings, which, Meg was learning, was more or less his way of expressing "I haven't the faintest idea."

"Well, then, if I'm a Namer, what does that mean? What does a Namer do?"

The wings drew together, the eyes closed, singly, and in groups, until all were shut. Small puffs of mist-like smoke rose, swirled about him. "When I was memorizing the names of the stars, part of the purpose was to help them each to be more particularly the particular star each one was supposed to be. That's basically a Namer's job. Maybe you're supposed to make earthlings feel more human."
—From *A Wind in the Door*

Reflect

❖ Who has named you, and with what names?

—— **Meditation** ——

Stars

It was you who taught me
that disaster
means dis-aster,
separation from the stars.
And in this city
where the lights make them
so difficult to see,
your words help to ward off
disaster for me.
Flung across the
shadows of soul
they dance,
pinpoints of light
drenching my sky.

I think, Madeleine,
there is one star
who bears your name.
—Jan L. Richardson

—— ❖ ——

Blessing: *Go in peace, named and loved by God. May the One who fashions all stories dwell gracefully with you in the unfolding of your own.*

 She-Who-Sees-God
The Unnamed Mother of Samson

Invocation: *Open my eyes, O God, to perceive your fiery presence; open my heart, divine visitor, to receive you with wisdom and grace.*

Text: Judges 13:2-25

Context: According to scripture, few people behold the face of God and live to tell about it. Yet an unnamed woman receives such a vision as well as a spirit that recognizes the meaning of the encounter. While confusion exists over the identity of the messenger—it seems to be an angel, but Manoah and his wife understand it to be God—certainly a powerful revealing of the divine takes place.

Although the text names Manoah repeatedly, it fails to record the name of his wife, one of the only women in scripture to receive an annunciation. The messenger appears not once but twice to the wife rather than to Manoah. Her feisty, perceptive dispelling of Manoah's fear at the end of the story suggests to the reader why God has chosen this woman to give birth to a son who will be even more fiery than she.

This woman's openness, trust, and vision present a striking counterpoint to Manoah's zealous attempt to control a situation beyond his comprehension. She reminds us that while we bear a responsibility to ask questions, true power and understanding often lie in standing still long enough to be touched by the flames of wisdom.

—— MONDAY ——

In his dogged efforts to contain and comprehend his experience rationally, Manoah risks missing the message altogether. His mistake lies not in asking too many questions but in asking them of the wrong people. He implores God to provide information while his wife's ears still ring with the messenger's words. Had he entreated her to speak further with him, what would she have revealed? What lay in the eyes of this woman who had beheld divinity, who had received the sacred announcement, who had been entrusted with the care of the one she now carried? What would have been dis-covered for Manoah if he had gazed upon her a moment longer?

That's the trick of revelation: it appears where we least expect it. We beseech heaven for a sign when it burns in our midst; we seek God's face and miss its contours beneath our own fingertips.

—Jan L. Richardson

Reflect

Imagine sitting in the field with this woman.

❖ What do her eyes reveal to you?

❖ What does she tell you her name is?

—— TUESDAY ——

Revelation is a process with two main elements, but these are not the divinity and divinely revealed truths, events, or insights. Rather, the two main elements in revelation are the divinity revealing and humans listening and responding. Revelation is a *relation* between subjects, knowing subjects. Revelation is a meeting between persons. Revelation is what happens in the "in between" of personal relationships. . . .

From this perspective, if one asks, even within the context of theological teaching on revelation, *"What is revealed?"* the entire tradition of Christian theology teaches that it is the Ultimate which is revealed, or more comprehensively, the direct object of the verb *reveal* is divinity/humanity/reality. Instead of saying Christianity or Judaism or Buddhism or the Bible *has* a revelation, it is more correct to say Christianity or Judaism or Buddhism or the Bible *is* a revelation, or in personal terms, a community of people engaged in and becoming aware of a disclosure of Being in the present. . . . This points finally to the reality that revelation is temporal, and that it is occurring *now* or not at all in the fleshly, individual, communal lives of children and adults. Possibly, it is occurring as well in the nonhuman and animal worlds too; in all of the earth forms.

—Maria Harris in *Teaching and Religious Imagination*

Reflect

❖ In what relationships, human and nonhuman, do you sense God's revelation?

❖ What is it about those relationships that enables revelation to occur?

The relationality of revelation means that it is not one-way. We cannot receive and remain unchanged. In the story Samson's mother, the one who receives the revelation becomes, in turn, the one who reveals. By the end of her story, she reveals not only God but something deep within herself. She unveils, dis-covers her own power: the power to speak, the power to name what she perceives; the power to describe the holy; the power to name—if not herself, then the one to whom she gives birth. She is a woman on the edge; where before she has measured her words, she now speaks with abandon. Her words come freely and boldly. She has seen into the flames and knows—perhaps all too well—what lies in them.
—Jan L. Richardson

Reflect

❖ What enables *you* to be revelatory, to unveil, to dis-cover yourself and the holy within you?

——— **THURSDAY** ———

Her Face

It was my seventh summer. I think everything and everyone slept that hot afternoon in Little Rock. The day, the dust, the sun were red; the roses were wide open. I lay with my dog in a cool place on the north side of my grandparents' clapboard house. Hydrangeas flourished there, shaded from the heat. The domed blue flowers were higher than our heads. I held the dog, stroking her into sleep. But she held my gaze. I watched the dog and she watched me, a balance of equal weights. As I looked into her eyes I knew that I would never travel further than into this animal's eyes. They were as deep, as bewildering, as unattainable as a night sky. Just as mysterious was another movement, the rush of water deep within me, the sound in my ears resounding from my breast. I gazed into the dog's eyes and I listened to the sound of the water inside and I understood: "This is God."

I spent the rest of the afternoon digging a hole. I spaded and shoveled the hole for many days until its walls collapsed, my act of worship exhausted.

Soon after this, in an elementary school in Chicago, I came upon a photograph in a book; it was a small statue of a woman. The recognition was immediate and certain; I knew this was she whom I had heard in the water and whose face I had sought within the dog's eyes. This discovery brought a sense of well-being and gratitude which has never diminished.

But she had no face. She was crowned with waves of water, covering her head, overshadowing the face. It was her entire body which spoke, her breast-belly body, a thick bulb rooted, pushing up a halo of water, the water which moved within me. I've been looking for her face ever since. I had then, and still have one essential prayer: "Show me your face."
—Meinrad Craighead in *The Mother's Songs: Images of God the Mother*

Reflect
- ❖ Where do you look for the face of God?
- ❖ When have you been surprised to touch or perceive or glimpse its contours?

—— **FRIDAY** ——

Contact Lenses

Lacking what they want to see
makes my eyes hungry
and eyes can feel
only pain.

Once I lived behind thick walls
of glass
and my eyes belonged
to a different ethic
timidly rubbing the edges
of whatever turned them on.
Seeing usually
was a matter of what was
in front of my eyes
matching what was
behind my brain.
Now my eyes have become
a part of me exposed
quick risky and open
to all the same dangers.

I see much
better now

and my eyes hurt.
—Audre Lorde in *The Black Unicorn*

Reflect

❖ When is it terrifying, burdensome, dangerous, painful for you to see, to perceive?

—————— **SATURDAY** ——————

I wonder what Samson's mother saw there in the flame of the altar before the angel ascended. I wonder if she saw how fire would come to haunt her son. In the fire, did she see visions of the dust, the rubble to come? I wonder if she wondered, much later, in a time beyond the time when she passes out of our record of the story, why it had all come to this.

I wonder if she saw simply nothing but holy fire burning into her brain and searing her memory. I wonder if she went around with flames in her eyes ever after. I wonder if she ever sat alone in that field again.

—Jan L. Richardson

Reflect

❖ What do you imagine Samson's mother-to-be saw there in the flame of the altar?

❖ What memories do you suppose she carried with her from that place?

—————— **SUNDAY** ——————

"I learned that her name was Proverb."

And the secret names
of all we meet who lead us deeper
into our labyrinth
of valleys and mountains, twisting valleys
and steeper mountains—
their hidden names are always,
like Proverb, promises:
Rune, Omen, Fable, Parable,
those we meet for only
one crucial moment, gaze to gaze,
or for years know and don't recognize

but of whom later a word
sings back to us
as if from high among leaves,
still near but beyond sight

drawing us from tree to tree
towards the time and the unknown place
where we shall know
what it is to arrive.
—Denise Levertov in *Breathing the Water*

Reflect

❖ What are you still learning from past encounters, distant revelations?

❖ How are they still unfolding in your life?

—— **Meditation** ——

Revelation

In these days of first fires,
I wonder how to tell you
that I burn them
not for light
to see
but for warmth
enough to feel
the form of your face,
to embrace
the shape of your name.
—Jan L. Richardson

—— ❖ ——

Blessing: *Go in peace and journey with wonder in the God who has showed to you the holy in your midst.*

39 Contours of the Holy
Sacred Spaces

Invocation: *Hallow this space with your presence, gracious God. In friend, in stranger, in earth, in sky, help me trace the contours of the sacred.*

Text: Psalm 148

Context: I grew up in the country, in a home in the middle of a large field that my grandfather gave to my father and mother after they were married. Next to the house was a huge tree, a full-grown water oak that held a succession of swings and gave shade to the holes that my brother and sister and I dug as kids.

The oak tree began to die while I was in college, and soon it permanently lost all its leaves and occasional pieces of its limbs. Around this same time I took up the habit, whenever I visited home, of stealing outside at night with a blanket and gazing at the stars. The oak tree kept me company, a silent witness to the stars' journeys. In the deep night, the barren tree had a wise beauty that became particularly evident when the moon rose through its branches. It was a place of instant peace, of imagining, of connection, of prayer. Although a storm finally felled the tree, this place remains one of my first and clearest images of sacred space.

In her book *Sacred Dimensions of Women's Experience*, Elizabeth Dodson Gray writes, "What hallows a space is what happens there." From the contours of our inner selves to the places in which we live, play, and work to our home planet and beyond, we dwell in and move through spaces that take on meaning according to how we engage them. Sacred space is born of relationship, of care, of what we give and receive. These readings invite you to consider where, and in whom, you find your sacred space.

—— **MONDAY** ——

I grew up in the Southwest deserts of Arizona, New Mexico, and West Texas. I understood in my very bones, the connectedness between water and parched land. I learned to be attentive to the seemingly little things of life—desert flowers, the smell of creosote bushes after a sudden, summer rain's washing, the subtle changes in land colors as the sun journeyed its daily course, the open and vivid blue skies. I know the quick and awesome movement of the spirit in the huge clouds that come into the desert sky, dump water and rush out—all in an afternoon.

As a child, I remember lying alone on the desert mattress and watching the vast universe unfold with glitter, shape, depth and mystery. Night gently opened her stargazing doors to me and the desert floor cooled in greeting.

—Susan Beehler in *Wellsprings: A Journal for United Methodist Clergy-women*

Reflect

❖ What is your primal space, the place of your first memory?

——— TUESDAY ———

This season has been a long one of transition for me. As I moved out of my familiar apartment in Atlanta last summer into a home that Mrs. Wilkins has owned for forty years, as I watched my parents begin to move out of the only home I knew growing up, and as I ponder my imminent return to Florida, I have struggled with where "home" is. For me, home has happened in moments. In the sacred spaces shaped by the hands of friends and family, in the sharing of meals, in the blessing of my room with their festive art and laughter and presence, in their sheltering arms, I have found sacred space to call my own.

—Jan L. Richardson, from a letter, 1993

Reflect

❖ In what ways is your home space, sacred space?
❖ What persons or moments have made it so?

——— WEDNESDAY ———

Much of my awareness of sacred space and experiences with times that were holy have been with you. I am struck by the power in Naming, the power that comes from naming a time or a place holy and sacred—recognizing it as special and having a meaning bigger than that which was created separately by those involved. . . .

Mary Catherine Bateson writes, "Relationships need the continuity of repeated actions and familiar space." In my mind it is these deliberate efforts we make with one another that allow us to assign meaning to our days and our connections. . . .

Now, I think about how I would describe this collaborative creation of sacred space to another who was seeking it within a relationship or a community. I wonder, could she understand my words without hearing the longer stories which accompany them? Could she know this vision without sharing the Journey? Could she feel my longing without our bodies close, touching, sharing warmth, sharing strength?

For the birth of a New Creation, for this sacred space, we give her Names. The stories she will read and live. We pray for ones who will share her Journey and pray for ones to hold her close.

—Kary Kublin, from a letter

Reflect

❖ How would you describe this "collaborative creation of sacred space" to another seeking it?

❖ What deliberate efforts, repeated actions, and familiar spaces have nurtured the sacred in your relationships?

------ **THURSDAY** ------

[*Loreena McKennitt writes this concerning the song "Courtyard Lullaby":* *"The photographs which appear in this booklet were taken at a sixteenth-century hunting lodge in Portugal, where Elisabeth Feryn and I stayed for a week. Within the lodge was a courtyard, marked at each corner by orange trees. The feel of the place reminded me of the Unicorn tapestries which hang in The Cloisters in New York City. The tapestries and the lodge are both rich with earthy, pre-Christian iconography—depicting the mysterious life and death cycle of the seasons. It was in this courtyard that this piece was conceived."*]

Courtyard Lullaby

Wherein the deep night sky
The stars lie in its embrace
The courtyard still in its sleep
And peace comes over your face

"Come to me" it sings
"Hear the pulse of the land
The Ocean's rhythms pull

To hold your heart in its hand"

And when the wind draws strong
Across the cypress trees
The Nightbirds cease their songs
So gathers memories.

Last night you spoke of a dream
Where forests stretched to the east
And each bird sang its song
A Unicorn joined in a feast

And in a corner stood
A pomegranate tree
With wild flowers there
No mortal eye could see

Yet still some mystery befalls
Sure as the cock crows at morn
The world in stillness keeps
The secret of babes to be born

I heard an old voice say
"Don't go far from the land
The seasons have their way
No mortal can understand."
—Loreena McKennitt in *The Visit*

Reflect
It was in listening to this song and reading Loreena's notes that I conceived this week's theme.
- ❖ What images of space do her words evoke in you?
- ❖ How do the spaces around you influence what emerges from within you?

—— **FRIDAY** ——

Not My Own

sometimes i feel like i've got no home
i love these mountains
but they're not my own

they were taken a short time ago
by the men with the guns
from the ones with the bows
and hate spread over the land
another culture killed
by the white man's hands
and hate spread over the land

how can i call this country mine
why would i want to identify
with the murder of millions and genocide
no this land is not my own

my ancestors had no home
they lived in countries
that were not their own

they were driven like beasts
branded in blood
the rulers said not good enough
slaves they were slaves they've been
but they swore they'd never go back again
no those lands were not their own

how can i call those countries mine
why would i want to identify
with the murder of millions and genocide
no those lands were not their own

sometimes i feel like i've got no home
this man's world is not my own

we were burned for being women of strength
brought to the fire by the church and state
for the ways of the fathers we would not take
and it goes on and on to this very day
still this world is not my own

and they taught us well ourselves to hate
we lost our names hid our strength
said yes, it's god's will men dominate
now we're fighting on thru to a better way
but still this world is not my own

how can i call their culture mine
why would i want to identify
with the murder of millions and genocide
no this world is not my own

sometimes i feel like i've got no home
this weary world is not my own
—Karen Beth, from *Karen Beth: The Edge of the Horizon* (LP and tape)

Reflect

When I heard Karen Beth sing this song in concert, she spoke of her great love for her home in the Catskill Mountains and also of her awareness that the land was not truly her own, that it had been wrested from others before her.

❖ What threatens sacred space?
❖ Who occupied your space before you?

——— SATURDAY ———

For years I have looked ahead, searching for holy places down the road and trying to reach them as soon as possible. Now I believe instead that this ground is sacred, and wherever I stand at this moment is holy. The women who are my companions have opened my eyes to the holy in the ordinary. Deena Metzger wrote in *Heresies I*: "Each day is a tapestry, threads of broccoli, promotion, couches, children, politics, shopping, building, planting, thinking interweave in intimate connection with insistent cycles of birth, existence, and death." We can become so focused, as I have been, on our accomplishments that we will not even see the holy, sacred, healing grace of God present all around us as we travel. And if we do not stop and look, our woundedness and alienation and fatigue will grow, and we will never be able to hear our own voice. We need to rest and allow our spirits to be healed and made whole along the way, not so that we can do better or travel farther but so that we will make the journey in our own good time. And sometimes we ought to linger, perhaps for a long time, until the beauty of that place has shaped us from the inside.

—Judith E. Smith, from "This Ground Is Holy Ground" in *Weavings: A Journal of the Christian Spiritual Life*

Reflect

Imagine your "inner space," the geography of your soul.

- ❖ How is it shaped by the sacred spaces you encounter along the journey?
- ❖ What is holy about the space you are in right now?

—————— **SUNDAY** ——————

This Earth: What She Is to Me

As I go into her, she pierces my heart. As I penetrate further, she unveils me. When I have reached her center, I am weeping openly. I have known her all my life, yet she reveals stories to me, and these stories are revelations and I am transformed. Each time I go to her I am born like this. Her renewal washes over me endlessly, her wounds caress me; I become aware of all that has come between us, of the noise between us, the blindness, of something sleeping between us. Now my body reaches out to her. They speak effortlessly, and I learn at no instant does she fail me in her presence. She is as delicate as I am; I know her sentience; I feel her pain and my own pain comes into me, and my own pain grows large and I grasp this pain with my hands, and I open my mouth to this pain, I taste, I know, and I know why she goes on, under great weight, with this great thirst, in drought, in starvation, with intelligence in every act does she survive disaster. This earth is my sister; I love her daily grace, her silent daring, and how loved I am *how we admire their strength in each other, all that we have lost, all that we have suffered, all that we know: we are stunned by this beauty,* and I do not forget: what she is to me, what I am to her.
—Susan Griffin in *Woman and Nature: The Roaring inside Her*

Reflect
- ❖ What stories do you and the earth share with each other?
- ❖ What spaces do you create together?
- ❖ What are you to each other?

—————— **Meditation** ——————

All Hallows

In Her hollows
she hallows
all spaces within;
whole-making,

holy-making,
She draws us in.

In our hollows
we hallow,
breathing earth,
birthing sky;
wholly making
our spaces,
we bid Her come.
—Jan L. Richardson

—— ❖ ——

Blessing: *Who may know the shape of the sacred, and who can tell the lines of the holy? May you, O friend, find its form through the shadows; may you cry out, "It is here!"*

40 Holy Hospitality
Dorothy Day

Invocation: *God of the poor, may I know you in each person. Make my life a place of hospitality, O God, where you are pleased to dwell.*

Text: Matthew 25:31-46

Context: Born in Brooklyn, New York, in 1897, Dorothy Day became one of the most influential forces in Roman Catholicism in the United States. She never earned a degree, she never joined a religious order; as a laywoman she became a bearer of justice, committed to seeing and ministering to Christ in all people.

From an early age, Dorothy Day felt drawn by the struggle of industrial workers to secure better wages and working conditions. Not convinced that the church was doing enough for them, Dorothy became involved with other organizations that seemed more committed to their struggle. She joined the Industrial Workers of the World, held a brief membership in the Socialist Party, and had Communist affiliations that she said helped her to find God in God's poor, abandoned people.

A longing for love as the basis for social justice, coupled with the birth of her daughter Tamar Teresa, led to Dorothy's conversion and baptism in the Roman Catholic church in 1928. While continuing to work as a writer, in 1933 she met Peter Maurin, a French peasant who proposed that they start a paper to bring the church's social teachings to the common person. That May they published their first issue of *The Catholic Worker*. Within three years its circulation went from 25,000 to 150,000. Combining their outspokenness on issues of faith and political and economic justice with a commitment to live out their beliefs, Dorothy, Peter, and others eventually opened thirty-two Houses of Hospitality and farms. In the city, the Houses became places of refuge for the poor, ill, and others who fell through the cracks of society; in the country, the farms became places of retreat and centers for education.

Arrested several times for protesting, largely dependent on others for support, and often criticized for her unbusinesslike practices, Dorothy maintained that her ministry was not a business but a movement. Dorothy died in 1980, but *The Catholic Worker* movement continues her commitment to ministry, justice, and education. The paper, founded by Dorothy and Peter, still sells for a penny a copy.

─── **MONDAY** ───

The experiences that I have had are more or less universal. Suffering, sadness, repentance, love, we all have known these. They are easiest to bear when one remembers their universality, when we remember that we are all members or potential members of the Mystical Body of Christ. . . .

A conversion is a lonely experience. We do not know what is going on in the depths of the heart and soul of another. We scarcely know ourselves.
—From *Union Square to Rome*

Reflect
❖ What suffering, sadness, repentance, and love have you known?
❖ How do these experiences link you with others—even in the midst of the lonelinesses in which we live?

─── **TUESDAY** ───

Love and ever more love is the only solution to every problem that comes up. If we love each other enough, we will bear with each other's faults and burdens. If we love enough, we are going to light that fire in the hearts of others. And it is love that will burn out the sins and hatreds that sadden us. It is love that will make us want to do great things for each other. No sacrifice and no suffering will then seem too much.

Yes, I see only too clearly how bad people are. I wish I did not see it so. It is my own sins that give me such clarity. If I did not bear the scars of so many sins to dim my sight and dull my capacity for love and joy, then I would see Christ more clearly in you all.

I cannot worry much about your sins and miseries when I have so many of my own. I can only love you all, poor fellow travelers, fellow sufferers. I do not want to add one least straw to the burden you already carry. My prayer from day to day is that God will so enlarge my heart that I will see you all, and live with you all, in [God's] love.
—From *House of Hospitality*

Reflect
❖ How do your sins give you clarity about the badness in others?

❖ How does your ability to love illuminate humanity's goodness?

—— WEDNESDAY ——

(December 1945) For a total Christian, the goad of duty is not needed—always prodding one to perform this or that good deed. It is not a duty to help Christ, it is a privilege. Is it likely that Martha and Mary sat back and considered that they had done all that was expected of them—is it likely that Peter's mother-in-law grudgingly served the chicken she had meant to keep till Sunday because she thought it was her "duty"? She did it gladly; she would have served ten chickens if she had them.

If that is the way they gave hospitality to Christ, it is certain that is the way it should still be given. Not for the sake of humanity. Not because it might be Christ who stays with us, comes to see us, takes up our time. Not because these people remind us of Christ . . . but because they *are* Christ, asking us to find room for Him, exactly as He did at the first Christmas.

—From *Dorothy Day: Selected Writings*

Reflect
❖ In what faces have you seen Christ knocking at the door of your life?
❖ How do you practice hospitality to Christ through them?

—— THURSDAY ——

I know that if anyone started asking Teresa [Dorothy's daughter] any questions she would not be able to answer them. She has an aversion to answering questions. My only knowledge of her spiritual processes is through her conversations, either with other children or with me. She will volunteer information, but she will not have it drawn from her by direct questioning. . . .

And yet when I hear her talk, hear her wise little comments on things I say, I feel certain as to her spiritual knowledge.

About prayer, for instance, Freddy said that he did not know how to pray. Questioned by Teresa, he said that he merely repeated prayers after his mother. All he had to do to pray was to think every now and then of God, Teresa told him. "Just remember Him," she said. "Like after I go to Communion in the morning, then lots of times during the day I suddenly remember that I've got God. That's a prayer, too."

—From *House of Hospitality*

Reflect

❖ Who are the wise children who have taught you?

Today practice Teresa's prayer, remembering that you've got God.

─── **FRIDAY** ───

(July–August 1940) There is poverty and hunger and war in the world. And we prepare for more war. There is desperate suffering with no prospect of relief. But we would be contributing to the misery and desperation of the world if we failed to rejoice in the sun, the moon, and the stars, in the rivers which surround this island on which we live, in the cool breezes of the bay, in what food we have and in the benefactors God sends.

—From *Dorothy Day: Selected Writings*

Reflect

❖ In the midst of the poverty and hunger and war in the world, what specific things give you reason to rejoice?

❖ How do you, in turn, take this rejoicing into the places of poverty and hunger and war?

─── **SATURDAY** ───

(February 1979) We had hard baked potatoes for supper, and overspiced cabbage. I'm in favor of becoming a vegetarian only if the vegetables are cooked right. (What a hard job cooking is here! But the human warmth in the dining room covers up a multitude of sins.) Another food grievance: onions chopped up in a fruit salad, plus spices and herbs! A sacrilege—to treat foods in this way. Food should be treated with respect, since Our Lord left Himself to us in the guise of food. His disciples knew Him in the breaking of bread.

—From *Dorothy Day: Selected Writings*

Reflect

❖ What bothers you in the process of searching for justice and love?

❖ What eases the frustrations of the search?

─── **SUNDAY** ───

Postscript

We were just sitting there talking when Peter Maurin came in.

We were just sitting there talking when lines of people began to form, saying, "We need bread." We could not say, "Go, be thou filled." If there were six small loaves and a few fishes, we had to divide them. There was always bread.

We were just sitting there talking and people moved in on us. Let those who can take it, take it. Some moved out and that made room for more. And somehow the walls expanded.

We were just sitting there talking and someone said, "Let's all go live on a farm."

It was as casual as all that, I often think. It just came about. It just happened.

I found myself, a barren woman, the joyful mother of children. It is not easy always to be joyful, to keep in mind the duty of delight.

The most significant thing about *The Catholic Worker* is poverty, some say.

The most significant thing is community, others say. We are not alone any more.

But the final word is love. At times it has been, in the words of Father Zossima, a harsh and dreadful thing, and our very faith in love has been tried through fire.

We cannot love God unless we love each other, and to love we must know each other. We know [God] in the breaking of bread, and we know each other in the breaking of bread, and we are not alone any more. Heaven is a banquet and life is a banquet, too, even with a crust, where there is companionship.

We have all known the long loneliness and we have learned that the only solution is love and that love comes with community.

It all happened while we sat there talking, and it is still going on.

—From *The Long Loneliness: The Autobiography of Dorothy Day*

Reflect
- ❖ What is your long loneliness?
- ❖ Where has it been eased?

—— **Meditation** ——

The Open Door

Those who leave
the door open

often are said
to have been born
in barns.
And you, Dorothy,
left the door open
so long,
daily inviting Christ,
himself born in a barn,
to come in.

He entered
again and again.

Dorothy,
when you left,
you left the door
wide open.
—Jan L. Richardson

——— ❖ ———

Blessing: *By your life may others come to know the hospitality of the One whose door remains always open.*

41

Holy Poverty
Saint Clare of Assisi

Invocation: *Come, Sister Poverty! Be my guest; from you may I learn the blessedness of letting go.*

Text: Luke 6:20-21

Context: Born in Assisi, Italy, around 1194, Clare was the third of five children born to the well-to-do Favorone family. From an early age she displayed both a devotion to God and a strong skepticism of the prevailing powers. In *Clare of Assisi: Early Documents*, Regis Armstrong relates a story about Clare on Palm Sunday in 1212. When the young women of the town "customarily dressed in their finest and proudly processed to the Bishop for a palm branch," Clare did not go forward but stood in her place, waiting for the Bishop to come to her. That same Sunday, Clare, who had befriended a radical young preacher named Francis, secretly went to Our Lady of Angels, the Portiuncula, where she made a commitment to Francis and his spiritual brothers to embrace their life of devotion and poverty.

Clare lived in several monasteries, moving more than once to avoid pressure from her family, who had sought to arrange a marriage for her. Other women joined her, including her mother, and Clare became the leader of the "Poor Ladies of San Damiano," later to be known as the "Poor Clares." Recognized as followers of Francis, Clare and her sisters shared his passion for poverty, humility, and charity to all, particularly those on the margins of the affluent society in which Clare and Francis had grown up.

Although tradition attached to Clare the identity of *la pianticella* (the little plant) of Saint Francis, she embodied her own distinct vision, which continued to shape Franciscan life after Saint Francis's death. Her few surviving writings reveal a deep commitment to a God-centered life, a life that tried to give up anything that would hinder relationship and intimacy with those whom God had created.

The following excerpts of Clare's writings come from the book *Francis and Clare: The Complete Works.* Clare's writings and the writings that intersperse hers in this week, during which we celebrate her feast day (August 11), beckon us to ponder what separates us from one another. She also invites us to embrace poverty as a way of life that frees us not simply from material possessions but from all things that create harmful divisions among us.

O blessed poverty,
>who bestows eternal riches on those who love and
>embrace her!

O holy poverty,
>to those who possess and desire you
>God promises *the kingdom of heaven*
>and offers, indeed, eternal glory and blessed life!

O God-centered poverty,
>whom the Lord Jesus Christ
>Who ruled and now rules heaven and earth,
>*Who spoke and things were made*,
>condescended to embrace before all else!

Reflect

Clare and Francis offered an image of poverty embodied as a woman. Imagine Sister Poverty. Invite her to be your companion this week, asking you the questions that these readings raise.

❖ What does Sister Poverty look like?
❖ In whom have you seen her?

—— **TUESDAY** ——

For Francis and Clare, imitation of the poor Christ was not exhausted by walking barefoot and owning only one cloak. It also meant poverty of spirit. Sometimes it seems we shrink from notions like poverty of spirit because we see only the negative, dehumanizing face of poverty around us. We should, rightfully, recoil at a spirituality that would hold up self-loathing or victimization as an ideal. But poverty of spirit does not refer primarily to this. It refers to a freedom of spirit, an inner life unencumbered by excessive psychological baggage.

What inner poverty is genuinely about is loving well. It is about intimacy. Francis and Clare and other great lovers in the tradition knew that true intimacy with God and others means allowing oneself to know and be

Holy Poverty ~ 325

known. It means letting down the barriers of self defense that separate us. It means becoming unselfconsciously naked, so that we might joyfully enter into true intimacy with another.

—Wendy M. Wright in *The Vigil*

Reflect

❖ How free, how poor is your spirit today?

―――― **WEDNESDAY** ――――

If so great and good a Lord, then, on coming into the Virgin's womb, chose to appear despised, needy, and *poor* in this world, so that people who were in utter poverty and want and in absolute need of heavenly nourishment might become *rich . . .* in Him by possessing the kingdom of heaven, then *rejoice and be glad* (Hab 3:18)! Be filled with a remarkable happiness and a spiritual joy! Contempt of the world has pleased You more than [its] honors, poverty more than earthly riches, and You have sought to store up greater *treasures in heaven* rather than on earth, *where rust does not consume nor moth destroy nor thieves break in and steal. . . . Your reward,* then, *is very great in heaven* (Mt 5:12)! And You have truly merited to be called *a sister, spouse, and mother* (2 Cor 11:2; Mt 12:50) of the Son of the Father of the Most High and of the glorious Virgin.

You know, I am sure, that the kingdom of heaven is promised and given by the Lord only to the poor . . . for [s]he who loves temporal things loses the fruit of love. Such a person *cannot serve God and [money],* for *either the one is loved and the other hated,* or *the one* is served *and the other despised* (Mt 6:24).

You also know that one who is clothed cannot fight with another who is naked, because [s]he is more quickly thrown who gives [her]his adversary a chance to get hold of [her]him; and that one who lives in the glory of earth cannot rule with Christ in heaven.

Reflect

❖ What possessions do you hold, or are you held by?

―――― **THURSDAY** ――――

Sitting there, listening, I remembered why I admired this story-teller—Richard Ward always returned me to the story differently. This time he told of the rich young ruler who left Jesus, dejected because he could not bear to part with his great possessions. (See Mark 10:17-22.) This wasn't simply about economics, Richard maintained. It's a call to give away what we are wealthy in.

For Richard, who is wealthy in stories, it has been a call to give those stories away, to draw people into the story of God and of one another. For many who are wealthy in money, it indeed is a call to give away material possessions, to restore the imbalance of monetary wealth in the world. For others, wealthy in time, education, skill, compassion, and whatever other gifts they possess, it is a call to give away that wealth for the healing of the earth.
—Jan L. Richardson

Reflect
- ❖ What are you wealthy in?
- ❖ How are you giving it away?

—— FRIDAY ——

Place your mind before the mirror of eternity!
Place your soul in *the brilliance of glory!*
Place your heart *in the figure of the* divine *substance!*
And *transform* your whole being *into the image* of the Godhead
    Itself
    through contemplation!

So that you too may feel what [God's] friends feel
    as they taste *the hidden sweetness*
    which God . . . has reserved
    from the beginning
    for those who love [God].

Since you have cast aside all [those] things which, in this deceitful and turbulent world, ensnare their blind lovers, love Him totally Who gave Himself totally for Your love. His beauty the sun and moon admire; and of His gifts there is no limit in abundance, preciousness, and magnitude. I am speaking of Him Who is the Son of the Most High, Whom the Virgin brought to birth.

Reflect
- ❖ Where are you placing your mind, your soul, your heart?
- ❖ What is being transformed in you?

—— SATURDAY ——

The words of a visitor to India, a materially impoverished country, recall Wendy Wright's words about the true nature of poverty of spirit: intimacy that grows among persons willing to be mutually connected with one another.

During each of our visits to schools, churches, families, we were always offered food and drink and a place to freshen up. India was a great teacher in the art of hospitality. People treated us with great respect and cared for us with genuine sincerity. Western concepts of self-reliance, self-sufficiency, and individualism are foreign to Indians whose lives are based on interdependence. Much of India lacks the state-of-the-art technology that is taken for granted by much of the Western world, technology that allows one person to do the work of many and that seduces us into thinking that we can be self-reliant. Indians depend on each other and work together to accomplish tasks and often to survive. Taking care of each other is a prevailing attitude. Neighbors and friends are often understood to be extended family. Helping each other is simply expected.
—Sandra Smith, from a letter

Reflect
- ❖ What in your culture feeds a sense of self-reliance?
- ❖ How does this sense of self-reliance affect your spirituality?
- ❖ Is spirituality something you attain on your own, or does it emerge out of relationships and a sense of community?

—— SUNDAY ——

What you hold, may you [always] hold.
What you do, may you [always] do and never abandon.
But with swift pace, light step,
    [and] unswerving feet,
    so that even your steps stir up no dust,
go forward
    securely, joyfully, and swiftly,
on the path of prudent happiness,
    believing nothing,
    agreeing with nothing
    which would dissuade you from this resolution
    or which *would place a stumbling block* for you on the way,

so that you may offer *your vows to the Most High*
in the pursuit of that perfection
to which the Spirit of the Lord has called you.

Reflect

❖ What are you being challenged to let go of, materially and/or
spiritually, in order to lighten your step?

—— **Meditation** ——

Sister Poverty Has Her Say

*You also know that one who is clothed cannot fight another
who is naked.*

—Saint Clare

This is how we must fight:
bared
skin to skin
close enough
to feel the warmth
of flesh exposed,
near enough
to see my face
reflected in your gaze.
—Jan L. Richardson

—— ❖ ——

Blessing: *May the God who holds you, ever sustain you, strengthening
you to give care to creation.*

42 Journey through Good-bye
Grandfather Tales

Invocation: *Bless my remembering, O God, of the men whose stories are woven with mine. In places of hurting or of happiness, grant me wholeness.*

Text: Psalm 112:6-9

Context: My father's father, Mark Richardson, was a gentle soul. Like his father before him, Gramps was a farmer. He and his two brothers worked the same land that my great-grandfather had given his life to. He raised vegetables (until World War II), oranges, cattle; and, with my grandmother Flora, five children.

When he semiretired from the farm, Gramps took up carpentry and became a skilled craftsman. For his children and grandchildren, he built beautiful desks, dressers, bookcases, shelves; for each granddaughter, a hope chest. He always had a stash of lazy susans, trivets, napkin holders, toys, and other smaller creations ready to share with the wide circle of friends who stopped by to visit.

Some time after my grandmother died, Gramps's memory began to slip. Over the next few years, he was slowly robbed not only of much of his short-term memory but also of memories of years before. The latter seemed the ultimate injustice as he struggled to place the faces and names of family and friends who had been an intimate part of his life for years.

But Gramps's persistent gentleness and humor never changed. Even in his final days, in the rapid physical deterioration following blood clots that led to the amputation of most of a leg, the spark of his spirit still remained evident. It is a spark that shaped and, I pray, runs through me.

From Gramps I learned much about living well and saying good-bye well. Three summers have passed since that last good-bye in the summer of 1991, and as we journey through another summer, I remember those days with a granddaughter's heart.

—— **MONDAY** ——

Driving home from Atlanta at the end of the term, I am anxious. So many good-byes behind me to friends who are moving on, and I'm aware of the good-byes still to come.

I arrive home to the sight of the Moon Tree, my star-gazing companion, in a heap on the ground. My parents had told me of this; they also had told me of Gramps, of the clots, of the amputation. They greet me with the news that he almost died yesterday morning. He'll come home soon; nothing they can do. Hospice is being brought in.

The next morning Mom and I go to the hospital. Before we leave, I walk out to the Moon Tree. It has been dead for years, but still it stuns me, seeing it reduced to a heap, limbs a foot and a half wide ripped clean. The trunk broke almost level with the ground.

I walk among the remains, touching the tree for the first time in ages. Given its fragility, it was too dangerous to walk under it while it still stood. I move my hand along its wasted limbs, its wounds, wondering if this visit will be something like my visit with Gramps.

He too was standing when I last saw him.

—Jan L. Richardson

Reflect

❖ When have you seen the brokenness within you being mirrored in brokenness around you?

—————— **TUESDAY** ——————

Gramps is home; the family has gathered, waiting. We know death is coming in a little or a longer while. Gramps sleeps a lot. Family members hover throughout the house, talk quietly, speak with him during his moments of wakefulness.

Saturday night we gather around the table. Generations have eaten here, fed by strong women who knew how to ease a body's hunger. Toward the end of the meal someone brings Gramps to the table. Mostly he sleeps, his head resting against his hand. Occasionally he rouses himself, gazing at the great-grandson who plays at his feet.

—Jan L. Richardson

Reflect

❖ What memories do you hold of the gathering of the generations, of the threads of connection?

—— WEDNESDAY ——

The day after the family feast. I'm heading to Lakeland, where I will be ordained in two days. Leaving later than I had planned, I pull onto the highway, deciding to forego a stop at Gramps's. I'm nearly to McIntosh before I stop, turn around, and head back to Evinston.

I pull up in Gramps's drive, walk into his room. He hasn't been responding much. His eyes are open. I take his hand, say words I won't remember later. I do tell him I'm on my way to be ordained. He's been one of my biggest supporters. I remember preaching my ordination sermon at the little church in Evinston a few months before, watching Gramps doze near the front. He wasn't remembering much of anybody or anything by then. Afterwards a friend told me, "Your grandfather came up to me and said, 'That was *my* granddaughter up there preaching the sermon.'"

Gramps doesn't say anything when I tell him where I'm headed. But I think he knows.

—Jan L. Richardson

Reflect

- ❖ What about the deaths in your family . . . how have you been there, physically or otherwise?
- ❖ How did it feel to wait for the death?

—— THURSDAY ——

That night I am restless. I am remembering, remembering, and weary with good-byes. At 3 A.M. I wake, stay awake until morning.

I see familiar faces in Lakeland, friends among those who have gathered for annual conference. I double as a delegate and a sign language interpreter. Walking down from the stage after an interpreting stint that morning, I find Preacher Paul waiting for me. He and the Richardsons have loved one another since before I was born.

Paul puts his arm around me, tells me Gramps died that morning, holds me as I cry.

Later I call Mom and Dad. "Gramps died around 3:00 this morning," they tell me.

—Jan L. Richardson

Reflect

- ❖ Who have been the news-bearers in your life?

- ❖ How has your relationship with them affected their telling of the news?

FRIDAY

Ordination is a blur, a celebration mixed with sadness. Somehow I know that among those hands laid on me are those of Gramps. I leave conference early for the memorial service.

We gather at Gramps's home afterward. My nearly one-year-old nephew is going wild, so I spirit him away for a walk outside. I carry Scott out to one of the cattle pastures behind the house and talk to him as we stand at the fence.

We walk around the yard, ending up in Gramps's shop. I breathe in the familiar smell, a mixture of scraps and boards of lumber, machines, carpenter's glue, wood shavings, stain, and decades of dust. It has always smelled this way.

"This is where Gramps made all his stuff," I tell Scott. I desperately want him to remember, knowing he won't. But his great-grandfather runs in his blood.

—Jan L. Richardson

Reflect

- ❖ What stories and memories of places has your family passed down from generation to generation?
- ❖ How will you pass them on?

SATURDAY

Moving into my house in Orlando, I finally get to use all the furniture Gramps made me. The pieces sat in my room at my parents' house during years of college and seminary. Now they grace my home. Desk and bookshelves in the study, hope chest in the bedroom, dresser in the guest room, étagère in the living room.

I find an extra lazy susan I didn't know I had. One goes in the dining room. Another generation, another table. The other I tuck away for one of Gramps's great-grandchildren.

—Jan L. Richardson

Reflect

If you are at home, look around your space.

- ❖ What possessions have you received from others?
- ❖ What stories and spirits inhabit them?

─── SUNDAY ───

Sitting around one evening, I talk with Kary about how I'm still trying to make this place home. I tell her about a project my sister suggested for the bedroom, a folding screen to divide part of the room. Minutes later we're in the car heading for the hardware store with measurements and a hastily sketched design in hand. We walk out later with lumber, screws, hinges, sandpaper, stain, brushes, and Kary's brand-new cordless drill ("I've been needing one!").

Two days, another trip to the store, and several revisions later, we're beholding a beautiful folding screen that I wouldn't want anyone to examine too closely but that *we* have created. (I later had to convince various family members that no, it wasn't a kit.) We carry it into the bedroom, drape sheets over it to get the effect of the real material that it will frame one day.

"Gramps would be proud," I say with a smile.
—Jan L. Richardson

Reflect
- ❖ Who has taught you about the delight of creating?

─── Meditation ───

Going Home
   For Gramps

We were all together
celebrating your grandson's engagement
when you walked up
to one of your daughters.

"I'm ready to go now,"
you told her.

"But Daddy,
this is your house!"

You were confused, a little
(perhaps less than we thought),
so you asked,

"Well, then when
are all these people
going home?"

We laughed, but now I know
there is some home
we are always going to,
and there is some land
we never leave.
—Jan L. Richardson

———— ❖ ————

Blessing: *May God meet you on all the paths of your remembering and
lead you to lands of restoration.*

43 Namer of God
Hagar

Invocation: *O God who sees, give perception to my soul.*

Text: See daily readings

Context: One of the longer stories in Hebrew scripture, the tale of Hagar appears in bits and pieces throughout the larger narrative concerning Sarah, Abraham, and the beginnings of the people who would become the nation of Israel. That we seldom hear Hagar's voice compounds the fragmentation of her story. The text records her speech only rarely. As an enslaved woman, she lives on the margins not only of her society but of the text as well.

However, when pieced together, the text reveals a startling story of power and terror. Caught between Sarah and Abraham in a struggle for power, Hagar intimately knows the choices facing those who encounter abuse. Yet the object becomes subject in this story as Hagar is the first in scripture to receive an annunciation. She is the only person in scripture who dares to name God, and she becomes the mother of a great nation.

Hagar's story occasions discomfort because it illumines the divisions that exist among women along lines including race and class. It invites us to consider the injustices that we as women perpetuate against one another, often in the name of keeping peace with the men in our lives.

——— **MONDAY** ———

Read Genesis 16:1-5.

Through her slave's womb, Sarai sought esteem and honor for herself.

But the tables were turned on Sarai. . . . Instead of esteem, Sarai received contempt. Instead of respect, Sarai was ridiculed. And by her maid, no less!

Whether Hagar's contempt for Sarai was real or imagined on Sarai's part, we can only guess. (After all, the story is told more from Sarai's point of view than Hagar's.) But one thing is certain: Hagar's elevation as Abram's pregnant concubine must have served only to point up Sarai's downfall as the wife who could bear him no children.

As the woman carrying the child of the wealthy landowner, the status of the pregnant slavewoman in the house of her mistress drastically changed. The relationship between the mistress and maid required renegotiation. Before, Hagar had been a defenseless slave. Now, as the pregnant concubine of the prosperous but old man Abram, Hagar was protected. She ceased to be Sarai's slave and became Abram's wife.

Perhaps the pregnancy awakened something in the slavewoman, something that previously lay dormant.

Perhaps it was her sense of self-worth.

Perhaps it was her sense of purpose and direction.

Or, perhaps, it was the prospect of being loved unconditionally by her child. (Pregnancy has had that effect on more than one woman.)

Whatever the reason, Hagar could no longer see Sarai and her relationship to her mistress in the same way as before, for Hagar was able to give the old man Abram something his wife Sarai could not. Consequently, Hagar transformed before her mistress' eyes. Her attitude about herself changed as well. The child growing inside her was proof that she was more than a slave: she was a woman.

—Renita J. Weems in *Just a Sister Away*

Reflect

Think of pregnant women you have known, or yourself, if you have experienced pregnancy.

❖ How has that experience altered the self-image and self-esteem of you or the other women?

—————— **TUESDAY** ——————

Read Genesis 16:6.

If we as black women appear, to some, to be reading too much of our own brutal history into the biblical story, let it be pointed out that whatever the nature of the punishment Sarai imposed, it was evidently harsh enough to convince the slavewoman to run away. Hagar chose the unknown dangers of the wilderness over her pallet in her mistress' house.

The story of the Egyptian slave and her Hebrew mistress is hauntingly reminiscent of the disturbing accounts of black slavewomen and white mistresses during slavery. Over and over again we have heard tales about the wanton and brutal rape of black women by their white slavemasters, compounded by punitive beatings by resentful white wives who penalized the raped slavewomen for their husbands' lust and savagery.

There are also the pitiful stories of slavewomen who willingly conceded to their slavemasters' sexual advances: first, as a way of protecting their husbands, children, and loved ones from being beaten; second, as a way to keep themselves and those close to them from being sold away; or, third, as the only way of elevating their social rank in order to protect themselves from vicious overseers and mistresses.

The painful memory of black and white women under slavery and the web of cruelty that characterized their relations continue to stalk the relationships between black and white women in America even to this day. Slavery was abolished in America a mere one hundred twenty-five years ago; but evidently one hundred twenty-five years is not long enough to abolish the memories and attitudes that slavery arouses in a nation. Unless a miracle occurs, it is sad to say that it will probably take another one hundred twenty-five years to erase the pain and antagonism bred from two hundred fifty years of the cruelest brutality one race could inflict upon another—especially in the name of God.

And, for some peculiar reasons, when it comes to women, those memories have proven especially hard to erase.

—Renita J. Weems in *Just a Sister Away*

Reflect

❖ How many women of other races do you know?

❖ What is the nature of those relationships—friends, coworkers, employee/employer, etc.?

❖ Do you think each of you would describe the relationship similarly or differently?

──── **WEDNESDAY** ────

Read Genesis 16:7-16.

The Seed Is the Light of the Earth
For Muriel Rukeyser, October 1981

In the absence of light
we maintain our eyes cannot see.
We believe our pupils dilate
to a maximum degree and no more.
We are certain our bodies do not glow
with the cold phosphorescence of the bog,
of water, unfathomed, under pressure,

our own, or beyond our making. We assure
ourselves we are exonerated because
we cannot float through the night
graceful with inherent sonar. We think
anatomy keeps us from the dark forest.

I tell you here, in this dark, this
indistinct country, comes our shaped
and fleshed evolution. That step
on the unlit path stretches us,
and those who may come after.
With each hesitant journey
we open, blazing beacon fires,
flashing lanterns from high, distant
hills. Dark surrounds us. We are
paradox. We carry our own light
and move in love through the dark,
as the seed loves the earth enclosing it.
—Christina Pacosz in *Looking for Home: Women Writing about Exile*

Reflect
- ❖ What did Hagar see that enabled her to keep moving?
- ❖ What "step on the unlit path" stretches you?
- ❖ What do you carry; what sustains you in the dark?

—— **THURSDAY** ——

Read Genesis 21:1-14.

Quite frankly, the kinds of atrocities some mothers have committed against other mothers and their children continue to stun me. I am often amazed at the extent to which otherwise intelligent, otherwise moral women (and men) will renounce intelligence and morality to protect some perceived rights they feel their children have in relation to other mothers' children.

I am reminded of the sight of scowling, rabid mothers picketing and yelling vile insults at innocent school children whose only offense is that they have been infected with the AIDS virus and want to continue to go to school. Then, there is the sight of white mothers from Little Rock, Chicago, and Boston snarling and hurling obscenities at innocent black children en route to schools they have been forced by the courts to desegregate. What is there about these children that these women hate so much? What kind of fear

is this that explodes into madness? I doubt whether the day will ever come when I am no longer appalled by human evil.
—Renita J. Weems in *Just a Sister Away*

Reflect
This litany of fear, of hatred, of injustice stretches in time before and beyond Hagar and Sarah.
❖ What words would you add to this litany?
❖ Do you find any language of hope in the midst of this litany?
❖ How do you respond when you feel overwhelmed by human evil?

— **FRIDAY** —

Read Genesis 21:15-21.

Wilderness Chant

Strong with your heart
deep with your soul
close with your breath
fast with your hand

drenched with your cries
healed with your sight
a way out of no way
in this parched land.
—Jan L. Richardson

Reflect
❖ When has a way out of no way been made for you, when it seemed that even the things or people you held most tightly were in jeopardy?

— **SATURDAY** —

At some time in all our lives, whether we are black or white, we are all Hagar's daughters. When our backs are up against a wall; when we feel abandoned, abused, betrayed, and banished; when we find ourselves in need of another woman's help (a friend, neighbor, colleague, relative, stranger, another man's wife); we, like Hagar, are in need of a woman who will "sister" us, not exploit us.

In those times we are frequently just a sister away from our healing.

We need a woman, a sister, who will see in our destitution a jagged image of what one day could be her own story. We need a sister who will respond with mercy. We need a sister whose genuine mercy—not pity which is episodic, random, and moody—is steadfast, consistent, and free.

Betrayal. Exploitation. Denial. Resentment. Suspicion. Distrust. Anger. Silence. How do we get past these memories? How do we reach beyond the enormous gulf of distrust on both our parts and forge friendships and coalitions?

It will not be easy.

In fact, it will be very difficult.

It will require a deliberate effort on our part to listen when it is easier to dismiss.

At times, it will mean that we must be as willing to confront and confess the evil in us, as a community of women, as we are to point to evil in the world.

It will require a resolve to work with one another both in spite of and because of the pain.

It will require a willingness to respect the genuine differences in one another and to see them as the strength of our coalition, not the bane of our existence.

As black and white women in America, as Israeli and Lebanese women, as white South African and black South African women, as Asian and European women, as the wives of terrorists and the wives of victims of terrorists, working for righteousness in splendid isolation from one another is a luxury we cannot afford.

Injustice in our lands relies upon the perpetual alienation of women from one another and upon relentless hostility between women. Indeed, our estrangement from one another continues to compromise the integrity of our witness as God-fearing women.

The future of our families depends upon our ability to bridge over the memories of our scars.

The future of our people depends upon our willingness to tunnel through the tragedies of our past encounters.

The future of our world depends upon our resolve to walk headlong into that which makes us different as diverse tribes of a vast world and to march straight into that which binds us as people of God.

If we don't, who will?

—Renita J. Weems in *Just a Sister Away*

Reflect

❖ How easy is it to confront and confess the evil within us?

❖ What will it require in your life to confront and confess this evil?

—— **SUNDAY** ——

A Litany of Bridges

Leader: We who are in exile pray for bridges.
         We who are torn pray for mending.
         We who are alone pray for community.

         Without warning, we have become exiles from our own holy
         stories, without place and without name.

All: We who are in exile pray for bridges.

Leader: We stand outside the holy words, lacking the key that fits.

All: We who are in exile pray for bridges.

Leader: Grant us the gift of holy language so that we may recognize our
         Names when we come before you in prayer.

All: We who are in exile pray for bridges.

Leader: Without warning, we have been torn away from our own
         reflections.

All: We who are torn pray for mending.

Leader: We have lost the holy faces which mirror our own.

All: We who are torn pray for mending.

Leader: Grant us the sight to create anew visions of holy womanhood.

All: We who are torn pray for mending.

Leader: Without warning, we have been dishonored, beaten, raped,
         disbelieved, and degraded.

All: We who are torn pray for mending.

Leader: Grant us sacraments of healing for women's wounds, old and
         new.

All:	We who are torn pray for mending.
Leader:	Without warning, we have been pushed to the side, with only the brave and tired to lead us into the light.
All:	We who are alone pray for community.
Leader:	We have been blinded into looking at differences among us in scorn rather than in celebration.
All:	We who are alone pray for community.
Leader:	We have alienated ourselves from each other, forgetting that each woman's struggle is everywoman's burden.
All:	We who are alone pray for community.
Leader:	Grant us the power of love and forgiveness, drawing us all into your wide heart and under your wide wing.
All:	We who are in exile pray for bridges.
	We who are torn pray for mending.
	We who are alone pray for community.

—Heather McVoy, written for a service of the Tallahassee Women-Church, Tallahassee, Florida

Reflect

❖ What bridges are you praying for and building?
❖ What mending are you praying for and doing?
❖ What community are you praying for and creating?

—— **Meditation** ——

Why must woman stand divided?
Building the walls that tear them down?

. . . .

A woman is a ritual
A house that must accommodate
A house that must endure
Generation after generation. . . .

—Genny Lim, from "Wonder Woman" in *This Bridge Called My Back*

The Ritual

I see them at the door,
years later, lifetimes later,
of the house they occupied
in anger and in exile
in jealousy and dis-ease
spent on each other,
caught in their larger web.

They gaze at each other,
remembering across the span,
remembering children now grown,
remembering dreams now changed.

I want them
to go through the door,
to break bread
at the dusty table,
to share wine
from the cracked cup,
to dream
of building this house anew.

I want Sarah
to teach Hagar
how to laugh
and Hagar
to teach Sarah
how to see.

But look.
They are waiting for us
to begin.
—Jan L. Richardson

——— ❖ ———

Blessing: *May you begin, beloved of God, to laugh, to see, to build new bridges, to dream new dreams.*

44 **Streams of Liberation**
Miriam

Invocation: *Lead me to your wellsprings, O Source of Life. May I drink deeply of your wisdom and delight in your waters that birth freedom.*

Text: See daily readings

Context: Miriam's story runs like an underground stream through the story of the Exodus of the people of Israel. Her story emerges at pivotal times, then she sinks back into the hidden currents of the story. Yet her appearances, both in scripture and in legend, testify to Miriam's influential role in the Exodus journey. One of the only women in scripture identified as a prophet, Miriam contains within herself a wellspring of vision, passion, and commitment to action.

Miriam's frequent connections with water shape our passage through this week. Drawing on scriptural accounts and Jewish traditions, these readings move us along the path of her journey toward freedom for her people and herself.

—— MONDAY ——

[*A Jewish legend says Miriam foresaw the birth of Moses in a dream. In Israel's memory, Miriam's connection with water begins with the waters of Moses' birth. The waters that flow from her mother inaugurate Miriam's own participation in the Exodus. Perhaps the waters of Miriam's dream are the source of the river that sustains her throughout her life.*]

Miriam's Dream

The mouth of the river,
she does not whisper;
she does not settle her lips
   into a thin line
while she composes her thoughts;
she does not grin
she does not chuckle.

The mouth of the river,
she rages
she cries out from her watery depths
she moans over rocks
she yells over stones
she screams
she laughs
she bellows

from the circle of her mouth,
from the *O* of her lips:

O daybreak
O freedom
O life.
—Jan L. Richardson

Reflect

- ❖ What do you remember of your childhood dreams—night dreams or daydreams?
- ❖ What are the connections between those dreams and the ones you dream now?

—— **TUESDAY** ——

Read Exodus 2:1-4.

Miriam's Lullaby

Mother's tears fill up this river;
sorrow washes through the deep.
For your life her arms are empty;
for her courage, now you sleep.

Hush, my darling, I am watching;
cease your crying, close your eyes.
Angels fill your head with dreaming
while the freedom waters rise.

Gently on the waters rest you,
unaware of raging depths;
innocent of power within you,
power to free and power to bless.

Hush, my darling, I am with you,
calling on the spirits wise;
may they guard and may they guide you
while the freedom waters rise.
—Jan L. Richardson

Reflect

Imagine yourself on the bank of the river with Miriam.

- ❖ When have you released someone or something precious to you?
- ❖ What would you and Miriam say to each other?

—— WEDNESDAY ——

Read Exodus 2:5-9.

Encounter

We are not the same
but we stand in the river

we stand not the same
but we move with the tides

we move not the same
but we ache with all longing

to bless and bring forth
the waters of life.
—Jan L. Richardson

Reflect

- ❖ What connects these two very different women?
- ❖ What waters move through the two women, enabling them to create together?

—— THURSDAY ——

Read Exodus 15:19-21.

Song from the Other Side of the Sea

My father, my brother, my lover, my son
drowned in the waters at Yahweh's strong hand

while songs echoed back from the opposite shore,
while Miriam led in the victory dance.

Miriam, prophet, do you foresee
a time when your freed ones will build other walls?
Miriam, sister, do not forget
that freedom for one must mean freedom for all.

No gift can I offer from this barren shore
to strengthen you on this journey begun.
My river of tears is all I have left
of my father, my brother, my lover, my son.
—Jan L. Richardson

Reflect

Even as Miriam led the women in rejoicing by the sea, women on the other side wept for their lost ones.

❖ How will it become possible for us to share a common vision of freedom—one in which all may live?

—— FRIDAY ——

Read Numbers 12:1-16.

Miriam Speaks with Anger in the Wilderness

Miriam says: look where you got me.
Anger says: now you stand on the edge.

Miriam says: look at this flesh.
Anger says: now you know your beauty cannot save you.

Miriam says: these tears burn me.
Anger says: they are born of cleansing fire.

Miriam says: you drain me.
Anger says: I have wells you know not of.
—Jan L. Richardson

Reflect

❖ Why do you think God punished only Miriam?
❖ What did Miriam think about during those days in the wilderness?
❖ What sustained her?

Read Numbers 20:1-5.
[Miriam was so vital to the Exodus journey that Jewish legend attributes the loss of water to Miriam's death.]

The Leavetaking

Death, for those left behind,
is not so much a
wrenching away
as a drying up,
a parching
as bones
tendons
muscles
nerves
flesh,
robbed of sustenance,
turn to salt
and stiffen,
knowing their loss,
aching for return.
—Jan L. Richardson

Reflect
- ❖ What do death, loss, and leavetaking take from you?
- ❖ Imagine saying farewell to Miriam. With what words, actions, memories do you leave each other?

—— **SUNDAY** ——

[Legend tells us that as the people of Israel journeyed, a well appeared at different times along the way. This well, known as Miriam's Well, continues to appear whenever people are in need, bringing the waters of life.]

Miriam's Well

Where the visions take flesh
where the seeds bear fruit
where the thirsty drink deeply
where the hungry feast

where the dreamers embrace
where the prisoners run free
where the children laugh
where the wounded heal
where the creatures play
where the dry bones dance.
—Jan L. Richardson

Reflect

❖ What might Miriam's well look like in your life?
❖ What thirsts, dreams, hopes does it sustain?

—— Meditation ——

Invitation

Miriam,
I wanted to write this
    by the river,
but for two solid weeks
    it has rained.
The river would not wait;
it vaulted its banks
came to my door
knocked on my windows
pounded my roof
and clenched its hands
    around my spirit.
I thought I was trapped
    till I heard its refrain:

sister, come and dance.
—Jan L. Richardson

—— ❖ ——

Blessing: *May your dreams overflow your boundaries; may you dance on newfound shores; may you drink deeply of healing visions and rest beside liberating streams.*

45 Generation to Generation
Grandmothers, Mothers, Daughters

Invocation: *Faithful God, from generation to generation you bless your people with mercy. Share your strength with me, that I may tell out the stories of those who shaped my life.*

Text: Luke 1:50

Context: "God's mercy is for those who fear God, from generation to generation," Mary sang after her kinswoman Elizabeth blessed her (Luke 1). Hannah, Mary's foremother in faith, first sang such a song (1 Samuel 2:1-10). Across the generations, the song connected these two women who shared a similar call from God.

From generation to generation our lives connect, and the lives of our grandmothers and mothers give shape to our own songs of joy, of lament, of praise, and of pain. Often the threads of our relationships are tangled, and the process of weaving meaning from them may be fraught with anger and loss. Yet by their presence or their absence, their tender care or their failures, our foremothers influence who we are.

The writers this week invite us to ponder the connections that pass to and through us; connections that inspired the songs our grandmothers and mothers have sung. With wisdom may we remember them; with hope may we pass them on.

—— MONDAY ——

One day my mother said, "Itka, come, I want to show you something." And I remember I was so excited with anticipation and curiosity and so frightened simultaneously to find out what was in that closet. She took out the key and opened it. "Look, my child." It was old leather-bound books—a whole closet of books. My mother was afraid the children might tear the books. She took out a book, and she said, "When you learn to read, you will discover a treasure here. You will be with the greatest minds. You can sit in Ciechanow, Poland, and you will see the whole world, and you will travel through the ages."

She took out a book. She took me on her knee. I can remember to-day—we sat near the window on a chair, and she started to read stories, and this became a daily ritual. And this gave me so much closeness to my mother. Because when we read she held me on her lap and I felt the warmth of the relationship and the story. I was a very curious child, and my mother always encouraged that curiosity.

—Itka Frajman Zygmuntowicz, with Sara Horowitz, from "Survival and Memory" in *Four Centuries of Jewish Women's Spirituality*

Reflect

❖ What first lessons do you remember from your mother or whoever reared you?

❖ What daily rituals gave meaning to your relationships with those who reared you?

——— TUESDAY ———

In a line-up of little old ladies, my grandmother would not stand out from the crowd. She is small, not much over five feet tall, and has curly gray hair.

The doctor who operated on her toes a few years back probably lumped her together in a mental category with all the other polite, retired ladies in his Gainesville practice. I imagine his eyes widening with surprise when Grandmother asked, "Now if I use my heel on the pedal, can I still drive the tractor?"

Grandmother, toes stitched and bandaged, had no time to sit around dealing in stereotypes or wallowing in self-pity. She had fields to plow and livestock to care for.

I see her practical hardiness evident in my mother's personality—a woman who pauses only to make the necessary adjustments when hardships surprise her.

More than any spoken words, Mom and Grandmother's attitudes toward their problems have taught me to live with the hurdles I encounter day to day.

—Brenda K. Lewis

Reflect

❖ What are the stories of the women in your history who have held surprises, who have revealed the unexpected?

Songs of Women (VI) (1927)

For poor brides who were servant girls,
Mother Sara draws forth from dim barrels
And pitchers sparkling wine.
Mother Sara carries with both hands
A full pitcher to whom it is decreed.
And for streetwalkers
Dreaming of white wedding shoes,
Mother Sara bears clear honey
In small saucers
To their tired mouths.
For high-born brides now poor,
Who blush to bring patched wash
Before their mother-in-law,
Mother Rebecca leads camels
Laden with white linen.
And when darkness spreads before their feet,
And all the camels kneel on the ground to rest,
Mother Rebecca measures linen ell by ell
From her rings to her golden bracelet.
For those whose eyes are tired
From watching the neighborhood children,
And whose hands are thin from yearning
For a soft small body
And for the rocking of a cradle,
Mother Rachel brings healing leaves
Discovered on distant mountains,
And comforts them with a quiet word:
At any hour God may open the sealed womb.
For those who cry at night in lonely beds,
And have no one to share their sorrow,
Who talk to themselves with parched lips,
To them, Mother Leah comes quietly,
Her eyes covered with her pale hands.
—Kadya Molodowsky in *Selected Poems of Kadya Molodowsky*

Reflect

Imagine these women; they too are our foremothers. Find their stories in scripture, and imagine the stories in between the lines.

❖ What do these women have to pass on to you?

───── **THURSDAY** ─────

Grandma's Song

Sitting on the front porch, I rock away my fears,
I'm ready for the world now, mama I've got to leave.
She said, "I don't know if I want you to go out there,
It's so cold, so cruel and sometimes it won't be fair,
But I know you've got to choose your own road."

I went to see my grandma and she was rockin' too.
She started talking 'bout the old days
And the things she used to do.
Then she started singing, "Swing low, sweet chariot,
Come on and let me ride."
She said "I'm waiting for that chariot to come on
And carry your grandma's aching bones on home."

I am on my own now and grandma she's gone home,
But I am not too sad, no, cause I know she's not alone.
I can still hear her singing, "Swing low, sweet chariot,
Come on and let me ride."
She said, "I'm waiting for that chariot to come on
And carry your grandma's aching bones on home."

Now when I feel the winds blow gently on my face
I can feel my grandma, she's come to warm this place.
And I know she's watching over me,
Seeing things that I cannot see.
I close my eyes and feel her hug my soul.
—Jacqueline R. Howard and Joyce L. Williams, from Joyce and
Jacque's *Higher Ground* (cassette)

Reflect

❖ Who sang to you as you grew up?
❖ What were the songs?

The image of God as Grandmother was given to me by Susan Savell at the 1987 United Methodist Clergywomen's Consultation. This engendered within me the image of my maternal grandmother. A Polish immigrant, she brought one of her most precious treasures with her from home: a family recipe for homemade bread. Part of her legacy to my mother and to myself is that same recipe. It is slightly altered from the original; my mother and I have put our own imprint on it. The image of three generations of women's hands, all kneading the same dough, gave birth to the following poem.

The Rising of the Loaf

"It takes lots of time," the Grandmother said,
"It takes lots of time to make health-full, whole bread.
You work from the dawning past the set of the sun,
But the rising of the loaf isn't done, isn't done—
The rising of the loaf isn't done."

"It takes lots of time," the strong Mother said,
"It takes lots of time to make holy bread.
You may think you've finished, but you've hardly begun,
For the rising of the loaf isn't done, isn't done—
The rising of the loaf isn't done."

"It takes lots of time," the wise Daughter said,
"It takes lots of time to make a-new bread.
For when it's completed, a new song will be sung,
But the rising of the loaf isn't done, isn't done—
The rising of the loaf isn't done."

"It takes lots of time," the Three said with one voice,
"But when the loaf's risen, we all will rejoice.
And we'll know what we've started has truly begun,
For the rising of the loaf will be done, will be done,
For the rising of the loaf will be done."
—Susan F. Jarek-Glidden in *Wellsprings: A Journal for United Methodist Clergywomen*

Reflect

❖ What objects, rituals, recipes, stories has your family passed down from generation to generation?

Late at night Mom taps on the door of my room in the home where we are vacationing. "If you're interested, there's a view I want you to see." I walk across the hall to her room. Through the floor-to-ceiling window I see the moon hanging low over the Alaska mountains, luminous through the cloud that blankets it. Together we gaze at the landscape, she who has returned, I who see it new and now have vision to match the years of stories she told me about this land.

Mom knows of all those times growing up when I stole out of the house to watch the sky, knows how much I miss it now that I'm in the city, knows how the sky haunts me, knows that yes, I am interested in this view, this sky, this night.
—Jan L. Richardson

Reflect
❖ What landscapes do you share with the women of your family?

────── **SUNDAY** ──────

During her first pregnancy, my sister went on bed rest after going into labor in her fifth month. In the same week, her husband's sister Nancy had a brain aneurysm and died several days later. Months later, Kary and I began to create a collection of lullabies for my newborn nephew. I had an image of Nancy and Scott, meeting in the passage as she was dying while he struggled to be born. "Nancy's Song" emerged from that image.

More than blood passes from generation to generation. To our sons, as well as our daughters, we seek to pass on stories, family histories, memories to connect them. And from them we learn as well. Perhaps the children bear memories and dreams we have never touched. May we learn to listen.

Nancy's Song

Baby in the night,
strange smile on your face,
I wonder who you're dreaming of;
does she wear a gentle face?

Through the gates of night,
does she whisper, does she call;

do you see someone in the starlight
whom we can't see at all?

Do you recognize
someone who shared your father's eyes,
whose blood flowed with a kindred beat
till it ran no more?

Child, how softly you sleep;
tell me, do you keep
a memory so deep
that pulses still with life,
with hopes and dreams
that she once bore?

Are there stories in your keeping
that only she could know;
are there pictures in your star-filled eyes
that only she could show?
In your journey to this circle
and hers to a place apart,
did you pass so close together
that she gave to you her heart?

Are there songs in the shadows
that only you can hear?
In the nighttime's deepest hours,
does she whisper not to fear?
When the morning sun is breaking
and pushing back the dark,
then do you see, with dawn-filled eyes,
why she gave to you her heart?
—Jan L. Richardson

Reflect

❖ Words, images, stories, songs . . . which ones do you want to pass on, whether or not you have children?

❖ To whom will you pass on the words, images, stories, and songs?

❖ How will you do it?

Lullaby for Caroline

When you see the sun go setting,
have no fear, child,
close your eyes;
mother sees it too and sings you
oh, my darling, do not cry.

When you see the moon come rising,
have no fear, child,
softly sleep;
grandma sees it too and sings you
oh, my darling, angels keep.

When you see the stars come shining,
have no fear, child,
hush your cries;
generations bless your slumber
oh, my darling, lullaby.
—Jan L. Richardson

Blessing: *May the God who comes anew in each generation give you peace in your remembering and heart for your journey.*

46 "The Sybil of the Rhine"
Saint Hildegard of Bingen

Invocation: *Lover of Wisdom, dwell with me. Giver of life, make sweet my prayers. Bearer of vision, may I perceive you in all creatures.*

Text: Habakkuk 2:2

Context: The last of ten children born to a noble German family in 1098, her parents offered Hildegard to God as a tithe and placed her in the hermitage of Jutta, a family friend, at the age of eight. Jutta taught Hildegard monastic disciplines, and after being joined by other women, they formed a nunnery that embraced the Benedictine Rule. After Jutta's death in 1136, Hildegard became abbess of the convent.

In 1141, at the age of forty-three, Hildegard received a dramatic vision and a call to "cry out and write." Although initially plagued by self-doubt, Hildegard painstakingly began to write down, with the help of assistants, an account of her vision. Ten years later she completed this work, entitled *Scivias (Know the Ways)*.

Hildegard went on to become a prolific writer. In addition to her other visionary works, *Liber vitae meritorum (Book of Life's Merits)* and *Liber divinorum operum (Book of Divine Works)*, Hildegard also wrote an encyclopedia of natural science entitled *Book of Simple Medicine* and a companion volume entitled *Book of Composite Medicine*. Animals, herbs, trees, gems, moral symbolism, healing charms, physics, cosmology, ethics, and doctrine were but a few of the subjects about which she wrote with authority. An accomplished musician, Hildegard also composed more than seventy liturgical songs, many of which are in use today.

Called "the Sibyl of the Rhine" by many in her day, Hildegard was sought for her wisdom and sage advice on matters ranging from theology to marital difficulties. Several hundred of her letters written to abbesses, abbots, priests, kings, bishops, the Pope, laywomen, and laymen survive. Unafraid to speak out against injustice on any level of the church or society, Hildegard made a few enemies as well. Yet she persisted in speaking, preaching, and writing until the end of her life, dying in 1179 at the Benedictine abbey she founded in Bingen.

—— MONDAY ——

[God speaks]

I, the highest and fiery power, have kindled every spark of life, and I emit nothing that is deadly. I decide on all reality. With my lofty wings I fly above the globe: With wisdom I have rightly put the universe in order. I, the fiery life of divine essence, am aflame beyond the beauty of the meadows, I gleam in the waters, and I burn in the sun, moon, and stars. With every breeze, as with invisible life that contains everything, I awaken everything to life.
—From *The Book of Divine Works*, Vision One

Reflect
Whisper Hildegard's words.
❖ What do you hear?
❖ What do you see?

—— TUESDAY ——

[Words of Peace]

The second figure, on her right, had an angelic face and wings capable of flying stretched out to each side. But she [Peace] was in human form, like the other virtues. And she said:

"I rebuff the attacks of the Devil, which come against me saying, 'I will not suffer tribulation, but I will rid myself of all my adversaries. I am not willing to fear any. Whom should I fear?' But those who utter this evil speech are cast out through me; for I have been appointed always to be glad and rejoice in all good things. For the Lord Jesus abates and consoles all pain, He Who bore pain in His own body.

"And, because He is the restorer of justice, I choose to unite myself to Him and sustain Him always, free of hatred and envy and all evils. And I also choose to present a joyful face to your justice, O God."
—From *Scivias*, Vision Six

Reflect
❖ What does Peace look like in your imagining?
❖ What words does she bear to you?

Wisdom, however, pours into the chambers, that is, into the spirit of human beings, the justice of true faith through which alone God is known. There this faith presses out all the chill and dampness of vice in such a way that such things cannot germinate and grow again. At the same time faith presses out for itself all the powers of virtue in such a way that a noble wine can be poured into a goblet and offered to us as a beverage. On this account believers should rejoice and be glad in true faith in an eternal reward. They should bear before them the pennants of the good deeds they have accomplished. Thirsting for God's justice, they should now suckle the holy element from God's breast and never have enough of it, so that they will be forever refreshed by the vision of God. For the holy element outshines all human understanding. When we grasp justice in this way, we shall surrender to it, taste virtue, and drink. We shall be strengthened by it as the veins of someone who drinks become filled with wine. We shall never go to excess like persons drunk on wine who lose control of themselves and no longer know what they are doing. In this way the just love God of whom they can never have too much but from whom they have bliss forever and ever.

—From *Book of Divine Works*, Vision Two

Reflect

❖ For what do you thirst?

❖ What gives you sustenance?

——— **THURSDAY** ———

Love says to you: "My desire is to abide with you and I would like you to bring me to your bed and be devoted to me in loving friendship. For when you compassionately touch and cleanse the wounds of others, then I am reclining on your bed. And when you meet simple, honest people with goodwill and in a godly way, then I am united to you in loving friendship."

—From a letter to Archbishop Eberhard of Salzburg

Reflect

❖ And what does Love say to you of her desire?

❖ In what touching of wounds, what sharing of joys, has Love inhabited your intimate spaces?

——— FRIDAY ———

Love streams down with the outpouring water of the Holy Spirit, and in this love is the peace of God's goodness. And humility prepares a garden with all the fruit-bearing trees of God's grace, containing all the green of God's gifts. Compassion, on the other hand, drips balsam for all the needs that adhere to the human condition. This sound of love rings in harmony with every hymn of thanks for salvation. Through humility it sounds in the heights where love beholds God and victoriously battles against pride. This love calls out in compassion with a pleading yet lovely voice. It gathers the poor and the lame around itself and begs so intensely for the help of the Holy Spirit that this same love is able to bring everything to fulfillment through good works. Love sounds in the tents where the saints shine on the thrones they have built for themselves in this world.
—From a letter to the five Burgundian abbots

Reflect
Let yourself rest in the garden that Hildegard describes, delighting in God's gifts, receiving sustenance for your needs. For this moment you don't need to think, you don't need to do. Just rest . . . just rest.

——— SATURDAY ———

And it is written: "The Spirit of the Lord fills the Earth." This means that no creature, whether visible or invisible, lacks a spiritual life. And those creatures that human beings do not perceive seek their understanding until humans do perceive them. For it is from the power of the seed that the buds sprout. And it is from the buds that the fruit of the tree springs forth. The clouds too have their course to run. The moon and the stars flame in fire. The trees shoot forth buds because of the power in their seeds. Water has a delicacy and a lightness of motion like the wind. This is why it springs up from the Earth and pours itself into running brooks. Even the Earth has moisture and mist.

All creatures have something visible and invisible. The visible is weak; the invisible is strong and alive. This [the invisible] seeks to get through to human understanding because human beings do not see it. And yet these invisible realities are forces in the workings of the Holy Spirit.
—From a letter to Bishop Eberhard II of Bamberg

Reflect

  ❖ What do you think of the spiritual life of creatures, of creation?
  ❖ What do their spirits have to say to ours?

—— **SUNDAY** ——

DE SANCTA MARIA
To Mary

Hail to you, O greenest, most fertile branch!
You budded forth amidst breezes and winds
in search of the knowledge of all that is holy.
When the time was ripe
your own branch brought forth blossoms.
Hail, greetings to you!
The heat of the sun exudes sweat from you
like the balsam's perfume.
In you, the most stunning flower has blossomed
and gives off its sweet odor to all the herbs and roots,
which were dry and thirsting before your arrival.
Now they spring forth in fullest green!
Because of you, the heavens give dew to the grass,
the whole Earth rejoices;
Abundance of grain comes from Earth's womb
and on its stalks and branches the birds nest.
And, because of you, nourishment is given to the human family
and great rejoicing to those gathered round the table.
And so, in you O gentle Virgin,
is every fullness of joy, everything that Eve rejected.
Now let endless praise resound to the Most High!
—From *Songs*

Reflect

  ❖ What rejoicing, fullness of joy, endless praise do you want to express?

—— **Meditation** ——

Prophecies

The young woman from Palestine was emphatic.

"Prophecy is *not* for sale!" She wasn't referring
to the cheapness some now pass off as prophecy,
the predictions of rapture and hellfire to come
that some embrace for solid ground in these
quicksands of time.

No, it was with the breath
of Miriam and Deborah, Isaiah and Amos that
she breathed, remembering those whose prophecies
stood not as a foretelling but a forthtelling—
speaking forth the truth about what was happening NOW,
telling out the tales that others wanted to ignore.

I doubt these prophets ever passed the hat
because what they said wasn't often popular, and
more than one risked death because they
refused to sell their prophecies, refused to
shape them into something that could more easily
fit their listeners' ears.

The young woman who has seen the rivers of blood
in her homeland has also heard the breath of Christians
at the door who believe that these are the days
of prophecies being fulfilled. Casting their lots
in the Holy Land, they gamble for the cloak of rapture
while the holy ones die all around them.

She just reminded me of you, Hildegard, that's all.
Prophecies and visions.
The real ones don't often make you rich.
—Jan L. Richardson

Blessing: *Go in peace, beloved of God. May the wind of God blow
within you, stirring your soul and awakening you to life.*

47 In the Garden
A Celebration

Invocation: *Created in your image, loving God, I come to you. Pass your healing hand over any wounds, any shame, any fears you find within me and lead me to the feast you have prepared.*

Text: Isaiah 58:11

Context: Communion is important to me, if you haven't already noticed. I have struggled mightily with images and words I have found at the table, even fasting from Communion for a time in hope of gaining more clarity. What has emerged is a conviction that the Christ whom we encounter at the Communion table calls us to bring our whole selves to that place and to *celebrate* the bodies into which Christ has poured his spirit—black, brown, yellow, and white bodies; sick bodies and well bodies; young, old, female, male bodies; bodies of differing sizes and abilities.

The daily readings that unfold this week find their basis in a Communion liturgy that I shared during a women's retreat one spring. The planners had invited the speakers to lead us in thinking about our changing bodies. In the informal liturgy that we celebrated in a circle on the final morning, I tried to weave together images of the blessedness of our bodies, the hope of resurrection and new life, and the spring that surrounded us.

—— MONDAY ——

The First Lesson

How beautiful you are, my love,
   how very beautiful!
Your eyes are doves
   behind your veil.
Your hair is like a flock of goats,
   moving down the slopes of Gilead.
Your teeth are like a flock of shorn ewes
   that have come up from the washing,

all of which bear twins,
    and not one among them is bereaved.
Your lips are like a crimson thread,
    and your mouth is lovely.
Your cheeks are like halves of a pomegranate
    behind your veil.
Your neck is like the tower of David,
    built in courses;
on it hang a thousand bucklers,
    all of them shields of warriors.
Your two breasts are like two fawns,
    twins of a gazelle,
    that feed among the lilies.
Until the day breathes
    and the shadows flee,
I will hasten to the mountain of myrrh
    and the hill of frankincense.
You are altogether beautiful, my love;
    there is no flaw in you.
—Song of Solomon 4:1-7

Reflect

❖   How often do you hear texts from the Song of Solomon in church? Consider reading the Song today or piece by piece this week. Sit with the images and let them speak as a counterpoint to the readings. Give particular attention to what the Song says about our bodies, created in the image of God.

——— **TUESDAY** ———

The Second Lesson

My beloved speaks and says to me:
"Arise, my love, my fair one,
    and come away;
for now the winter is past,
    the rain is over and gone.
The flowers appear on the earth;
    the time of singing has come,
and the voice of the turtledove
    is heard in our land.

The fig tree puts forth its figs,
   and the vines are in blossom;
   they give forth fragrance.
Arise, my love, my fair one,
   and come away."
—Song of Solomon 2:10-13

Reflect

❖ With body and soul, to where do you want to "arise . . . and come away"?

────── **WEDNESDAY** ──────

Proclamation

How little we hear these texts in the church! Yet how deeply they speak to the blessedness of our bodies, to the delight that being created in the image of God brings us. The poet was unabashed in sharing such delight, particularly in our first lesson.

Many of you have heard me speak of my friend Edward, heard the letter I wrote to him in which I spoke of longing to be able to touch him over the distance, not knowing how many more times we'd be able to do that in person, and wishing I had a balm to heal him in body and in spirit. Several weeks ago, during Lent, Edward died of complications from AIDS. I went to Atlanta for the memorial service, a service that Edward had planned himself. And among the scriptures that he chose to have read was this second one from the Song of Solomon. I was struck by the images of resurrection, of hope, of the passing of winter and the coming of spring. For me, it was a message from Edward—that something lies beyond, that new life continually waits to be reborn.

—Jan L. Richardson

Reflect

❖ What words have loved ones sent back to you—through scriptures, stories, songs, places?

────── **THURSDAY** ──────

Proclamation continued

I returned to Atlanta after Easter, a month after Edward died, and visited with Edward's friend Ray. One morning we went to the Atlanta Botanical Gardens and spent a couple of hours there. After walking through the gardens and eating lunch, we found a couple of chairs in the sunlight. There among the flowers, we talked. We spoke of missing, of loss. We dreamed of the future, of our hopes. We told stories. And we remembered. There in the garden, we remembered.

That time in the garden with Ray transformed me. To hear the words that Edward chose from Song of Solomon was one thing. But to see, with another who had been close to him, physical evidence of the persistence of new life and winter's turning to spring offered healing as nothing else had. It was an act of re-membering for me, of putting Edward's life back together, as well as my own.

The feast of Communion calls us to remember. We remember what Christ gave to us, and we remember all those, like Edward, who have shared in the feast with us. I believe that when we celebrate Communion, we celebrate not only with those physically present—those in this circle—but also with all who have shaped who we are, who have shaped us as the body of Christ. We remember, and we are re-membered.

—Jan L. Richardson

Reflect

❖ What do you long to be re-membered—put back together—within yourself?

❖ What spaces and times do you give yourself for remembering, for re-membering?

——— Friday ———

Blessing the Bread

The sacrament of Communion has everything to do with our bodies. Yet as women, we often have been taught to be ashamed of our bodies, to hide them, to be embarrassed about how they look and what they can or can't do. But on the night before Jesus died, when he shared a final meal with his intimate friends, he took bread, blessed it, broke it, and said, "This is my body, which is given for you. And as often as you eat this, do it in remembrance of me." In so doing, Jesus blessed and affirmed bodies as creative and holy vessels of new life.

—Jan L. Richardson

Reflect

- ❖ What are the first words you think of to describe your body?
- ❖ What messages have you grown up with about your body?

Blessing the Cup

As women, we often have been taught to be ashamed of our blood, to be embarrassed about "the curse," to believe in its uncleanliness. But on the night before Jesus died, he took the cup, blessed it, and said, "This is my blood, poured out for you and for many for the forgiveness of sins. Do this, as often as you drink of it, in remembrance of me." In so doing, Jesus blessed and affirmed the life-giving, creative power of blood.

—Jan L. Richardson

Reflect

- ❖ What words have you been taught about women's blood?
- ❖ Where is the blessing within those words?

————— SUNDAY —————

Sharing the Bread and Cup: Reflections

As we passed the bread and cup to one another, first in silence and then in song, I remembered how painful it was to watch Edward, after he was diagnosed with HIV, stop drinking from the cup and instead dip his bread into the cup. Although it was extremely unlikely that the virus could be spread through sharing the cup, I think it was Edward's way of showing concern for those who might not understand. It has been important to me to remember that there are hundreds of ways to celebrate communion in the body of Christ. We celebrate whenever we find ways to be the body of Christ with and for one another. Hundreds of years ago, St. Teresa of Avila wrote, "Christ has no body now on earth but yours; no hands but yours, no feet but yours." Communion happens wherever we work to re-member the body of Christ, to provide healing, to enable wholeness of body and spirit for our sisters and brothers. In doing so, we dream and work toward a day when all will once again eat of the same loaf and drink of the same cup.

—Jan L. Richardson

In the Garden ~ 369

Reflect

❖ How do you celebrate communion with others?

❖ To what places of healing and delight has this led you?

—— **Meditation** ——

Emergence
  For Edward

Flowers are born knowing
that it is okay to push
to grow
to open
to turn their faces
to the sun,
shameless
and wild.

And somehow I knew
it was okay
to open to you,
to turn my face
to your unexpected sunlight,
to brush against
your unimagined warmth.

And somehow I know
even in days
of killing frost
that somewhere
in another garden
we shall meet again.
—Jan L. Richardson

—— ❖ ——

Blessing: *May you always have a garden to return to and a feast to restore you for the journey.*

48 Wisdom in the Wilderness
The Desert Mothers

Invocation: *God of wilderness, God of wildness, lead me to the quiet places of my soul. In stillness, in openness, may I find my strength.*

Text: Psalm 63:1-8

Context: For centuries, the monastic life has attracted many people seeking to embody Christian faith in a radical way. As solitaries or as members of an organized monastic community, women and men have lived according to the rhythms of prayer and work—rhythms handed down through the generations.

We can trace the roots of monasticism to the early church in Egypt, where by the fourth century women and men had begun to establish communities in the desert. Significantly removed from the distractions of the city, they embraced lives of prayer, humility, simplicity, love, and celibacy. Each community was led by a teacher called the Amma (mother) or Abba (father).

In a time when childbirth endangered the lives of women of all classes and men typically controlled the lives of their families, the monastic life offered an appealing alternative to many women. Roberta Bondi notes in her book *To Pray and to Love* that this choice "was, at the most basic level, to step into a realm of freedom from slavery to her body as well as freedom from the control of male relatives." These women claimed Jesus' vision of the world in which a person's true identity came from living in the kingdom.

Although the monastics lived in the desert, their wisdom born of a life focused on love drew many city-dwellers. The few sayings of the Ammas that remain challenge us to examine our own routines of living, our own rhythms of prayer and work.

—— **MONDAY** ——

In the beginning there are a great many battles and a good deal of suffering for those who are advancing towards God and afterwards, ineffable joy. It is like those who wish to light a fire; at first they are choked by the smoke and cry, and by this means obtain what they seek [as it is said: "Our God is a consuming fire" (Heb. 12:24)]: so we also must kindle the divine fire in ourselves through tears and hard work.

—Amma Syncletica in *The Sayings of the Desert Fathers*, translated by Benedicta Ward

Reflect
❖ What practices of the spirit enable you to kindle the divine fire within yourself?

—— **TUESDAY** ——

There are many who live in the mountains and behave as if they were in the town, and they are wasting their time. It is possible to be a solitary in one's mind while living in a crowd, and it is possible for one who is a solitary to live in the crowd of his [or her] own thoughts.

—Amma Syncletica in *The Sayings of the Desert Fathers*

Reflect
❖ Where do you find solitude amidst the crowdedness of your life?

—— **WEDNESDAY** ——

Neither asceticism, nor vigils nor any kind of suffering are able to save, only true humility can do that. There was an anchorite who was able to banish the demons; and he asked them, "What makes you go away? Is it fasting?" They replied, "We do not eat or drink," "Is it vigils?" They replied, "We do not sleep." "Is it separation from the world?" "We live in the deserts." "What power sends you away then?" They said, "Nothing can overcome us, but only humility." "Do you see how humility is victorious over the demons?"

—Amma Theodora in *The Sayings of the Desert Fathers*

Reflect
Humility, one of those elusive qualities, resides more in letting go than in taking on and doing.
❖ How does humility emerge in your life?

—— **THURSDAY** ——

Humility as the early monastics describe it has nothing to do with passivity, nor anything to do with deliberately cultivating a poor self-image. Being a doormat is not being humble, nor is giving up the self in order to serve the needs, desires, and whims of another person who is not God. Humility is not sniveling, nor is it daydreaming gentle thoughts while the world's violence goes on around it.

Humility is difficult. Much of what is depicted in the literature seems nearly impossible to carry out and it certainly is without the grace of God's help. Humility itself is countercultural, as it was in the fourth, fifth, and sixth centuries. It wreaks havoc with all individualistic values: it is not a "live and let live" attitude. It does not say "it doesn't matter what you believe as long as you're sincere." It does not believe that Christian values are purely subjective, each person negotiating her or his own values with God in private. It calls for the renunciation of all deep attachments to what the world holds dear: goods, social advancement, the satisfaction of appetites at the expense of others, the right to dominate others in any personal relationship.

But if humility is hard, it is also powerful. Humility has to do with taking and accepting radical responsibility for the things that happen in life.
—Roberta C. Bondi in *To Love as God Loves*

Reflect
- ❖ How does this definition of humility compare with what you've learned about being humble?

Reflect on your own attachment "to what the world holds dear."

——— **FRIDAY** ———

If I prayed God that all [people] should approve of my conduct, I should find myself a penitent at the door of each one, but I shall rather pray that my heart may be pure towards all.
—Amma Sarah in *The Sayings of the Desert Fathers*

Reflect
- ❖ When have you spent time and energy being penitent at others' doors when you could have been dwelling in the space that God has prepared for you?

——— **SATURDAY** ———

It is good to live in peace, for the wise [one] practices perpetual prayer. It is truly a great thing for a virgin or a monk to live in peace, especially for the younger ones. However, you should realize that as soon as you intend to live in peace, at once evil comes and weighs down your soul through *accidie*, faintheartedness, and evil thoughts. It also attacks your body through sickness, debility, weakening of the knees, and all the members. It dissipates the strength of soul and body, so that one believes one is ill and no longer able to pray. But if we are vigilant, all these temptations fall away.

—Amma Theodora in *The Sayings of the Desert Fathers*

Reflect

❖ What are the things, or who are the people, that tug at your ability to live in peace?

—————— **SUNDAY** ——————

I have learned from the monastic teachers that prayer is a back and forth movement between us and God in the whole of our lives, between God's continual grace and our continual response. It is also a movement between our receptivity and friendly silence in God's presence and our continual reflection on the meaning of what we learn about God, ourselves, and others from the experience of our prayer as we grow in love.

I have learned that prayer is also a movement between us and the whole Christian community, ancient and modern, as we learn from it, critique it, find our feet in it, and are sustained by it. In our local communities prayer is the undergirding of our worship, our deep friendships, and sometimes even painful divisions. It connects us with the larger community of living Christians around the world whose lives are different from our own and who may not on the surface even share a form of Christianity similar to ours. Prayer also connects us with the body of Christ through the ages, the "cloud of witnesses" that continuously surrounds us, the prayers of those Christians who lived before us and who have left us the legacy of their prayers and insights.

I have learned that prayer also connects us with ourselves; it is the link between our new selves that are always being transformed into God's loving image and our old selves with which we must come to terms if we are to be transformed. By it we are able to discover who we are and move toward who we are to become. By it we become able to love, to care for the people who have been entrusted to us: our immediate neighbor and our far neighbors in the whole of God's world.

—Roberta C. Bondi in *To Pray and to Love*

Reflect

Grace and response. Receptivity and reflection. The individual, the community, and God.

❖ How is your prayer an ongoing movement between and among these?

❖ How do you long to pray?

—— **Meditation** ——

Rhythms

In the desert
it is easier to see
the unfolding of things.
With little shelter
one perceives how
day flows into night
and night gives birth to day.
And in this way
to survive is a process
and to live
means learning to dwell
in the gaps,
in the shifting of time
and space.

And so
this is about rhythms,
about choices;
about living
about dying
about dryness
about sustenance
about embracing
about letting go
about pursuing
about tarrying
about giving up
about taking on
about poverty
about true wealth

about restlessness
about peace
about hunger
about feasting
about emptying
about running over
about dwelling
about stillness itself.
—Jan L. Richardson

———— ❖ ————

Blessing: *Make me wise to your rhythms, O Holy One. May my life be a pleasing offering, a living prayer that connects me with you, with others, and with myself.*

49 Family Values
Ruth, Naomi, and Orpah

Invocation: *God of the journey, accompany me along the unfamiliar paths. Grace me with companions of the heart, that I may be at home in all places.*

Text: Ruth 1:1-18

Context: Three women stand together on a dusty road. As they talk, weep, wail, touch, and kiss, their movements reveal three distinct individuals who stand on the edge of their lives. In a pocket of solitude along this road, the women of this circle draw on their own visions and resources to decide for themselves the path each will take.

In this borderland between Moab and Bethlehem, between the known and the unknown, these women define themselves as they enact the choices they allow one another to make. Unrelated by blood, these strangers who have become family work out among themselves how they will relate to one another in the days to come.

Their choices challenge us to ponder what "family" means. For Orpah, ties of blood beckon her to return to her family of origin. For Ruth, ties of shared experience and history summon her to journey on with her family of choice. We need not consider either choice better, although Ruth's may be more surprising, in that she chooses a cross-cultural relationship with a woman rather than with a man of her own nationality.

These readings, which focus primarily on Ruth's choice, invite us to explore the challenges and possibilities of relationships among women. As we enter into the story of those who chose to travel together, we remember all women with whom we journey as companions.

 **MONDAY**

Orpah: The Return

Some say
I took the easy way,

but the return
was still a journey.

Some say
that my homegoing
was the path
much more secure,
but with each step
I wondered
what lay hidden
beyond each turn.

Some say
I could not bear
Naomi's unfamiliar road,
but ten years
and a newfound life
leave childhood paths
somewhat less certain.

Some say
I feared too much
the strange new land,
its foreign hills;
but they miss
my own adventure:
to reconcile
my once-known landscape
with the contours
of my changing self.

Some say
I took the easy way,
but I say
the return
is still a journey.
—Jan L. Richardson

Reflect

❖ When have you tried to return to what was once home?
❖ What happened?

From a cultural perspective, Ruth has chosen death over life. She has disavowed the solidarity of family; she has abandoned national identity; and she has renounced religious affiliation. In the entire epic of Israel, only Abraham matches this radicality, but then he had a call from God (Gen. 12:1-5). Divine promise motivated and sustained his leap of faith. Besides, Abraham was a man, with a wife and other possessions to accompany him. Ruth stands alone; she possesses nothing. No God has called her; no deity has promised her blessing; no human being has come to her aid. She lives and chooses without a support group, and she knows that the fruit of her decision may well be the emptiness of rejection, indeed of death. Consequently, not even Abraham's leap of faith surpasses this decision of Ruth's. And there is more. Not only has Ruth broken with family, country, and faith, but she has also reversed sexual allegiance. A young woman has committed herself to the life of an old woman rather than to the search for a husband, and she has made this commitment not "until death do us part" but beyond death. One female has chosen another female in a world where life depends upon men. There is no more radical decision in all the memories of Israel.

—Phyllis Trible in *God and the Rhetoric of Sexuality*

Reflect
Ponder the radical decisions made by women you know, or by yourself.

❖ What made the decisions radical?
❖ What gave you or them the strength for those decisions?

—— **WEDNESDAY** ——

Out of her love, Ruth acts, out of the passion of her heart. Her courage, just as the courage of . . . the Mothers of the Plaza de Mayo, comes from her heart, from her capacity to love in the face of fear and hopelessness. The courage to choose, to be a redemptive, liberating, whole-making presence in a world gone mad with greed, fear, and violence—that courage rests in our passions, our ability to love, not authority and power, but each other and those who suffer under structures that hurt them. For we must go where our hearts lead us. We must choose our people and our God on the basis of what we love, not on what we fear.

—Rita Nakashima Brock, from "The Courage to Choose/The Commitment to Being Chosen" in *And Blessed Is She: Sermons by Women*

Reflect

❖ If you could do absolutely anything, make any choice out of love and longing, what would you do?

❖ If you aren't doing it, why not?

—— **THURSDAY** ——

Companion: *com*, "together" and *panis*, "bread." The companion shares bread with another. In the fields of Israel during the first harvest after famine, Ruth gleans wheat for the making of bread. She shares bread with Naomi as her mother-in-law shares life, home, land, and God with Ruth. The prayer of companionship, sharing bread, releases the Holy into the world through a communion of Mystery present in the most common, in All-That-Is. . . . Bread represents whatever is most common, most essential, most necessary to life itself. It is so simple as to be almost overlooked unless it is missing. Without it we cannot live long. When we break and share bread together, we bring about companionship, extend life, and reveal the Holy One.

The Ruth-woman sings the song of bread. Her God is revealed in the eyes of the ones she companions. She is woman of the hearth incarnating in her life and work that first awareness women ever had of a Sacredness at the center of the circle of life—a Sacredness creating the circle. God is the seed women planted in primal times, the grain women harvested, the bread they baked and shared. Ruth is the mother of Eucharist, of Communion.

The Song

> I am Ruth.
> I remember.
> I never leave my land, for You are my Land,
>> Nor my people, for they are all that is born from Your Womb.
>> Oh great and holy Earth,
>> I remember you from the beginning
>> So that everywhere is my hearth and my home
>> And no field of grain is strange to me.
>> I will sow the seed, gather grain, and bake bread;
>> And I myself will be the bread I bake and break and share
>> As you are the seed and the earth where it is sown,
>> You are the oven of transformation
>> And the nourishment.
>> We are one body,

The Earth,
Contained in endless Love.
All present and alive in a crust of bread.
You are not Unknown,
You are the Bread.

—Christin Lore Weber in *Blessings: A WomanChrist Reflection on the Beatitudes*

Reflect

Ruth learned to live, to break bread, to sing in a strange land.

❖ When you have left a place to live in a new one or a strange one, what sustained you?
❖ How did you learn to live there?

—— **FRIDAY** ——

From a letter to a friend who wants to have a child and is debating between adopting a child or giving birth to a child herself.

Dear Lesley,

I've been thinking about our conversation concerning your desire to have children. You talked about the importance of continuing your mother's bloodline.

When I was a child at Matlow Creek Baptist Church I sang, "There's Power in the Blood"—a good old Baptist blood song. And there is power there. Throughout Christianity the blood has been involved with great meaning and power. But there is also power in the *story*. For me right now the greater power resides in the story.

It is in the stories of women that I find strength. The stories I work with and connect with and tell are powerful for me. There I find role models and sisters, and our stories mingle together to produce a rich tapestry of life.

Regardless of whether your children have your grandmother's blood, they will have her story. They will have your mother's story and your story. They will have Linda's story and Carol's story and Betsey's story. They will have all of our stories to draw strength from. We are all connected by our stories and by being a part of one another's story. Your children will be connected to your grandmother, and she will become a part of your story.

I don't know if any of this helps with your decision making, but I wanted to share it with you.

Shalom!
—Carolyn Mathis

Reflect

❖ It is said that blood is thicker than water, but what stories flow among you and others that connect you as family?

—— SATURDAY ——

But now, Elsa, look at us. New things are happening here too. Much of this has been started by women, in the peace movement, the women's movement, the quest for justice and a new life-style. I know how eagerly you study the books of feminist theologians. I also know that you have great hopes of a "global sisterhood," which was the motto of the women's pre-assembly meeting before the WCC [World Council of Churches] Sixth Assembly in Vancouver. When I spoke to the women who attended it from all over the world, I said that sisterhood is something we have to create and build; it does not simply exist because we happen to be women. I also said it can only come about if it is global, if it includes the human condition of our sisters in Asia, Africa and Latin America, in East and West.

Sisterhood means trying to develop independent relationships among women as something of equal birth and worth alongside brotherhood. I said that we need global sisterhood not against men but for our own sakes.

But what is sisterhood exactly? Is sisterhood something different from brotherhood? Does it have a different tone or range, does it reach higher or go deeper? Is it better, more enduring, more reliable, honest, generous, sensitive than brotherhood? Does it bind us, women, more closely together? Is it in fact true that sisterhood can only be global? Is sisterhood an indispensable stage on the road to full humanity for women and men together? And if so, why? So many questions, so many hopes. . . .

Dear Elsa, at the risk of sounding sentimental, I want to end my letter with this thought: Let us keep sewing away at the tear in the mantle of sisterhood so that we may turn it into something whole, something more honest, more all-embracing, more lasting in which we can wrap the cold, hungry, trembling earth and bring new life to the worried and confused people on it. Can we agree on that? Then let us try!

—Bärbel von Wartenberg-Potter, from "Letter to Elsa" in *We Will Not Hang Our Harps on the Willows*

Reflect

❖ What is sisterhood?
❖ What risks does intimate connection with the lives of other women bring, especially those whose lives seem different?

❖ What are the dark sides, the wounds, the challenges, and the blessings of such relationships?

—— **SUNDAY** ——

Arriving at Roxbury, arriving at Barbara's. . . . By the end of the evening of our first visit together, Barbara comes into the front room where she has made a bed for me. She kisses me. Then grabbing my shoulders she says, very solid-like, "we're sisters." I nod, put myself into bed, and roll around with this word, *sisters*, for two hours before sleep takes on. I earned this with Barbara. It is not a given between us—Chicana and Black—to come to see each other as sisters. This is not a given. I keep wanting to repeat over and over and over again, the pain and shock of difference, the joy of commonness, the exhilaration of meeting through incredible odds against it.

But the passage is *through*, not over, not by, not around, but through.
—Cherríe Moraga in *This Bridge Called My Back: Writings by Radical Women of Color*

Reflect
❖ Where are you building this passage?
❖ With whom are you building it?

—— **Meditation** ——

Two Step

Two step lightly
on the edge
of foreign lands,
seeking home;

two step tightly
in a pledge,
spinning visions
of their own.

Two step boldly,
crossing lines,
breathing life
through ragged bones;

two step wholly,

lives entwined,
breaking bread
and dancing home.
—Jan L. Richardson

———— ❖ ————

Blessing: *May each step of your journey be graced with the love of God who calls us to be kin with one another.*

50 I'll Take Freedom
Narratives of Enslaved Women

Invocation: *Creating and sustaining God, your love for your people has carried us through the ages. Open our eyes, O God, that we may see your strong hand of freedom; open our ears, that we may hear your words of justice; open our hearts, that we may forever remember the stories of your people.*

Text: Luke 4:16-19

Context: In 1619, a ship landed in Jamestown, Virginia. Aboard the ship were the first black Africans to be taken from their own country and brought as enslaved people to the land that eventually became the United States. More slave ships followed. James Mellon notes in his book *Bullwhip Days* that the slave trade, "which had begun as a trickle, quickly became a torrent, until by 1860 Abraham Lincoln felt compelled to declaim with distress and foreboding that almost one-sixth of the people then living in the so-called 'land of the free' were in fact slaves."

The African people and their descendants endured a wide variety of treatments under slavery in the "land of the free." Slaveholders frequently broke up families in the process of buying and selling those whom they treated as commodities. Often slaveholders used force in the form of whippings and beatings as well as restraints such as chains, bits, and haloes to control the enslaved people. While stories exist of slaves being treated "like family" or "almost as friends," even those most well-cared-for still were bound by a tenacious thread. And few, if any, were encouraged or even allowed to maintain the traditions woven through thousands of years of African heritage.

In many cases, the slaveholders treated the enslaved women as breeders and would pair them with male slaves chosen by the slaveholder in an attempt to produce even stronger, healthier slaves. Many enslaved women also found themselves at the mercy of their own master's sexual whims, and delivery of a mulatto child bearing the master's features was not uncommon. Such a delivery could generate both the verbal and physical wrath of the mistress of the plantation.

The surviving narratives of enslaved women reveal spirits that could not be bound. Little more than a century since the Emancipation Proclamation, their words challenge us not only to hear their own stories but also to ask ourselves where we stand in the continuing struggle for freedom.

—— **MONDAY** ——

'Bout de middle of de evenin', up rid my young marster on his hoss, an' up driv' two strange white mens in a buggy. Dey hitch deir hosses an' come in de house, which skeered me. Den, one o' de strangers said, "Git yo' clothes, Mary. We has bought yo' from Mr. Shorter." I c'menced cryin' an' beggin' Mr. Shorter not to let 'em take me away. But he said, "Yes, Mary, I has sole yer, an' yer must go wid' em."

Den, dose strange mens, whose names I ain't never knowed, tuk me an' put me in de buggy an' driv' off wid me, me hollerin' at de top o' my voice an' callin' my ma. Den, dem speculataws begin to sing loud, jes' to drown out my hollerin'.

Us passed the very fiel' whar Paw an' all my folks wuz wukkin', an' I calt out as loud as I could an' as long as I could see 'em, "Good-bye, Ma! Good-bye, Ma!" But she never heard me. Naw sah, dem white mens wuz singin' so loud, Ma couldn' hear me. An' she couldn' see me, 'cause dey had me pushed down out o' sight on de flo' o' de buggy.

I ain't never seed nor heard tell o' my ma an' paw, an' brothers, an' sisters, from dat day to dis.

—Mary Ferguson in *Bullwhip Days: The Slaves Remember*, edited by James Mellon

Reflect
Mourn . . . for all the families torn apart, then and now.

—— **TUESDAY** ——

Well, I was just a little girl, about eight years old, staying in Beaufort at de missus' house, polishing her brass andirons and scrubbing her floors, when one morning she says to me, "Janie, take this note down to Mr. Wilcox' wholesale store, on Bay Street, and fetch me back de package de clerk gave you."

I took de note. De man read it, and he say, "Uh-huh." Den, he turn away, and he come back wid a little package which I took back to de missus.

She open it, when I bring it in, and say, "Go upstairs, Miss!"

It was a raw cowhide strap, 'bout two feet long, and she started to pourin' it on me all de way upstairs. I didn't know what she was whippin' me 'bout, but she pour it on, and she pour it on.

Turrectly she say, "You can't say 'Marse Henry,' Miss? You can't say 'Marse Henry'?"

"Yes'm! Yes'm! I kin say 'Marse Henry'!"

Marse Henry was just a little boy 'bout three or four years old—come 'bout half way up to me. She wanted me to say "Massa" to him—a baby!
—Rebecca Grant in *Bullwhip Days*

Reflect
Pray . . . for those beaten into submission in Rebecca's day and ours.

———— **WEDNESDAY** ————

In the eleventh year of my age, my master sent me to another farm, several miles from my parents, brothers, and sisters, which was a great trouble to me. At last I grew so lonely and sad I thought I should die, if I did not see my mother. I asked the overseer if I might go, but being positively denied, I concluded to go without his knowledge. When I reached home my mother was away. I set off and walked twenty miles before I found her. I staid with her for several days, and we returned together. Next day I was sent back to my new place, which renewed my sorrow. At parting, my mother told me that I had "nobody in the wide world to look to but God." These words fell upon my heart with pondrous weight, and seemed to add to my grief. I went back repeating as I went, "none but God in the wide world." On reaching the farm, I found the overseer was displeased at me for going without his liberty. He tied me with a rope, and gave me some stripes of which I carried the marks for weeks.

After this time, finding as my mother said, I had none in the world to look to but God, I betook myself to prayer, and in every lonely place I found an altar. I mourned sore like a dove and chattered forth my sorrow, moaning in the corners of the field, and under the fences.
—Elizabeth, from "Memoir of Old Elizabeth, a Coloured Woman" in *Six Women's Slave Narratives*

Reflect
Remember . . . a time when you felt bereft and alone. Gather with those who did, and do.

—— THURSDAY ——

Marster neber 'low he slaves to go to chu'ch. Dey hab big holes out in de fiel's dey git down in and pray. Dey done dat way 'cause de white folks didn' want 'em to pray. Dey uster pray for freedom. I dunno how dey larn to pray, 'cause dey warn't no preachers come roun' to teach 'em. I reckon de Lawd jis' mek 'em know how to pray.

—Ellen Butler in *Bullwhip Days*

Reflect

- ❖ Imagine . . . what might they have prayed?
- ❖ What might those who live without freedom today pray?
- ❖ How do you pray with them?

—— FRIDAY ——

My white mother used to give it [oil for typhoid fever] to me, but she did not let me know what she was giving me, for she put some molasses in the oil and cooked them, so I should not know. I would not have known if I had not seen her one night have the old bottle in her hand putting the oil in the kettle, which she was making ready for me, and I looked up and saw what it was and, as young ones will do, did not want to take molasses and butter which I had been taking so long, for I had to take it on every night or I could not speak.

Later on she moved from the place where she was and bought another farm where it was not near the water, as the doctor thought that was not a good place for me to be, and I was not sick so much as I had been at the former.

The first hard spell of sickness on this farm was the fever that I was sick of at the time that she took sick of the yellow jaundice, and she turned as yellow as anything could be. She went home with that awful malady, thinking of me and of what my future should be in God's hands, to love and bless the world in which I should live if it should be the will of [God] who knows the future of all the people that live on this earth.

So God has been a father and a loving mother and all else to me, and sometimes there has been enough of trials in this life to make me almost forget that I had this strong arm to save me from these trials and temptations; but when I fly to [God] I find all and in all in [God].

—Kate Drumgoold, from "A Slave Girl's Story" in *Six Women's Slave Narratives*

Reflect

Remember . . . times you have flown to God.

❖ What have you found there, and whom?

SATURDAY

Glory! Glory! Yes, child, de Negroes are free, an' when dey knew dat dey were free—oh, baby!—dey began to sing:

> Mammy, don't yo' cook no mo',
> Yo' are free, yo' are free!
> Rooster, don't yo' crow no mo',
> Yo' are free, yo' are free!
> Ole hen, don't yo' lay no mo',
> Yo' free, yo' free!

—Fannie Berry in *Bullwhip Days*

Reflect

Rejoice! . . . in the songs of freedom, in celebration in the midst of struggle.

SUNDAY

What Ise lak bes', freedom or slavery? Well, 'tis dis away. In slavery, Ise owned nothin', an' never owed nothin', an', white man, Ise didn't know much. In freedom, Ise own de home, owe de people, an' raise de fam'ly. All dat cause me de worriment. In slavery, Ise have no worriment, but Ise take de freedom.

—Margrett Nillin in *Bullwhip Days*

Reflect

❖ Ponder . . . what would you be willing to do to stay free?
❖ What will you do to ensure freedom for others?

Meditation

I'll Take Freedom

I'll take Freedom.
Yes, I'll take her
across this burning field,
beyond this crushing border.

I'll take Freedom.
I'll take her whole,
waiting and past ready.

I'll take Freedom
far past those grabbing,
clutching, choking hands.

I'll take her
into the heart of the night,
fly with her across the sky.

I'll take Freedom,
take her even if it means
her sister Worriment
and her brother Fear come too.
But I won't hear them much
because Freedom
will be singing LOUD
and STRONG
and she will be LAUGHING
when I take her.

Oh, I'll take Freedom.
I'll take Freedom, yes.
—Jan L. Richardson

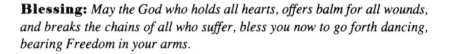

Blessing: *May the God who holds all hearts, offers balm for all wounds,
and breaks the chains of all who suffer, bless you now to go forth dancing,
bearing Freedom in your arms.*

51   Remembering in Two Voices
Joy Harjo and Kary Kublin

Invocation: *From your hand, creating God, come the shape of the land, the warmth of fire, the mystery of shadows, the feel of skin. From your mouth, mighty Spirit, flow the sound of thunder, the whisper of rain, the stillness of dawn, the humming of night. May I touch, O God; O Spirit, may I hear.*

Text: Psalm 143:5-6

Context: A member of the Creek (Muscogee) Tribe, Joy Harjo was born in Tulsa, Oklahoma, in 1951. She grew up there and in New Mexico, where she earned her bachelor's degree at the University of New Mexico in 1976. In 1978 she graduated from the University of Iowa with a Master of Fine Arts degree. A poet, associate professor of English at the University of Arizona, editor, filmmaker, scriptwriter, speaker, and tenor saxophone player, Joy has published three books of poetry: *What Moon Drove Me to This?*, *She Had Some Horses*, *In Mad Love and War*, and a chapbook entitled *The Last Song*. In 1989 she collaborated with photographer Stephen Strom to publish *Secrets from the Center of the World*. Her poetry breathes with the spirit of the people, the passions, and the places that have shaped her.

Kary Kublin is a doctoral student in speech/language pathology at Florida State University, an artist, and a writer. (See Week 28, "The Community of Two.") She has never met Joy; they do not know each other. Yet Kary's work also breathes with the spirit of the lives, people, and spaces that have influenced her.

This week I invite you to contemplate the poem "Remember," written by Joy for her book *She Had Some Horses*. The daily readings, written by Kary as meditative responses to the poem, call us to interact with both Joy's poem and with Kary's meditations. They beckon us, as they weave spaces and images of remembering, to ponder the things and the ways we remember. Remembering is itself a sacred act, for it reminds us who and whose we are. So remember and breathe with the spirit of the people, the passions, and the places that have given life and form to you.

Remember

Remember the sky that you were born under,
know each of the star's stories.
Remember the moon, know who she is. I met her
in a bar once in Iowa City.
Remember the sun's birth at dawn, that is the
strongest point of time. Remember sundown
and the giving away to night.
Remember your birth, how your mother struggled
to give you form and breath. You are evidence of
her life, and her mother's, and hers.
Remember your father. He is your life, also.
Remember the earth whose skin you are:
red earth, black earth, yellow earth, white earth
brown earth, we are earth.
Remember the plants, trees, animal life who all have their
tribes, their families, their histories, too. Talk to them,
listen to them. They are alive poems.
Remember the wind. Remember her voice. She knows the
origin of this universe. I heard her singing Kiowa war
dance songs at the corner of Fourth and Central once.
Remember that you are all people and that all people
are you.
Remember that you are this universe and that this
universe is you.
Remember that all is in motion, is growing, is you.
Remember that language comes from this.
Remember the dance that language is, that life is.
Remember.
—Joy Harjo in *She Had Some Horses*

—— **MONDAY** ——

sky

I know the date   it was probably the autumnal equinox when the stars
smiled at me   a story of surprise when I was born the second
unexpected twin   then as a cousin laughing in my sleeping bag giggling
to stay awake as the moon was slowly swallowed and formed again on
the other side of a living room window the night of the eclipse   knowing

her is pulling tide and present flow   she visits when they've all gone to
sleep

Reflect
Remember . . . that which calls you to look up . . . which encircles and lies
beyond you.

—— **TUESDAY** ——

sun

sleep is an easy habit but light intercedes silently   that must be dawn's
strength   to give and return without announcing that it's time to get up or to
go to bed   for circle turns to lay down beside me whispering good morning
and singing a lullaby

Reflect
Remember . . . sun days . . . morning wakings . . . stretching into the day.

—— **WEDNESDAY** ——

birth

searching photographs for points to connect the lines stitched in
grandma's sewing   I know of her life yet still long to see her face   and
my father's mother   oh sweet memory letting him cry   years after her
passing

Reflect
Remember . . . connections . . . the flowing of memories within family . . .
stories of your birth.

—— **THURSDAY** ——

earth

a suburban garden of tomatoes that was all   usually   let's try peas and
squash and a potato sprouted in my eighth grade science class   the lizards'
world becomes ring and green and wall   ladybug fly away home   grandpa's
lizard stories always had a happy ending

Reflect
Remember . . . your first awareness of earth . . . of life beneath the earth . . . of earth's stories.

——— FRIDAY ———

wind

the first time the shape of this longing was known to me it was the wind awake and playful skipping lightly across the canyon   I sat perched above wind was somersaults and swimming strokes announcing the birth

Reflect
Remember . . . wind blowing through your life . . . stirring longings, awakening you to play.

——— SATURDAY ———

you

I am fascinated by the word stranger   a person defined by context, by no context and strange-er still it is the universe a verse a song for one is many depending on where you stand

Reflect
Remember . . . strangers who have passed through your life . . . strangers who have become part of it.

——— SUNDAY ———

remember

she tells me words of motherly advice that insist on redeeming memories unknown to me   years were spent attending to the personal without repetition or poetry she is with me now shaping the prayers of one holding strong the holy rubbing smooth the sacred stones

Reflect
- ❖ Remember . . . what else?
- ❖ Who bids you to remember?

In the Morning

I am a night person.
Moonrise signals the
strongest beating of my heart
and Cricket sings the song
of my most wakeful hours.

But I think
I would like to meet you
in the morning,
to see you coming
through the mist
as the sun burns it
to day.

Following your eyes
as Crow circles overhead,
I think I would remember something
I had not seen before.
—Jan L. Richardson

—— ❖ ——

Blessing: *May the God who gives rise to new words from old memories now set you to motion, bidding you journey with grace in paths of beauty and blessing.*

52 Threatened with Resurrection
Julia Esquivel

Invocation: *God of life, breathe your resurrecting Spirit through lands wounded by violence and death. Fill the vessels of our hearts, O God, that we may sing with the hope of healing and new life.*

Text: Ezekiel 37:1-14

Context: In the thirty years of military dictatorships that followed the CIA-sponsored overthrow of the democratic government in Guatemala in 1954, tens of thousands of Guatemalans were killed. Hundreds of thousands more were dislocated in their own country or forced into exile. The victims, according to the Ecumenical Program on Central America and as recorded in *The Certainty of Spring*, were "peasants, trade unionists, priests, nuns, students, opposition figures—anyone suspected of 'subversive' activity."

As an advocate for human rights, Julia Esquivel knew these victims. The government banned her magazine *Dialogo*, which addressed Guatemalan life from a social and theological perspective. Governmental security forces abducted Julia herself for her critique of oppression by the government. Released after an international outcry, Julia went into exile in 1980 and continues to spend her time traveling, writing, and speaking about the pain and hope of her homeland.

Much of Julia's pain and hope weaves through her poetry. Her first book of poetry, *Threatened with Resurrection*, was published in English and Spanish by Brethren Press in 1982 and revised in 1994. Her second book, *The Certainty of Spring: Poems by a Guatemalan in Exile*, appeared in English in 1993. Of her poems, Julia says in *New Women, New Church*, an occasional publication of the Women's Ordination Conference, "They constitute a way of reaching out for my country despite the grief of living in exile. They are a 'heart's ease' which allows me to keep on going, working and if possible let me see some changes that humanize the lives of the poor and the wealthy." Replete with the faces, names, deaths, and dreams of her homeland and her people, Julia's poems reveal a passion for life and a conviction that a resurrection of hope, justice, and the spirit of the land is possible still.

I Am Not Afraid
of Death

I am no longer afraid of death,
I know well
its dark and cold corridors
leading to life.

I am afraid rather of that life
which does not come out of death,
which cramps our hands
and slows our march.

I am afraid of my fear
and even more of the fear of others,
who do not know where they are going,
who continue clinging
to what they think is life
which we know to be death!

I live each day to kill death;
I die each day to give birth to life,
and in this death of death,
I die a thousand times
and am reborn another thousand
through that love
from my People,
which nourishes hope!
—From *Threatened with Resurrection*

Reflect
❖ What frightens you?
❖ What nourishes hope within you?

Hope

In the darkest, most sordid,
hostile, bitter,

corrupt,
and nauseating places,
you do your work.
That is why your Son
descended into hell,
in order to transform that which IS NOT
and to purge that which BELIEVES ITSELF TO BE.
This is hope!
—From *Threatened with Resurrection*

Reflect

Psalm 139 says that God is everywhere, even in hell. Julia seems to be saying God is everywhere—perhaps *especially* in hell.

❖ What does God's presence tell us about where we are called to do God's work?

────── **WEDNESDAY** ──────

The Sigh

When it is necessary to drink so much pain,
when a river of anguish
drowns us,
when we have wept many tears
and they flow like rivers
from our sad eyes,
only then
does the deep hidden sigh of our neighbor
become our own.
—From *The Certainty of Spring*

Reflect

❖ Whose deep hidden sighs have become your own?

────── **THURSDAY** ──────

Indian Tapestry

When I go up to the HOUSE OF THE OLD WEAVER,
I watch in admiration
what comes forth from her mind:

a thousand designs being created
and not a single model from which to copy
the marvelous cloth
with which she will dress
the Companion of the True and Faithful One.

Men always ask me
to give the name of the label,
to specify the maker of the design.
But the Weaver cannot be pinned down
by designs,
nor patterns.
All of her weavings
are originals,
there are no repeated patterns.
Her mind is beyond
all foresight.
Her able hands do not accept
patterns or models.
Whatever comes forth, comes forth,
but she Who Is will make it.

The colors of her threads
are firm:
blood,
sweat,
perseverance,
tears,
struggle,
and hope.
Colors that do not fade
with time.

The children of the children
of our children
will recognize the seal
of the Old Weaver.
Maybe then
it will be named.
But as a model,
it can never again

be repeated.

Each morning I have seen
how her agile fingers
choose the threads
one by one.
Her loom makes no noise,
and men
give it no importance,
and nevertheless,
the design
that emerges from Her Mind
hour after hour
will appear in threads
of many colors,
in figures and symbols
which no one, ever again,
will be able to erase
or undo.
—From *Threatened with Resurrection*

Reflect

❖ What designs have been woven into your heart, never to be erased?

———— FRIDAY ————

Resolution

If
when you shed light on the lies
they hurt you—
then feel the pain!
You will not die!

If
when you speak the truth
they kill you—
die, then!
You will rise again!

If
when you fall

they trample you and crush you—
stand up then!
You shall walk!

If
all is over and
you cannot even draw another breath,
Return, and begin again!
—From *The Certainty of Spring*

Reflect

❖ What do Julia's words tell you of resurrection—of your own, of
the people, of God in the world?

—— **SATURDAY** ——

I Am Not Possessed!

For the many valiant women
of my Guatemala (John 8:49)

I am not possessed
I am not crazy
obsessed with an idea.

I am simply a woman
with a human heart.

I am a rebel
when faced with the cold and calculated
correctness of a bureaucrat.

He who is always bound
by the limits of "the correct"
"the objective" and "the prudent"
of an always-neutral balance.

The one who avoids taking risks
for the sake of his office
and his prestige.

I am the possessor of
(not possessed by)

the normality of a woman
that rejects and always will reject
the disorder constituted
by *machos*,
all of them potential generals.
By all those
who place the law
above life;
the institution
above humanity,
the personal project
above truth,
fear
above love,
ambition
above humility.

But I must admit
to those obsessed
with such criteria,
I am a red-hot coal
lighted by the fire
of a great love.

Brother,

Do you know the story
of the burning bush
that was never consumed?
—From *The Certainty of Spring*

Reflect

❖ What "crazy" or "obsessive" ideas (as labeled by others) have
sprung from your "simply human heart"?

❖ What power do you give to labels?

----- **SUNDAY** -----

They Have Threatened Us with Resurrection

It isn't the noise in the streets
that keeps us from resting, my friend,

nor is it the shouts of the young people
coming out drunk from the "St. Pauli,"
nor is it the tumult of those who pass by excitedly
on their way to the mountains.

It is something here within us that doesn't let us sleep,
that doesn't let us rest,
that won't stop pounding
deep inside,
it is the silent, warm weeping
of Indian women without their husbands,
it is the sad gaze of the children
fixed there beyond memory,
precious in our eyes
which during sleep,
though closed, keep watch,
systole,
diastole,
awake.

Now six have left us,
and nine in Rabinal,[*]
and two, plus two, plus two,
and ten, a hundred, a thousand,
a whole army
witness to our pain,
our fear,
our courage,
our *hope*!

What keeps us from sleeping
is that they have threatened us with Resurrection!
Because every evening
though weary of killings
an endless inventory since 1954,[**]
yet we go on loving
and do not accept their death!

---

[*] *Rabinal: town in the province of Baja Veracruz where massacre took place.*
[**] *Killings since 1954: year in which the government of President Jacobo Arbenz was overthrown by a CIA-backed mercenary army coup which initiated the unrelenting and ever-mounting repression by the military regimes in continuous power since then.*

Threatened with Resurrection ~ 403

They have threatened us with Resurrection
because we have felt their inert bodies,
and their souls penetrated ours
doubly fortified,
because in this marathon of Hope,
there are always others to relieve us
who carry the strength
to reach the finish line
which lies beyond death.

They have threatened us with Resurrection
because they will not be able to take away from us
their bodies,
their souls,
their strength,
their spirit,
nor even their death
and least of all their life.
Because they live
today, tomorrow, and always
in the streets baptized with their blood,
in the air that absorbed their cry,
in the jungle that hid their shadows,
in the river that gathered up their laughter,
in the ocean that holds their secrets,
in the craters of the volcanoes,
Pyramids of the New Day,
which swallowed up their ashes.

They have threatened us with Resurrection,
because they are more alive than ever before,
because they transform our agonies
and fertilize our struggle,
because they pick us up when we fall,
because they loom like giants
before the crazed gorillas' fear.

They have threatened us with Resurrection,
because they do not know life (poor things!).
That is the whirlwind
which does not let us sleep,

the reason why sleeping, we keep watch,
and awake, we dream.

No, it's not the street noises,
nor the shouts from the drunks in the "St. Pauli,"
nor the noise from the fans at the ball park.
It is the internal cyclone of a kaleidoscopic struggle
which will heal that wound of the quetzal
fallen in Ixcán,
it is the earthquake soon to come
that will shake the world
and put everything in its place.

No, brother,
it is not the noise in the streets
which does not let us sleep.

Join us in this vigil
and you will know what it is to dream!
Then you will know how marvelous it is
to live threatened with Resurrection!

To dream awake,
to keep watch asleep,
to live while dying,
and to know ourselves already
resurrected!
—From *Threatened with Resurrection*

Reflect

❖ What vigils do you keep?
❖ What calls you to dream awake, to keep watch asleep?
❖ What will you do with Julia's invitation?

—— Meditation ——

Corredores (Corridors)

Once, in the mountains,
in pursuit of snow in May
my friends and I drove
up and up

through one tunnel
and out,
through another tunnel
and then
suddenly, stunningly, magically
out onto a transformed mountain.
We had found snowfall's edge
and followed its lines, laughing.

Now I suppose it wasn't snow
that covered the mountains
of bodies of your people
or ice that froze the hearts
of those who built them.
I know that my mountain tunnel
and your dark corridor
are not the same.
Guatemala is hardly North Carolina,
though I would like to take you there.

But what I am trying to say
is a prayer
that beyond your dark corridors of death
you will find a stunning scene
and the edge of freedom,
and that together we may burst, laughing,
out from the tunnel
into a dazzling new day.
—Jan L. Richardson

——— ❖ ———

Blessing: *Go in peace, blessed to be a blessing. May the God of the poor, the Savior of the oppressed, and the Spirit of justice work within you, that you may be a bearer of warmth and love in the corridors that lead to life.*

53 All Hallows/All Horrors
Women Killed as Witches

Invocation: *God of the generations, you know the ages and hold all lives in your heart. Help us to remember the stories of pain so that we may give birth to different dreams.*

Text: Psalm 94:3-7

Context: Say "witch hunt," and many people in the United States immediately think of Salem Village, the town in Massachusetts where, by 1692, fourteen women and five men had been convicted and executed on the charge of practicing witchcraft. Yet the craze in Salem was not the first in New England, nor was New England itself an aberration in the Western world. Beginning with the Inquisition in Europe in the fifteenth century, women who once had been honored as healers, midwives, and wise elders began to be accused, imprisoned, tortured, burned, and hanged as evil, demonic, and dangerous devil-worshipers.

Although some men were convicted and executed as witches, the vast majority of those killed were women. Historians estimate that of the 100,000–2 million people who were executed in the witch hunts, women comprised at least eighty percent. (See *The Devil in the Shape of a Woman*, by Carol F. Karlsen.) In most cases the evidence against them was dubious, with accusations prompted by jealousy, fear, or confusion. Economic, political, and religious instability seem to have contributed to the witch hunts as people scrambled for solid ground by turning their inner fears outward. Those who lived on the margins—the eccentric, the old, the unmarried, the foreigner—often lived with the most risk of being accused.

Our modern Halloween derives in part from ancient festivals held on the eve of the Feast of All Saints (November 1), also known as All Hallows. While modern Halloween practices often play on our fears of the unknown, the evil, and the demonic, All Saints' Day, or All Hallows Day, calls us to remember those who died as victims of fear, ignorance, and malice. Traditionally a feast day to remember departed women and men of the faith, All Saints' Day is an appropriate time to mark the holocaust of women unjustly accused, tortured, and killed around the world.

The story of witchcraft is primarily the story of women, and this I suspect accounts for much of the fascination and the elusiveness attending the subject. Especially in its Western incarnation, witchcraft confronts us with ideas about women, with fears about women, with the place of women in society, and with women themselves. It confronts us too with systematic violence against women. . . .

This is not simply to call for recognition of the sheer numbers of women who have suffered in the name of witchcraft. That acknowledgment must be made to counter the trivializing and glossing of both witchcraft and women's history. Only by understanding that the history of witchcraft is primarily a history of women, however, can we confront the deeply embedded feelings about women—and the intricate patterns of interest underlying those feelings—among our witch-ridden ancestors.

—Carol F. Karlsen in *The Devil in the Shape of a Woman: Witchcraft in Colonial New England*

Reflect

Marcia Falk writes that "What we cannot remember, we must imagine." This week remember or imagine those who lived in fear for being different . . . and those who still do so today.

Mary Bradbury was one of the best-loved members of her community. Ninety-three neighbours had signed a statement that in half a century they had never known her to make trouble. . . .

Such testimony came from the circle of Mrs. Bradbury's affectionate acquaintance. Not everyone in Salisbury belonged to it; at its outer edges were people who took the view that her seeming goodness was a false front behind which she concealed abominations. The elder Ann Putnam, having lived in Salisbury in youth, and not having moved in Mrs. Bradbury's social set, knew all about the abominations. Her kinsman Richard Carr had as good as seen the woman turn herself into a blue boar; anyway he saw the boar rush out of a gate which Mrs. Bradbury had just entered and dash at the feet of his father's horse. Neither he nor another witness doubted that the boar was Mrs. Bradbury, and apparently neither did judges or jury when the story was duly relayed to them. . . .

Mrs. Bradbury was sentenced to hang—yet did not. Her friends found

means of spiriting her away and concealing her. The success of the concealment and the probably not ungrounded suspicion that local magistrates did not over-exert themselves to track her down gave rise in some quarters to discontent. It did not reassure common folk to feel that special privilege existed even among witches.
—Marion L. Starkey in *The Devil in Massachusetts: A Modern Enquiry into the Salem Witchcraft Trials*

Reflect
Remember or imagine those who have come to the aid of the accused.

WEDNESDAY

When Rebecca Nurse was found not guilty on charges of witchcraft, the courtroom erupted. "One of the throats of the girls issued a howling and roaring that was both more and less than human," Marion L. Starkey records in *The Devil in Massachusetts*. "Their bodies jerked and snapped in the unearthly choreography of their convulsions." Intimidated, the judge sent the jury back to rethink their decision. When they returned, they handed over a guilty verdict. Moments before she and four other women were to be hung, one of them, Sarah Good, cried out to a pastor who had accused her, "You're a liar! I am no more a witch than you are a wizard!"
—Jan L. Richardson

Reflect
Remember or imagine the fear on both sides—the powerlessness and the power that the fear wielded.

THURSDAY

By the end of the 1500s in some regions of Europe—southwest Germany, for example—the accusations and the hunting were out of control. No one could say who was a witch and who was not. In Rottenburg in 1602 even the chief prosecutor, Hans Georg Hallmayer, had confessed and had to be executed. The only way to end the random victimization seemed to be to end the whole process. And just as the learned and powerful had begun the panic, so they ended it. In southwestern Germany, in France, in Belgium, in the Netherlands, beginning as early as 1613, authorities refused to hear new accusations, made the rules of evidence stricter, stopped using torture, did not carry out executions, reversed sentences on appeal, and set fines for false accusations. Just as they had given the power and sown fear of those who held it, so now they began to deny it and to discredit those who claimed it.

—Bonnie S. Anderson and Judith P. Zinsser in *A History of Their Own: Women in Europe from Prehistory to the Present*, Volume 1

Reflect

Remember or imagine those who have helped turn the tide against fear and injustice.

—————— **FRIDAY** ——————

In 1697 Massachusetts proclaimed a solemn day of fasting and prayer in connection with the witchcraft trials, which had come to be recognized as a grave miscarriage of justice. One of the judges, Samuel Sewall, and a dozen of the witchcraft trial jurors publicly admitted the grievous errors they had made and asked forgiveness. In 1706 Ann Putnam, one of the first girls to be afflicted, did the same. In 1703 and 1711 the Massachusetts General Court reversed the attainders, by which the condemned were deprived of civil rights, inheritance, and property, against twenty-three of those convicted of witchcraft. They awarded financial compensation to some, finally bringing an end to one of the most tragic chapters in New England's history.

—Diana Ross McCain, from "The Witches of Salem 300 Years Ago" in *Early American Life Magazine*

Reflect

Remember or imagine acts of repentance, the power of justice.

—————— **SATURDAY** ——————

Three Hundred Years Later
    For Mary Ann

These are dangerous days for imagining,
days when burning bushes
are turned into pyres
and seers
are taken as scapegoats.

Three hundred years ago
they killed the heretics
in presses of stone

and at fiery stakes.

Three hundred years
after the fires went out
in this land,
the witch-hungry presses are still around,
now spewing glossy and slick
and just as mistaken.

And in this land
three hundred years later
there is still much at the stake,

more than jobs
more than positions
more than orthodoxy.

Three hundred years ago
those women knew what this is about:
about power
about naming
about claiming the holy things
as our own.

I tell you this:
three hundred years later
the women are crying out
that there is better news
for these days.
I have seen it
breaking bread at the table
embracing the brokenhearted
touching with oil the wounded and weary
laughing and dancing and singing and free.

It is beautiful, I tell you,
and it is strong,
and it is rising.
—Jan L. Richardson

Reflect
Remember or imagine those who today live with persecution for different ideas, dreams, and imaginings.

We remember all our sisters. . . . We weep for them. We do not forget them. And as we remember them, we dedicate ourselves to making a new world where we and our daughters can live free; a world where our granddaughters and our sisters' granddaughters and great-granddaughters may look back in wonder at some archaic, almost forgotten time when women died because men went to war.

—Chris Carol, adapted from a poem by Kate Nonesuch; from a Hallowmas Liturgy cited in *Women-Church* by Rosemary Radford Ruether

Reflect

❖ How do you want to be remembered or imagined?

❖ What will you do to keep from forgetting?

—— **Meditation** ——

Lament

Somewhere, someone knows the names.
They are not erased by
the gallows of fear
the sword of suspicion
the pyre of terror
the guns of prejudice
the stones of righteousness.

Names do not disappear.
They are written
in the roots of the trees
the veins of the rocks
crying out in the fire
water washing them over
and over again
flinging them onto some distant shore
into the heart of God
who remembers all.

The stones do cry out
and the wind
and the rain
and the fire of smoldering dreams;

all cry out:
remember
return.
—Jan L. Richardson

———— ❖ ————

Blessing: *May the God who is wise to human fears and failings strengthen you to remember, that by remembering you may give life to those who live in fear.*

My thanks to Helen R. Neinast for her assistance with this week.

54 The Touch of Freedom
The Bent-Over Woman

Invocation: *God of liberation, your spirit moves through people of all shapes, colors, and abilities. May I perceive you in the forms you take and the vessels you inhabit. May I know your embrace, that I might extend it to others.*

Text: Luke 13:10-17

Context: Immediately preceding Jesus' words on what the realm of God is like, this story suggests another place where the presence of God resides: in the bent-over body of this woman. Jesus sees deeply into the years of pain this unnamed woman has borne not only because of her physical condition but also from the community's attitude toward those whose bodies do not appear "normal." In Jesus' day, and often in ours, physical difference was considered a curse, a sign of an individual's sin. To come into physical contact with such a person placed one at risk of being cursed as well.

The story of Jesus' encounter with the bent-over woman is dramatic not only because of the healing that comes to the woman but also the healing that comes to the community. The community also receives Jesus' freeing touch as it begins to learn about the care God calls us to have for one another. With Jesus' touch of the woman's body, with her song of praise, and with the community's rejoicing, this story challenges us to consider how we participate in the diminishment of those around us and how we must provide the conditions for healing—physical, emotional, economic, relational—to happen for us all.

—— MONDAY ——

If you are physically able, do this:

Bend over. Stay there. Move. Try to clean your home. Make a phone call. Walk around. Talk to someone.

How long does it take to become uncomfortable?

Doing this exercise only approaches the pain the bent-over woman lived with for years. Yet we are called to approach it. We all carry some kind of difference within us, and we all possess in our imaginations the seeds of connection. Discovering what constricts us may provide clues to how others are constricted—and how we may share in keeping both them and ourselves bent over.

The two are tied together. As long as one person lives without freedom, then no one is truly free. And thus acts of healing toward others heal us too.

Stand up.

Rejoice!

—Jan L. Richardson

Reflect

❖ How did it feel to stand up?

——— TUESDAY ———

As a woman, I too have felt bent and distorted. As a matter of fact, I still often feel that way.

And it is the power of Jesus which liberates woman, in the space of the Kingdom of God. So that woman can stretch herself to full length, and glorify God.

This is what it's all about: liberation, power, glorification. How good is the work which is being done by bent and distorted people within a structure that leaves them no room for "stretching to their full length"? Are we so fearful, have we so little confidence in the power of Christ and the Kingdom of God, that we don't want all God's people stretching to their full length? Are we like the oppressors, who keep dangerous prisoners in tiger cages?

—Marianne Katoppo in *Compassionate and Free: An Asian Woman's Theology*

Reflect

❖ Are we like the oppressors?

❖ Who are we in the face of those who live at less than full length?

❖ How do we live at less than full length?

——— WEDNESDAY ———

[Maria de Groot] points out that, in Luke 13, the head of the synagogue really couldn't appreciate Jesus' healing the woman at all, as it was a sabbath day—and she sees a direct analogy with the attitude of today's church leaders, who are not overly enthusiastic either with "women on the sabbath and on Sundays, raised to their full height, taking the word and singing their own song, proclaiming from their own corporal recovery." In other words, they are very critical of women participating in salvation.

Jesus calls these spiritual leaders hypocrites, and throws the question right back at them: "If you free on the sabbath your ox and your donkey to let them drink, what then have you to say of my act regarding this woman? Is she not a daughter of Abraham?"

Jesus lifts up the woman to what she is. A daughter of Abraham, faced with the hypocrites who taught that they were the sons of Abraham. Yet who failed to grasp the essence of their own Torah. The woman is a daughter of Abraham, she does not have to become it by one or another achievement. For 18 years she has been bound by the power of evil—the power that Jesus calls Satan. And the hand of Christ is sufficient for complete liberation: there is no need for anything else. No approval of authorities, no proof from the woman's side. She is the daughter of Abraham, she is released.

—Marianne Katoppo in *Compassionate and Free*

Reflect

❖ What people, institutions, systems, and beliefs contribute to keeping women from living at less than full length?

❖ Ponder your experiences in the church. Where have you been helped to stretch, and where have you encountered resistance to release and liberation?

—— **THURSDAY** ——

The "problem" in this story lies not in the fact of the woman's disability but in her community's seeming unwillingness to heal her themselves. In this sense, they are more "disabled" than she. Their traditions, attitudes, beliefs, and stereotypes about people who look, walk, act, and live differently have dulled their compassion and their ability to be whole members of a whole community. They may pity her or feel sympathy for her, but such emotions do not release them or her from their broken relationship.

Jesus' touch does more than heal the woman of her physical condition. It breaks barriers; it shatters stereotypes; it goes against the expected norms of behavior. Everything he does calls attention to the woman and to his act: he calls to her; he touches her; he does this on a Sabbath. Not content to leave this woman in the shadows or to cure her quietly, Jesus wants his healing of the woman to spill over into the entire community. He calls the community beyond the boundaries of tradition, of physical ideals, of conformity in order to show them that being a community means creating the conditions for people to be who God created them to be, in whatever body they happen to be. It means touching others in a way that allows our deepest selves to be touched as well.

—Jan L. Richardson

Reflect

❖ When have you seen a community enlarge its boundaries to encompass those who have lived at less than full stretch?

❖ What is necessary for a community to do this?

——— **FRIDAY** ———

The bent-over woman could not straighten up by her own strength and power. She could not heal herself. We, too, must acknowledge that in our world there are victims of injustice and unfair laws and traditions who cannot heal themselves. Under their burden of our privileged places, they cannot stand upright. If they could have changed the situation themselves, they would not be so old while they are yet so young. They would not be dying before they have had a chance to live.

Jesus challenges us to make their struggle our struggle. His life and death instruct us that it is not two different struggles; it is one common struggle. Because the same God created us, we belong to one another. As long as anyone remains bent over, no one stands fully upright. When one is lifted, we are all lifted—and we all rejoice at the glorious things Jesus has done. When one is empowered, we are all empowered. Then what is left to do?

We praise God!

—Helen Bruch Pearson in *Do What You Have the Power to Do*

Reflect

Imagine you are a bystander in the story.

❖ What do you see?

❖ How do you respond?

——— **SATURDAY** ———

One day I got a massage from someone I hardly knew: [quoted material is from journal entry] "The tight spot in my abdomen. I cried as soon as she rubbed it.

And held it. Where I hold out love. Where I hold out God. And the heart center so tight, hunched in, curled over. What if God loved me? This is what it would be like if God loved me . . . a glimpse, a long flash, a short being in God's love—and maybe, in time, with crying out the clenches of fear in my gut and the shudder of protection in my heart-chest-back, maybe someday I will allow love. From God, from people, from grass, potatoes, dogs, even pavement." I had to get up from the table. I couldn't feel that for very long.
—Ellen Anthony, from "Somebody Has to Die" in *Weavings: A Journal of the Christian Spiritual Life*

Reflect

❖ Where do you "hold out love," "hold out God"?

❖ When is it difficult for you to receive a healing touch, to stretch into the love of God?

—— **SUNDAY** ——

Prayer for All Things Rising

For all things rising
    out of the hiddenness of shadows
    out of the weight of despair
    out of the brokenness of pain
    out of the constrictions of compliance
    out of the rigidity of stereotypes
    out of the prison of prejudice;

for all things rising
    into life, into hope
    into healing, into power
    into freedom, into justice;

we pray, O God,
for all things rising.
—Jan L. Richardson

Reflect

❖ What do you sense rising in your life?

❖ As you rise into life, into freedom, into hope, whom will you enable to rise?

The Renegade Touch

Here
smaller than the palm
of my hand
pressed to the small
of your back
I touch
the site
of your feeling's flight.

My fingers press,
as if to trace the lines
of torn nerves
turning to new patterns.

The shape of your body
challenges mine;
to get close
is a dare;
to embrace,
a dance.
—Jan L. Richardson

—— ❖ ——

Blessing: *Arise, beloved daughter of God. May you know what it means to live at full stretch in body and spirit. Go in peace, freed by the power of God in you to widen the circle of healing.*

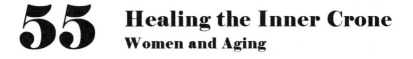

55 Healing the Inner Crone
Women and Aging

Invocation: *From age to age, O God, you bless your people with tender care. In our every age, Eternal Wisdom, bless us with your constant companionship and your fiery presence.*

Text: Psalm 71:17-19

Context: I once heard Maria Harris, a keenly perceptive educator and writer, speak of our need to discover our "inner elder." In the last decade, many persons have begun to heal from painful pasts as therapists and counselors urged them to "discover the inner child." Yet Maria was the first person I have ever heard suggest that we turn our attention to imagining our inner elder, our inner wise one, our inner crone as well.

In a culture that spends much of its time marketing and consuming ways to ward off old age—or at least its visible effects—Maria's suggestion borders on revolutionary. What would it mean for us not only to seek out the elders around us but also to seek the elder within? What insights might we gain in daring to imagine ourselves older and to ask questions of what that means for us now? Perhaps if we spent time now imagining our "inner crone," we would greet her more joyfully as she emerges in our lives.

This year has grown old, and we along with it. Soon Advent will come, and time will spiral once again. The God of the ages knows our own aging, knows intimately the changing seasons of our lives. In every time and through each season, God dwells with us, embracing us in each step of the sacred journey.

—— MONDAY ——

I remember when I said out loud to myself, "You're old!" I do not recall the exact date, but I remember the event vividly. In retrospect, I believe that I uttered my declaration of independence in defiance of a television commercial that I had just heard in which someone had exclaimed that she was not old, was not going to be old, and, in short, seemed to be promising to live forever. I was indignant at her denial of an inevitable reality, and I said to the commercial, "You're so busy trying to recapture the fantasy of youth that you're wasting the reality of age and the life it has given you!"

When I went to the mirror, looked myself straight in the eye, and said, "I'm old!" it became real. But the corners of my mouth were turned down, and my frown was grim and joyless. Those two words went downhill all the way to the bottom. Then I said it again; my eyes gleamed, the corners of my mouth turned up in a wide grin, and my voice rang out as if in a proud declaration. That day I learned something important to my being eighty-five—for "oldness" is very special and very precious; it is not to be denied. We have to make age work for us; we can't treat it as an enemy.

—Elizabeth Welch in *Learning to Be 85*

Reflect
- ❖ What do you think of aging, of being old?
- ❖ What does your community, your society think of it?

———— **TUESDAY** ————

I am still every age that I have been. Because I was once a child, I am always a child. Because I was once a searching adolescent, given to moods and ecstasies, these are still part of me, and always will be. Because I was once a rebellious student, there is and always will be in me the student crying out for reform.

This does not mean that I ought to be trapped or enclosed in any of these ages, the perpetual student, the delayed adolescent, the childish adult, but that they are in me to be drawn on; to forget is a form of suicide; my past is part of what makes the present Madeleine and must not be denied or rejected or forgotten.

Far too many people misunderstand what *putting away childish things* means, and think that forgetting what it is like to think and feel and touch and smell and taste and see and hear like a three-year-old or a thirteen-year-old or a twenty-three-year-old means being grownup. When I'm with these people I, like the kids, feel that if this is what it means to be a grownup, then I don't ever want to be one.

Instead of which, if I can retain a child's awareness and joy, and *be* fifty-one, then I will really learn what it means to be grownup. I still have a long way to go.

—Madeleine L'Engle in *A Circle of Quiet*

Reflect
- ❖ What do you think it means to be grown-up?

❖ What awarenesses and joys, thoughts and feelings, touches and tastes, sights and hearings do you want to carry with you?

───── **WEDNESDAY** ─────

The first step, I think, is to recognize that all of these aspects of old age which I have mentioned—illness, diminution of energy, increased dependence on others, the threat and certainty of death—are simply more extreme expressions of that same finitude which is our bodiliness and the indispensable ground of joy. Pain and illness are not strangers to the young; our reserves of bodily energy have always been limited; we are dependent upon others throughout our lives; and death has always been a certainty. In youth it is easier (at least for some) to turn away from the facts of our finitude, to pretend that they are unimportant. When we grow older, it becomes difficult to keep up the pretense.

—Valerie C. Saiving, from "Our Bodies/Our Selves: Reflections on Sickness, Aging, and Death" in *Journal of Feminist Studies in Religion*

Reflect

❖ What pretenses have your body, your experiences, your journey called you to shed?

❖ What has filled or changed the spaces once occupied by pretense?

───── **THURSDAY** ─────

Silent Story

Rattling, a racket,
a rattling I heard
and spun to pale kitchen curtains
tearing back their thin veneer.

My stare, blue bleary, locked her eyes,
brown, clear as a child's,
while metal gates slammed down my mind,
barring heart's admission.

Hunger's incessant jab
tattooed the crosshatched face,
street-wise, no pillow for her head;
hands a wreck exposed,

were given stone instead of bread.

Plowing through the alley,
her rusted cart scrapes by my door:
bags of scant stuff bunched in brutal openness.

She clatters across broken cobbles
while I, in kitchen cozy,
smooth close the veil between our worlds,
but can't shut out my sister's secret:
she shelters Christ the Crone.
—Maureen Noworyta in *The Journal of Women and Religion*

Reflect
❖ What do you see here?
❖ What do you think of such an image?

—— **FRIDAY** ——

Teasing and reminiscing late into the night, the [Delany] sisters [Bessie and Sadie, 102 and 104, respectively] sometimes feel like schoolgirls. Once, Miss Sadie relates with relish, a neighbor complained about the ruckus. "She couldn't see what two old women would find so much to be laughing about."
—From an interview by Kiley Armstrong

Reflect
❖ What do you long to laugh about when you are an old woman?
❖ With whom do you want to raise a ruckus?

—— **SATURDAY** ——

We sat there together [after Camille's mother died] in the room not saying very much, occasionally speaking to each other, mainly just being silent together. Eventually I walked over to the bed where she lay and I touched her hand. At that moment something very strange occurred to me. Death has always seemed such a mystery to me, something that I could not fathom; but in that moment something else happened. At that moment I remembered almost fifteen years ago when I had the same mysterious feelings holding my newborn daughter in my arms. I was amazed. I was in awe. I thought then as I thought two weeks ago, this is a *mystery*. I don't understand this. Holding my newborn daughter in my arms, watching her very tentative movements and feeling amazed and awed by this little life in my hands; standing there holding my dead mother's hand and watching the stillness, that too was amazing and I was awed.

Surely the two mysteries of life are birth and death. These events we can never understand fully. . . . What we can do is tell the story of our birth, of our life, and of the lives and deaths of those we love, what they mean to us and what they meant to us, how they touched us and how they shaped us. It is in telling the story and telling our story that we begin to share with each other. We begin to see we all have anxieties, that we all have strengths and weaknesses and lonelinesses. But along with that is amazement and wonder and mystery, if we let ourselves experience it.

—Camille Littleton Hegg in *Women of the Word: Contemporary Sermons by Women Clergy*

Reflect

Think of the stories you know of birthing times and dying times.

❖ What connects these stories of birthing times and dying times?

—————— SUNDAY ——————

What else is there left? Oh, yes, so many longings I still feel, vividly, acutely, now that the time is used up. They have not faded but hang suspended in my heart.

—Zhang Jie, from "An Unfinished Record" in *Love Must Not Be Forgotten*

Reflect

❖ Whatever your age, what longings still hang suspended in your heart?
❖ As this year draws to a close, what is your inner crone looking like and saying to you?

—————— Meditation ——————

Crumbs

Breaking bread with the
wise old one I hope lives
in me,
I tuck away a piece,
thinking to save it
for later.

Sometimes I forget
that by her dreaming,
by her laughter,
it is she
who feeds me
now.
—Jan L. Richardson

———— ❖ ————

Blessing: *May you embrace the wisdom of each age with wit, with grace, with power, and with faith.*

56 Taste of Power Transformed
Queen Vashti

Invocation: *You dwell with us, O God, in power and in beauty. Be incarnate in me, that my actions may heal and free with beauty and with power.*

Text: Esther 1:5-22

Context: In the Christian church, Christ the King Sunday marks the end of both ordinary time and the liturgical year. While many who observe this day focus on the majestic images of Christ, we remember that in his life Jesus tried to turn his society's understanding of power upside down. He showed again and again that his own power, God's power, lay in connection, in simplicity, in just relationships, in healed lives, in love.

Queen Vashti knew something of power as well. As a queen, she daily breathed the power that came from her position and her marriage. Yet when faced with the manipulative power of her husband, Vashti acted out of a power all her own. Risking her marriage, her status, and her life, Vashti said no.

Vashti summoned the power to defy the prevailing powers at a feast. In this week, let us join her table, listening to her story as we consider what it means to share power with one another. As we close this year, let us sit with all the women who have journeyed with us through these seasons: Hagar, Mary, Julian, Etty, Dorothy, the *madres,* and all the rest. May they continue to share their power as we turn with wisdom toward another year in our sacred journey.

------ **MONDAY** ------

There comes a time when even a queen has to put her royal foot down and say, "Enough is Enough." . . .

Let us not fool ourselves. The Old Testament story does not suggest that Queen Vashti was unhappy being a queen, nor that she was unappreciative of the privileges which came with being a queen, nor that she despised her husband, despite his shortcomings. In the times in which she lived, Vashti, no doubt, was well aware that it was more prudent to be married than unmarried, more comfortable to be a queen than a peasant.

But Vashti's story is not simply a recounting of one of many instances in a marriage where one spouse acts insensitively toward the other, or where one inconveniences the other. Something more was at stake in the king's request than the queen's personal comfort. Queen Vashti found nothing flattering in her husband's desire to show off her beauty before his drunken guests. She refused, even in the face of banishment, to comply with his dehumanizing command.

—Renita J. Weems in *Just a Sister Away*

Reflect

❖ What words, images, requests, or demands have left you feeling less than human, less than whole?

❖ What propels you to move beyond those feelings?

—————— **TUESDAY** ——————

The Call
(Written with special affection for Queen Vashti)

We are
to be
the mannequins

thin, mute
and haughty

set before windows
to be seen
marveled at
appreciated

locked
where spots of anchored light
will fall.

Somewhere alone
wanders
the woman in me
far away from the dollar toys
and dull of window eyes.

Come along,
come along
New-Born.
I have room for you
in the soul
of one person
singing.
—Greta Schumm in *Images: Women in Transition*

Reflect

Imagine the woman who wanders in you.

- ❖ What is she leaving?
- ❖ Where is she going?

───── WEDNESDAY ─────

Women need to know that they can reject the powerful's definition of their reality—that they can do so even if they are poor, exploited, or trapped in oppressive circumstances. They need to know that the exercise of this basic personal power is an act of resistance and strength. Many poor and exploited women, especially non-white women, would have been unable to develop positive self-concepts if they had not exercised their power to reject the powerful's definition of their reality. . . . Sexism has never rendered women powerless. It has either suppressed their strength or exploited it. Recognition of that strength, that power, is a step women together can take towards liberation.

—bell hooks in *Feminist Theory: From Margin to Center*

Reflect

- ❖ What does bell mean by "basic personal power"?
- ❖ In an age where victims rightly cry out against injustice, how can we move beyond a stance of victimization toward exercising the power we do have?
- ❖ How does Vashti do this?

───── THURSDAY ─────

Vashti refused to leave the banquet where she was ministering to and cele-brating with women, the forgotten ones of her day. She refused to allow the king, her husband, to display her body to his drunken friends as if it were some prized possession of his. In her refusal Vashti defied the controlling powers of her day.

Patriarchal authority cannot tolerate such defiance, however. There is no room for questioning the way things are or for diversity of any kind. The reaction of the king and his advisors is much like we experience today. They were threatened by her and fearful that they might lose their power and control over other women. They decided to silence her, to banish her, making an example of her, lest other women follow her lead and defy their husbands also.

But Vashti *can* be a model for us, thousands of years later. Vashti's refusal echoes through time, sustaining women who seek to resist the definitions and expectations of those considered powerful. We are Vashti's sisters. And today, as we dance Sarah's circle, we need also to sing Vashti's song—a song of justice and equality for all.

—Carolyn Mathis

Reflect

❖ What songs and acts of resistance, great or small, does Vashti's courage prompt in you?

----- **FRIDAY** -----

A Psalm Celebrating Beauty

Choir 1   She walks in beauty
as the night,
veiled in the folds of mystery,
concealing the deep, dark secret source
of her integrity,
revealing only what will inspire,
so is she who walks with God.

Choir 2   She rises in beauty
as the dawn,
radiant with newly awakened light,
clear as far as the eye can see,
slowly, surely, enticing all
into the orb of her energy,
so is she who rises with God.

Choir 1   She sits in beauty
like a stone, certain of her appointed place,
fundamental and firm to the insecure,

unafraid to sit alone,
so is she who sits with God.

Choir 2   She stands in beauty
like a tree,
deep-rooted, so no catastrophe
can wipe her memory from the land,
nor fell her
when she takes a stand,
so is she who stands with God.

Choir 1   She is with Beauty constantly,
she who enters the cosmic force
of quintessential harmony,
savoring all she has come to be,
so is she who is with God.

Choir 2   She is beauty incarnate,
the kind
transcending sinew, stature, skin
to thrill the participating mind
and fill the senses.
Who will find
a clearer image of the Deity
than she who is in God?

—Miriam Therese Winter in *WomanWitness*

Reflect

Imagine one choir as Vashti and the women around her table and the other choir as yourself and women you know. Read the psalm again with this image, hearing these voices.

❖ What do you see in their faces, hear in their words?

❖ What do these women have to say to one another?

—— **SATURDAY** ——

According to one legend, Vashti was killed for defying her husband. Her murderers maintained that it was the only way to deter the other women from following her threatening example.

But what if she lived? What if those women whom she hosted at her feast understood her refusal, having longed to do what she did? What if they shared their own power, returned her care of them by making Vashti's escape to a safe place possible?

Joan Chittester, in her book *Job's Daughters: Women and Power*, speaks of power as a *charism*—a gift, a grace to be shared. When persons offer saving, healing care to those bound by the whims, desires, and demands of others, this offering is a charism. This power is grace-full and care-full.

Perhaps the women who feasted with Vashti returned this power to her. Perhaps it is this power that Vashti calls us to return to one another now.
—Jan L. Richardson

Reflect
- ❖ What do you think happened to Vashti?
- ❖ What care would you extend to her, as she reveals her face in women today?

—— **SUNDAY** ——

May the lives of the Vashtis of the Old Testament, of the past and present centuries inspire us and encourage us to keep saying no to the dominant culture, the oppressive structure and dehumanizing power. May we allow the Holy Spirit to rekindle the potential and the gifts in us; to empower us to become who we are and who we are yet to be. May the emergence of beauty, the image of God in us, break all the barriers and prejudices which imprison us. Such experience of becoming aware of ourselves; recognizing and accepting our own dignity and value would in turn help us to appreciate and value the gifts in others. Consequently, we shall be moved to [prophesy] and advocate for all those who are deprived of love, freedom, justice and peace. . . .

May we not allow ourselves to be overwhelmed by the issues and the problems. But, instead, uplift and support each other in exploring creative ways of dealing with them.
—Esther Byu, from "A Message of Encouragement and Hope for the New Year" in *Women's Link*

Reflect
- ❖ What image or images of power and transformation do you want to carry with you, to embody in this coming year?

❖ What do you want to take with you from Vashti's feast for the journey ahead?

Before you go, allow yourself to rest here for a time . . . with these women, at this table, along your sacred journey.

―――― **Meditation** ――――

House of Grace
  For Nancy Lee

"It's children playing outside" you said,
but it wasn't their sound I was trying
to discern as we sat after dinner
in the house of a woman named Grace.
It was the sound of the canal
outside the window, and the bay
just beyond.
I thought it was rain
on this day we had spent
so clear.

On your sofa as you prepared this meal
I had read your words about
woman care, about woman caring,
and your words spilled over
into my plate, filling me in
this feast.

At dinner you spoke of exodus,
of letting go,
of your refusal to give up
your body, your soul to the spectacle
and it nearly cost you your life.

But here in this house, as you embrace
the second half of your life, you speak
of what delights you now:
the feel of wood beneath your palm as you dust
putting on clean sheets to prepare for a guest
picking grapefruit that's just right for breakfast
and these feasts . . .

Now you are awakened each morning
by the power in you to choose.

I love these days in the gap with you;
you, not knowing quite where you're going
but being quite sure what you've left behind,
and me, smiling
for dancing water
for children at play
for power transformed
in the house of a woman
named Grace.
—Jan L. Richardson

———— ❖ ————

Blessing: *Be blessed, you who were born in the very image of God. Be blessed, you who feast with grace and with care. Be blessed, you who dare to dream new dreams. In this turning of seasons, in this turning of life, be blessed!*

Permission
Acknowledgments

❖

The publisher gratefully acknowledges permission to reprint the following copyrighted material:

Paula Gunn Allen: "Womanwork" from *A Cannon between My Knees,* 1981. Used by permission of Strawberry Press.

Alta: Excerpt from "7:3" in *The Shameless Hussy.* Copyright © 1981, 1994 by Alta. Used by permission.

Bonnie S. Anderson and Judith P. Zinsser: From *A History of Their Own,* Volume 1. Copyright © 1988 by Bonnie S. Anderson and Judith P. Zinsser. Reprinted by permission of HarperCollins Publishers, Inc.

Ellen Anthony: "The Extra Room" and excerpt from "Somebody Has to Die." Used by permission.

Gloria Anzaldúa: From the Forward to the second edition of *This Bridge Called My Back,* edited by Cherríe Moraga and Gloria Anzaldúa. Copyright © 1983. Used by permission of Kitchen Table: Women of Color Press and the author.

Marie Assaad: From *New Eyes for Reading.* Copyright © 1986 World Council of Churches, Geneva, Switzerland. Used by permission.

Marjory Zoet Bankson: From *Braided Streams: Esther and a Woman's Way of Growing.* Copyright © 1985 by LuraMedia, Inc. Used by permission of LuraMedia, Inc., San Diego, CA.

Marjorie Bard: From *Shadow Women: Homeless Women's Survival Stories.* Copyright © 1990 by Marjorie Bard. Used by permission of Sheed & Ward. (1-800-333-7373).

Mary Catherine Bateson: From *Composing a Life.* Copyright © 1989 by Mary Catherine Bateson. Used by permission of Grove/Atlantic, Inc.

Susan Beehler: From *Wellsprings: A Journal for United Methodist Clergywomen,* Winter, 1989. Used by permission of the author.

Karen Beth: "Not My Own." Copyright © 1982 by Karen Beth. Used by permission.

Roberta C. Bondi: From *To Love as God Loves.* Copyright © 1987 Fortress Press. Used by permission of Augsburg Fortress; from *To Pray and to Love.* Copyright © 1991 Augsburg Fortress. Used by permission of Augsburg Fortress.

Rita Nakashima Brock: From *And Blessed Is She: Sermons by Women,* edited by David A. Farmer and Edwina Hunter. Copyright © 1990 by David A. Farmer and Edwina Hunter. Reprinted by permission of HarperCollins Publishers, Inc.

Rosemary Radford Ruether: From *Women-Church: Theology and Practice of Feminist Liturgical Communities*. Copyright © 1985 by Rosemary Radford Ruether. Reprinted by permission of HarperCollins Publishers, Inc.

Valerie C. Saiving: From "Our Bodies/Our Selves: Reflections on Sickness, Aging, and Death" in *Journal of Feminist Studies in Religion*, Volume 4, Number 2 (Fall, 1988). Used by permission of the journal and Scholars Press.

Judy Scales-Trent: "On that Dark and Moon-Less Night" from *Double Stitch: Black Women Write about Mothers and Daughters*. Used by permission.

Nancy Hastings Sehested: From *And Blessed Is She: Sermons by Women*, edited by David A. Farmer and Edwina Hunter. Copyright © 1990 by David A. Farmer and Edwina Hunter. Reprinted by permission of HarperCollins, Inc.

Gehan Shehata: Excerpts from letters. Used by permission.

Dorri Sherrill: Excerpts from "The Annunciation," "Imaging a Christian Feminist Theodicy," and "The Power to Choose." Used by permission.

Rita Silk-Nauni: From *A Gathering of Spirit: A Collection by North American Indian Women* edited by Beth Brant. Copyright © 1988 by Rita Silk-Nauni. Used by permission of Firebrand Books, Ithaca, NY.

Chris Smith: From "Feminist Spirituality" in *Wellsprings: A Journal for United Methodist Clergywomen*, Spring, 1990. Used by permission of the author.

Judith E. Smith: From "This Ground Is Holy Ground." Reprinted from *Weavings: A Journal of the Christian Spiritual Life* (Sept/Oct 1992) Volume 7, Number 5. © 1992 by The Upper Room. Used with permission.

Sandra Smith: Excerpt from a letter. Used by permission.

Dorothee Sölle: From *Revolutionary Patience*. English translation © 1977 by Orbis Books. Used by permission of Orbis Books and The Lutterworth Press.

Marion L. Starkey: From *The Devil in Massachusetts*. Copyright © 1949 by Marion L. Starkey. Reprinted by permission of Curtis Brown, Ltd.

Barbara Brown Taylor: From "Magnificat" in *Mixed Blessings*. Copyright © 1986 by Barbara Brown Taylor. Used by permission of Cherokee Publishing Company.

Phyllis Trible: From *God and the Rhetoric of Sexuality*. Copyright © 1978 Fortress Press. Used by permission of Augsburg Fortress.

Bärbel von Wartenberg-Potter: From *We Will Not Hang Our Harps on the Willows*. Copyright © 1987 World Council of Churches. Used by permission; from *The Power We*

Celebrate by Musimbi R. A. Kanyoro and Wendy S. Robins, eds. Copyright © 1992 Lutheran World Federation, published by WCC Publications, World Council of Churches, Geneva, Switzerland. Used by permission.

Elaine Wainwright: From "Companions on the Journey" in *Women-Church,* Number 9, Spring, 1991. Used by permission of *Women-Church,* an Australian journal of feminist studies in religion, GPO Box 2134, Syndey NSW 20001, Australia and the author.

Margaret Walker: "I Want to Write" and "For Mary McLeod Bethune" from *October Journey.* Copyright © 1973 by Margaret Walker Alexander. Used by permission of Broadside Press.

Anna Lee Walters: From "A Teacher Taught Me" in *Voices of the Rainbow,* ed. by Kenneth Rosen, published by Seaver Books, New York, NY. Copyright © 1975 by Kenneth Rosen. Used by permission of Arcade Publishing,

Benedicta Ward, trans.: From *The Sayings of the Desert Fathers.* Used by permission of Cassell PLC.

Christin Lore Weber: From *Blessings: A WomanChrist Reflection on the Beatitudes.* Copyright © 1990 by Christin Lore Weber; from *WomanChrist.* Copyright © 1987 by Christin Lore Weber. Reprinted by permission of HarperCollins Publishers, Inc.

Renita J. Weems: From *Just a Sister Away.* Copyright © 1988 by LuraMedia, Inc. Used by permission of LuraMedia, Inc., San Diego, CA.

Elizabeth Welch: From *Learning to Be 85.* Copyright © 1991 by Elizabeth Welch. Used by permission of The Upper Room.

Macrina Wiederkehr: From *Seasons of Your Heart: Prayers and Reflections.* Copyright © 1991 by Macrina Wiederkehr. Reprinted by permission of HarperCollins Publishers, Inc.

Miriam Therese Winter: From *WomanWitness.* Copyright © 1992 by Medical Mission Sisters. Reprinted by permission of The Crossroad Publishing Company; from *WomanWord.* Copyright © 1990 by Medical Mission Sisters. Reprinted by permission of The Crossroad Publishing Company.

Wendy M. Wright: From *The Vigil.* Copyright © 1992 by Wendy M. Wright. Used by permission of The Upper Room.

Flora Slosson Wuellner: From "Transformation: Our Fear, Our Longing." Used by permission.

Dhyani Ywahoo: From *Voices of Our Ancestors: Teachings from the Cherokee Wisdom Fire.* Copyright © 1987 by Dhyani Ywahoo. Used by permission of Shambhala Publications, Inc.